De Lingua Belief

De Lingua Belief

Robert Fiengo and Robert May

A Bradford Book
The MIT Press
Cambridge, Massachusetts
London, England

© 2006 Massachusetts Institute of Technology

All rights reserved. No part of this book may be reproduced in any form by any electronic or mechanical means (including photocopying, recording, or information storage and retrieval) without permission in writing from the publisher.

MIT Press books may be purchased at special quantity discounts for business or sales promotional use. For information, please e-mail special_sales@mitpress.mit.edu or write to Special Sales Department, The MIT Press, 55 Hayward Street, Cambridge, MA 02142.

This book was set in Sabon by Interactive Composition Corporation. Printed and bound in the United States of America.

Library of Congress Cataloging-in-Publication Data

Fiengo, Robert, 1949–
  De lingua belief/Robert Fiengo and Robert May.
    p. cm.
  "A Bradford book."
  Includes bibliographical references and index.
  ISBN-13: 978-0-262-06257-2 (alk. paper)
  ISBN-10: 0-262-06257-7 (alk. paper)
  1. Language awareness. 2. Language and languages—Philosophy. I. May, Robert, 1951– II. Title.

P120.L34F54 2006
401—dc22

2006040347

10 9 8 7 6 5 4 3 2 1

To Barbara, and to Carlen and Julian, with love and thanks.

... we [are] studying language as an instrument or a tool, attempting to describe its structure with no explicit reference to the way in which this instrument is put to use. The motivation for this self-imposed formality requirement for grammars is quite simple—there seems to be no other basis that will yield a rigorous, effective, and "revealing" theory of linguistic structure. The requirement that this theory shall be a completely formal discipline is perfectly compatible with the desire to formulate it in such a way as to have suggestive and significant interconnections with a parallel semantic theory. What we have pointed out ... is that this formal study of the structure of language as an instrument may be expected to provide insight into the actual use of language, i.e., into the process of understanding sentences.

—Noam Chomsky, *Syntactic Structures*

Contents

Acknowledgments ix

Introduction 1

1 Beliefs about Language 7
  1.1 Foundational Questions 7
  1.2 Syntactic Identity and Referential Identity 25
  1.3 Anaphora, Context, and Referential Intentions 34

2 Names and Expressions 51
  2.1 Distinguishing Names and Expressions 52
  2.2 Beliefs Concerning Language 56
  2.3 Belief Ascription and Attributed Assignments 63
  2.4 Singularity 70
  2.5 Identity Puzzles 75
  2.6 Concluding Remarks 80
  Appendix: The Propositional Status of Assignments 82

3 Identity Statements 99
  3.1 Two Intuitions about Identity Statements 99
  3.2 On What It Is That Bears Reference 107
  3.3 The Logical Form of Identity Statements 112
  3.4 Names, Expressions, and Rigidity 118

4 Paderewski 139
  4.1 The Puzzle 139
  4.2 Linguistic Information 142
  4.3 Bridging the Gap 145
  4.4 The Puzzle Deepens 148
  4.5 The Identity Puzzle 152

4.6 Informativeness and the Reverse Puzzle   154
4.7 A Demonstrative Puzzle   158
4.8 Demonstrative Reference   164
4.9 Concluding Remarks   168

References   173
Index   177

Acknowledgments

The research in this book has gestated for almost a decade. Over that time, we have had an opportunity to discuss our work with many of our colleagues, and we have profited greatly from these interactions. Among them, we would like to single out Barbara Abbott, Kent Bach, Barbara Bevington, Johannes Brandl, Sylvain Bromberger, Graeme Forbes, Richard Heck, Chris Hom, Kent Johnson, Jeff King, Ernie Lepore, Brian Loar, Peter Ludlow, Ruth Marcus, Richard Mendelsohn, Stephen Schiffer, Gila Sher, and Christopher Tancredi to thank for taking the time to provide us with their comments, thoughts, and encouragement. We would also like express our gratitude to our students in our seminars during this period at The Graduate Center and UC Irvine for their discussion and feedback.

Chapter 1, "Beliefs about Language," incorporates with permission of the publisher and editors, respectively, passages from our papers "Anaphora and Identity," first published in S. Lappin, ed., *The Handbook of Contemporary Semantic Theory,* Blackwell, Oxford, 1996, and "The Semantic Significance of Syntactic Identity," which appeared in H. Bennis, P. Pica, and J. Rooryck, eds., *Atomism and Binding,* Foris Publications, Dordrecht, 1997. Chapter 2, "Names and Expressions," first appeared in *The Journal of Philosophy,* 95, 377–410, 1998, and is reprinted here, with slight revisions and an appendix new to this volume, with the permission of *The Journal of Philosophy.* Chapter 3, "Identity Statements," is a revised version of a paper that appeared initially in G. Preyer and G. Peter, eds., *Logical Form and Language,* Oxford University Press, Oxford, 2002, and appears by courtesy of the Oxford University Press. Chapter 4, "Paderewski," is new to this volume.

Introduction

Speakers, in the course of their conversations, use language to talk about language. Doing this is by no means an unusual occurrence; it is rather a prevalent and commonplace aspect of our everyday linguistic practice. Talk about language may be about many different things; we may ask what words mean, or what the right word is for a certain purpose. We may worry about whether we have made ourselves clear, or whether we have correctly expressed what we meant to say. That we can make such inquiries implies that we have a certain degree of conscious access to the various kinds of knowledge and the complex array of skills that underlie our ability to speak. While this access is by no means complete, we nevertheless often do form on this basis beliefs about linguistic matters of considerable subtlety, both about ourselves and about others.

The topic of this book is beliefs of this sort, beliefs speakers have about the language they know and use: *de lingua* beliefs. That speakers have linguistic beliefs is undeniable. For instance, readers of this book all have the belief that they are speakers of English; people have very definite beliefs about what language they speak, and what language other people speak. These beliefs are useful beliefs. Conversation is greatly enhanced when the participants all believe they are speaking the same language. Believing that one speaks English is a very substantive belief to have—it is not the same as believing that one speaks French—and it is also a very complex one, under which many subbeliefs may fall. These too may play an important role in our use of language. For instance, we have conscious command of the relation between the expressions of our language and what they refer to, of whether we have managed to refer to the same thing twice by the use of such expressions, and of whether two (distinct) expressions refer to the same thing. Admittedly, we sometimes get these things wrong. Nevertheless, success in communicating depends on getting them right, because for conversants to agree that they are all talking about the same things depends in large part on their believing that they share beliefs such as that "Frege" refers to Frege, and not Russell, and that "Cicero" and "Tully" refer to the same person, or that "chair" means chair, and not table, and that "bellies" and "tummies" mean the same thing.

It might be thought that while beliefs like those we are describing reflect an underlying linguistic reality, they are nonetheless epiphenomenal, a mere sideshow to the underlying principles and conditions that *explain* our knowledge and use of language. This would not be to say that ascertaining the grounds speakers have for linguistic beliefs, and how they come to hold them, is a topic without interest. To the contrary. Unfolding the nexus of linguistic, communicative, conventional, and intentional factors that give rise to such beliefs is a topic of some subtlety, to which we will devote considerable attention. In our view, however, the significance of *de lingua* beliefs goes considerably beyond this. As we have already indicated, beliefs of this sort are essential for explaining at least some aspects of the success of communication, and it is with their explanatory roles, we believe, that the ultimate interest in linguistic beliefs resides. Our goal in the chapters to follow will be to endeavor to understand how *de lingua* beliefs infiltrate our use of language, in doing so trying to reveal their genesis as well as to unravel the explanatory roles they play.

Our analysis of *de lingua* beliefs will be conceptual. We call it conceptual, not philosophical, because its intent is to reveal aspects of the conceptual structure of an underlying scientific theory. In this regard, our inquiries will be much like Frege's. For Frege, the concern was with the analysis of the conceptual structure of the underlying theory of logic. But although that theory failed, as consequently did his logicist program, nevertheless many of the notions he employed that constitute much of what we think of as Frege's philosophical contribution, most notably, the distinction between sense and reference, have persisted, but now detached from the conceptual mileau in which they were conceived. In large part because of the power of the applications that Frege made of these notions, primarily to statements of identity and belief, they have become matters of persistent philosophical curiosity, largely in the philosophy of language, and have engendered issues at considerable remove from Frege's conceptual concerns.

Part of our purpose in this book is to recapture these cases under a conceptual analysis. As they were for Frege, they will be for us important test cases for the validity of central theoretical concepts, and also as in the case of Frege, these concepts will be at the heart of characterizing the sort of things the theory is about. But for us, the underlying theory is not logic, but linguistic theory; the relevant objects not numbers, but the expressions that make up the sentences of a language. They are cases, we believe, that reflect the nature of concepts that we find at the foundation of empirical theories of language.

In this vein, the project we envisage is one of considerable extent and complexity, in large part because the beliefs that speakers can have about language are themselves quite extensive and complex. Consequently, our approach is not meant to be exhaustive; rather, we have chosen to restrict our attention to linguistic beliefs of two specific sorts:

1 Beliefs about the semantic values of linguistic expressions
2 Beliefs about the syntactic identity of linguistic expressions

Our choice to focus on these sorts of linguistic beliefs is not random. One reason for doing so is that in a very general sense, beliefs of these sorts are intimately involved in what it means to say of speakers that they properly know, and are able to properly use, their language. Without doubt, beliefs speakers have about reference and coreference of the sort we remarked on above, beliefs that directly depend on (1) and (2), reflect fundamental aspects of our underlying linguistic competence, as well as how we employ that competence to further our communicative ends. A second reason is that we can explore such beliefs in the context of cases that, for the reasons just cited, are well known in the philosophical and linguistic literature—the informativeness of identity statements, and the failure of substitutions in attributions of propositional attitudes. Although the extent of the discussion of these cases is vast, there is a persistent insight about what is at issue, namely, that speakers can fail to believe of two distinct expressions that they are coreferential, even though they are. They fail to have certain *de lingua* beliefs. Part of our goal in this book is to understand this failure, and its connection to the apparent breakdown of an otherwise intuitive principle of meaning—that we expect terms with the same reference to make the same contribution to content in all contexts in which they occur. Now tilling for new insight in these areas where matters of reference and coreference take center stage might seem like trying to grow corn from hardscrabble earth, but we think not. Once we understand what it is to hold *de lingua* beliefs falling under (1) and (2), and to believe that others hold them too, and have explicated the roles they play in the referential use of language, there will be considerable new insight to be had about these famously puzzling phenomena.

Although each of the essays that form the chapters of this book can be read as a self-contained study, they all have a common dialectic and reflect shared themes. By way of orientation, we can broadly divide these themes topically along the dimensions to which we have already alluded: understanding (1) the nature and genesis of linguistic beliefs, and (2) the explanatory roles such beliefs play in language use. The first theme takes flight by posing the question of the objects of linguistic beliefs: What *are* the linguistic entities that such beliefs are about? How are they to be characterized and individuated, so that we can tell when we have the same or different beliefs? These questions we take to be of a fundamentally grammatical order, their answers to be sought within the provinces of linguistic theory, wherein we seek descriptions of the resources available to speakers for generating linguistic beliefs. To properly understand *de lingua* beliefs, we must first understand the structure of the language they are about, for it is through the ontology of language that we will be able to say whether *de lingua* beliefs are the same or different. Beliefs about language can be imposed on us in various ways; the structure of the language itself, the rational use of language to communicate, the conventions of naming, and speakers' referential intentions can all give rise to linguistic beliefs, as we will see. But that they are *linguistic* beliefs depends on our prior characterization of the language they are about, and to do this is to concern ourselves with linguistic theory.

The first theme broached in these essays, then, focuses on what linguistic beliefs are, and under what circumstances it is appropriate for speakers to hold them. The second theme builds on the first, addressing the question of how attributing such beliefs to speakers accounts for properties of their use of language. The answer to this latter question flows from a key insight, namely, that when certain conditions are met, the content of beliefs about the reference of expressions can be taken to be part of what we *say* by our utterances, part of the propositional content; to put it a little differently, they can be part of the *interpretation* of our utterances, by ourselves and by others. By "part of" here we mean *formal* part—that is, as constituents of the logical form that expresses this interpretation, that represents what we say. From this, as we will see, it follows that logical forms may contain mention of, and hence reference to, expressions otherwise used. When such mention is within the context of a propositional-attitude verb, the result is, we believe, a *de dicto* attribution, as this notion has been traditionally understood, and we will label them as such, (as opposed to *non–de dicto* beliefs, inclusive of, but not to be identified with, *de re* beliefs). Our beliefs about the identity conditions of expressions will come into play at this point, in assessing the logical forms of our sentences, including those of the sort just mentioned. Our recognition of whether the same linguistic expression is repeated in such forms will fix the circumstances under which two expression-tokens may be taken to corefer, for sometimes it is tokens of distinct expressions that corefer, while at others it is tokens of the same expression. Which way it is will matter. It will matter because whether sentences can be taken to have logical forms in which substitution can be validly carried out, or are informative, will depend on our beliefs about how anaphoric relations between expressions are ultimately fixed (or not) by the structure of the language we speak.

It might seem that the project we have been introducing is somewhat quixotic, given the central explanatory role played by linguistic aspects of beliefs. Perhaps the best-known occasion in which language figured so prominently is in Carnap's discussion of propositional attitudes in *Meaning and Necessity* (1947). But even as its author admitted, this was not a wholly successful venture, withering primarily under the attacks of Church, so much so that today virtually any account that gives language pride of place is largely discredited. Nevertheless, our goal is to resurrect such a view, and to rectify the neglect that linguistic structure—syntax—has received, particularly in philosophical discussions of reference. Indeed, as Putnam pointed out early on, in response to what was perceived as one of the central difficulties of Carnap's theory, so-called Mates cases, this is not wholly fair. We can make no judgment about such cases, Putnam rightly emphasizes, until we have a proper analysis of their logical structure, and to know this we must ascertain whether the same expression (or variable) is repeated or not. Putnam has set us in the right direction, for reasons that are not hard to see. Unless we get the identity conditions right, we will not know what sort of sentence or sentences we are confronting analytically. We would not have a definite fix on the structure—the *logical forms*—of the sentences we use in making our utterances. The common sense here is that in order for the analytic questions to be clearly posed, much less answered, the first thing on the table must be a proper accounting of linguistic structure that allows us to know whether one is encountering two occurrences of the same expression or not. It is right here, at the beginning, that we find the contribution of natural-language syntax to the understanding of philosophical problems. Because information about the linguistic identity of expressions is exploitable by speakers in the context of belief attributions and identity statements, we can have an account of substitution and informativeness that is at heart formal. So, although our theory does place significant and substantial formal constraints on how speakers can report, attribute, or interpret the contents of mental states, and so constrains the information that can be propositionally expressed, it is nevertheless independent of any specific theory of propositions or depiction of the content of mental states.

As a guide to our readers, we should mention that the ideas we will be pursuing find their roots in our previous monograph, *Indices and Identity,* and our current work represents an outgrowth of the primarily linguistic research presented there. Readers of that work will recognize its central theme, that the relation of expression identity to coreference is essential for understanding pronominal anaphora, wending its way through the chapters of this book, and the research developed there (and elsewhere in the linguistics literature) is intended to provide the empirical terra firma for the current investigations. We have assumed, however, no familiarity with our prior book here. Moreover, readers may approach the current volume as a monograph, or as a collection of essays. Those who choose the former strategy will be privy to the chronological unfolding of our thinking, the second, third, and fourth chapters having been written in that order for the most part, the first chapter having been written last. For those who choose the latter approach, and wish to read chapters selectively, or in a different order, we have left in overlapping material, at pain of some repetition, so that each chapter may be read on its own as an independent essay.

1
Beliefs about Language

1.1 Foundational Questions

Our inquiries commence with a basic, and we think uncontroversial, assumption about the use of language: it is a rational activity. Thus, speakers, in making their utterances, do so purposively and in an informed way, with the intention of satisfying communicative goals. To achieve these goals, speakers choose to utter the sentences they do because they believe that those sentences best express what they want to say, although for any given task, language may provide a variety of sentences that might be used to perform it. It is this point of view—that, in the normal course of events, speakers say what they say for a reason—that marks the starting point of our inquiries.

From the perspective we are taking, the use of a sentence can be likened to the use of a tool. Suppose that we wish to join two pieces of wood with a nail. To do so, we need to choose a tool from the chest by which we can best accomplish this goal. A hammer will do the trick nicely; indeed, it is a tool optimally constructed for the task at hand, given its shape and mass. Other tools might work, but less well. The handle of a screwdriver, for instance, could be pressed into service, but this would be a decidedly odd choice in most circumstances, given that it is designed to drive screws, not nails; nevertheless, one might have one's reasons for eschewing the hammer in favor of the screwdriver. But either way, if things go well, the end result is that the boards are joined with a nail.

To an extent, language use proceeds in a parallel way. Suppose we wish to say it is raining outside. To do so, we need to choose a sentence by which we can best accomplish this goal. The sentence "It is raining outside" will work nicely; indeed, it is the sentence that is optimally constructed for the task at hand, precisely because what it means is that it is raining outside. Other sentences might work, but less directly. One might utter "I'm getting wet," expecting one's interlocutor to draw the conclusion that it is raining outside, though the sentence does not mean that it is raining outside. One may have one's reasons for indirection. Either way, the speaker will have communicated that it is raining.

Suggestive as the analogy between tool use and language use is, we should not lose sight of the disanalogies, for language use presents complications not found with the simpler case of tool use. These arise, first and foremost, from the fact that language use is embedded in conversation. For communicative language use, there must be at least a speaker and a hearer. For language use to succeed, these interlocutors must be on the same wavelength; they must share certain assumptions. A speaker's choice of a sentence to utter will be made against the background of his or her beliefs about these shared assumptions; it would be pointless for a speaker to utter a sentence without believing that the hearer was in a position to comprehend the intended meaning. These background assumptions can be roughly divided into two sorts. There are those that go along with the assumption that the speaker and hearer are speaking the same language, and there are those that stem from the particulars of the context of utterance, including who is making the utterance, to whom, when, and where it is being made, and the beliefs interlocutors have about their shared factual knowledge. This distinction is roughly what people have in mind when they distinguish between the conventional and conversational settings of an utterance.

As we see things, then, language use is a matter of rational choice on the part of speakers; it is a solution to a tool-use problem of a sort. Central to what determines whether a sentence is right for the job is its meaning; this is true even in cases of indirection, or exploitation of the maxims, as Grice had it. Apprehension of that meaning is the basis for the belief that the chosen sentence will do what it is supposed to do in the circumstances in which it is employed, and that it will be comprehended as doing so by hearers who speak the same language, hearers who, to extend our metaphor, are in possession of the same toolkit. Speakers who utter "It is raining outside" believe that hearers will comprehend this to mean that it is raining outside, and so they believe they can utter this sentence in order to satisfy their intention to communicate that it is raining outside. Hearers, for their part, will presume that the speakers' choice of a sentence to utter is made on rational grounds, given the speakers' goals that it was appropriate to utter a sentence that means that it is raining outside. The hearers' judgment of appropriateness may be simple or complex. Speakers may have uttered "It is raining outside" simply because they wanted to communicate that it is raining outside, and nothing more. But they may also have uttered this sentence with the intention of communicating something more, so that their utterance, with the meaning it has, was intended to invite the hearers to initiate a chain of reasoning, by which, if successful, the speakers will have succeeded in implicating something by their utterance that it did not literally mean.

Given that rational speakers make a choice, what are the things they are choosing among? What *resources* do they have available for this choice? We have already tipped our hand on this question; to get across what we want to say, and to understand what others say to us, we have to utilize the *linguistic* resources placed at our disposal. That is, for an utterance, speakers choose among sentences of their language. But how do we characterize a language? The standard way to answer this question is to assume that we have a device G, and that sentences, as defined by G, are used by speakers. The resource issue is thus fundamentally a linguistic issue; it requires determining the grammar of a language. G serves to define sentencehood, and sentences, as we have emphasized, are the objects of certain *attitudes* of speakers—speakers believe of sentences, by virtue of their linguistic properties, that by uttering them they can say what they want to say. (Utterances in this light are tokens of linguistically *structured* entities, as fixed by G, taken with respect to dated, located, and oriented occasions of use.) We rely on G to individuate the objects of these beliefs, to give us the criteria by which we can say whether the sentences we use are the same or different.

Now suppose, as we will throughout, that we have speakers who know G, and are in a position to rationally use the sentence "Frege had a beard." To do so by making an utterance, however, speakers must believe that it will express what they want to say, namely, that Frege had a beard. Establishing the conditions sufficient for holding this belief is no doubt a very complex matter, but regardless of this complexity, there are certain beliefs that speakers must hold *at a minimum*—they must believe that "Frege" refers to Frege, that Frege satisfies "had a beard," and that

"Frege had a beard" is true if and only if Frege had a beard. Having these beliefs, and believing that others have them, is essential to the cooperative enterprise; as such they are constitutive of rational use of language. If speakers did not have these beliefs, we would be hard-pressed to maintain that they could rationally use the sentence "Frege had a beard" to say that Frege had a beard; they would lack beliefs necessary to underwrite this activity.

The linguistic beliefs we are describing are what we call as a class *de lingua*. They contrast with beliefs that are not linguistic, usually called *de re*. Of the *de lingua* beliefs, there are some that are usually called *de dicto*, that term being traditionally restricted to uses in which a name refers to an object. (We will refine this relation shortly.) While one of the central issues we will be addressing in this book is how *de re*, *de lingua*, and *de dicto* beliefs are to be distinguished, we can nevertheless already employ the terminology to distinguish the *de re* belief of Frege that he had a beard, the *de dicto* belief that "Frege" refers to Frege, and the *de lingua* belief that by uttering "Frege had a beard" one says that Frege had a beard. Speakers who have all of these beliefs are in a position to rationally decide (given perhaps additional considerations of information and context) whether to say "Frege had a beard," given their communicative goals and intentions.

In orienting our thinking about *de lingua* beliefs, it will be useful to center the discussion around three foundational questions:

Origin: What are the sources of linguistic beliefs?
Pertinence: What are the things linguistic beliefs are about?
Identity: How do we recognize when the same linguistic belief is being expressed over again?

What we have said thus far has been meant to address the question of *origins;* our answer has been that *de lingua* beliefs arise as an essential aspect of our rational use of language. But now the second question—that of *pertinence*—looms large. What are *de lingua* beliefs about? What, for instance, is the belief that "Frege" refers to Frege about? In a way, the answer is straightforward; given that at least part of the content of this belief is a relation between a linguistic term and a value, this relation and its arguments are what the belief is about. Thus, if our interest is to know what we bring to bear whenever we talk about people by name, then whatever else might be involved, this will involve knowing which linguistic shape or form refers to which person. But with this interest, we had better get straight right away just what sort of linguistic shape or form this is, if we are to give a substantive answer to the question of *pertinence*.

Apropos of this interest, it will suit our expository goals to limit our attention to beliefs such as that "Frege" refers to Frege, which we will call, to introduce terminology we will employ throughout, beliefs of *Assignments*. In learning the names of people, we acquire Assignments, and sometimes, to our embarrassment, we forget them. We can be conscious of them, although we need not be; we acknowledge this when we try to bring back to consciousness what someone's name is. Sometimes we have to decide *which* name to use when referring to someone. We might ask ourselves: "Should I call her 'Nancy' or 'Mrs. Smith'?" and the decision can often be delicate. Moreover, we can attribute Assignments to others; not only do we know what names we give to people, we know what names other people give to people. And we know that sometimes these are different. We say such things as "Can you imagine? She calls Burton 'Barton'!" Or the victim of bigamy might say: "I only knew him by the name 'Donald Fenster.'" Here we implicitly say about other people that they know certain Assignments and that they use them when referring. We can also report errors, as when we say "Max believes that 'Grundlagen' refers to a beer." It can even happen that, since we can be consciously aware of these matters, when we talk about the beliefs of others, we include Assignments in our belief attributions, and so mention the terms in which the belief is held. This is one sort of belief attribution that has been called *de dicto*.[1]

As conceived, Assignments involve the specification of a certain relation between linguistic entities and semantic values; the content of the belief that "Frege" refers to Frege includes a relation between "Frege" and its referent. But what exactly are the terms of this relation? The natural response is to say that it is a relation between a domain of *names* in a language and a counterdomain of *objects* in the world. Up to now, we have spoken this way ourselves. But is it the right way? We think not. While the proper description of the counterdomain is a well-worn philosophical chestnut, it is not our intention here to join this debate, and it will do for present purposes to leave it be. Rather, where we take exception is with the description of the domain, for it is much too imprecise. Now, this may seem an odd claim, for admittedly it is no violation of common usage to say that names refer. But do they? Let's consider.

Suppose we say that "Nixon" refers. Fine, but to whom? Richard? Trot? Some other person altogether? In response, we commonly say that the name is ambiguous, there are actually many Nixons and the name "Nixon" might refer to any of them. It all depends on circumstance. Now all of that, though vague, is, in a flatfooted sense, perfectly true. Suppose someone suddenly turns to you and, out of the blue, demands "Who does 'Nixon' refer to?" Replies of various sorts come to mind, but it is clear that this is a very unfair question. There is, or was, a very famous Nixon, of course, but many of us are aware of others, such as Trot Nixon, the baseball player, and it is unclear what the right answer might be. Even worse would be the question "Who does 'John' refer to?" Appreciation of the unfairness of such questions is perhaps what leads to the conclusion that names are ambiguous.

It is, however, but a short step from these flatfooted truths to some real mistakes. Take the claim that the name "Nixon" has more than one referent. Where should we look to evaluate the truth of this? If we ask ourselves whether we can think of more than one person named "Nixon," we find that indeed there is more than one. So, if understood as a claim about the number of bearers of the name "Nixon," the thesis is true. But we might take the thesis differently. We might take the thesis as saying that the name "Nixon," *as it appears in discourse,* has more than one referent. And that is far from true. A person who utters "Nixon was a Republican" never intends to be taken as saying that any old person named "Nixon" was a Republican. In fact, the sentence "Nixon was a Republican" *cannot* be used to say that any old person named "Nixon" was a Republican. No one intends ambiguity through the use of a name. A speaker who says "Nixon was a Republican" intends to say that some particular person named "Nixon" was a Republican, either Richard, or Trot, or perhaps some third person altogether. (Nobody who says "Nixon was a Republican" will allow that its truth depends only on there being someone named "Nixon," perhaps a person that the speaker has no knowledge of, who was a Republican. Nobody uses names to talk about nothing in particular.) And while it might be that, on hearing someone say "Nixon was a Republican" you might not know whether he is talking about Richard, or Trot, or someone else, you would never consider the possibility that the speaker meant that any old person name "Nixon" was a Republican. For, again, the sentence cannot be used that way. The right tool for this pretty strange job, or at least *one* right tool, is: "Any old person named 'Nixon' was a Republican." (Of course, this is not to be paraphrased as "If a person was old and named 'Nixon,' he was a Republican.") "Someone named 'Nixon' was a Republican" will not do, since that is taken to be an unambiguous statement about some *particular* person named "Nixon," though, after being told that this person named "Nixon" was not a Republican and that that person named "Nixon" was a Republican, one might get exasperated and say "Well, surely SOMEone named 'Nixon' was a Republican," and this *is* about nobody in particular.

In part, the possibility of confusion here depends on an ambiguity in the term "ambiguity," or at least an ambiguity in what "ambiguity" is ascribed too. If "ambiguity" is to mean *has more than one bearer,* and if it is applied to names in isolation, then names, including the name "Nixon," are ambiguous. But there is another way to understand "ambiguity," as meaning *has more than one referent*. In this case, however, we are no longer concerned with names in isolation, but rather with their occurrences in discourse—that is, within the context in which terms are used referentially. Contrary to the prior cases, occurrences of *expressions* in discourse are *unambiguous*; no occurrences of expressions in discourse, including expressions containing the name "Nixon," are ambiguous. To be sure, different expressions may sound the same by virtue of containing (tokens of) the same name, and sometimes we may not know which unambiguous expression we are confronting. Nevertheless, it remains that we have one expression of the name "Nixon" that unambiguously refers to the president, and a linguistically distinct expression that unambiguously refers to the baseball player.

This brings us in contact with an old insight. Frege said: "We can inquire about reference only if the signs are constituent parts of sentences expressing thoughts" (*Grundgesetze*, II, §97). He was on the right track. We would only alter this to say: "We can inquire about reference only if the signs are constituent parts of sentences *used in discourse* to express thoughts." To avoid confusion, we must distinguish names, which have bearers, from the occurrences of expressions containing names in discourse, which have referents. If we do, we may say that it is not really names that have reference, but linguistic expressions that occur in sentences used in discourse, which, of course, may contain names. This is to say that Assignments are relations between syntactic expressions and values, and given that these are expressions containing names, if such expressions refer at all, they refer, at least in normal circumstances, to the bearers of those names. As such, names do not refer, but the expressions that contain them do.

The distinction we are drawing here between names and expressions is one we will insist on as we proceed; we will elaborate on it in each of the subsequent essays. What we need to observe about it here at the outset is that it belies a deeper linguistic distinction, that between the vocabulary and the syntax of a language. Names are vocabulary items and expressions are syntactic items that may contain names; it is the latter that make up the domain of Assignments, not the former. Now, the vocabulary of a language is standardly characterized as a *lexicon,* a nonrepeating list, each entry of which is uniquely specified by certain linguistic properties. Among these are phonological, morphological, and syntactic properties; what is *not* among these properties is reference. Since Chomsky's influential discussion in *Aspects of the Theory of Syntax,* it has been assumed that the information in a lexical entry determines where a lexical item can occur in syntactic structures. It cannot possibly matter that "Frege" refers to Frege, and not to Russell or Wittgenstein. (Although it might matter that it refers to a person, and not a rock, it could not matter which *particular* person it refers to.) While names, *qua* lexical items, have various linguistic properties through which they are individuated, and that determine in part how they may be syntactically expressed, their reference is *not* among these properties. To the extent that we persist in speaking of names as referring, it is only in the derivative sense of their occurring in expressions; names, strictly speaking, do not refer, only expressions containing them do. In saying this we do not deny that names have bearers; indeed, it will be important to us that speakers have beliefs about this. Moreover, we do not deny that these latter beliefs may have conceptual content sufficient for describing the referent; it will be of no matter to our concerns whether they do or not. What we do deny, however, is that such referential information is part of lexical information; that this information is part of our *lexical* competence. Names, to repeat, are lexical items, and as such, are *not* the "linguistic vehicles" of reference.

There are many questions of a very fundamental sort about Assignments that naturally pop up at this point. One line of questioning pertains to the substance of Assignments, to what sort of propositions they are. For instance, do they state only arbitrary linguistic facts? Are they trivial in some way or another? Are they informative? What is their metaphysical status, are they necessary or contingent? These are important questions and others are easily imaginable; we need to know the answers to these questions to fully understand the explanatory role Assignments will play. These questions, however, are premature—we have yet to even illustrate the explanatory role—and so we will postpone answering them until this is done (in chapter 2). What is not to be postponed is a remaining *formal* issue that needs to be settled about Assignments. This is the third question that we posed above, the question of *identity*. How are we to recognize when we are in the presence of distinct Assignments, or two occurrences of the same one?

The answer to this question is straightforward: Assignments are the same if they contain the same relations between the same arguments; otherwise, they are different. Indeed, since the relation is constant, the only difference that could matter would be a difference in the arguments, either in the expressions themselves or in their values. Assignments to "[Frege]"—we indicate expressions by enclosing them in brackets—are distinct from Assignments to "[Russell]." So too are Assignments to "[Cicero]" and "[Tully]," although here there is only a mismatch between one of the arguments; they agree on their values. These two sorts of mismatches are the only ways Assignments can differ. Hence we can say that Assignments are the same if and only if they contain the same expression (with the same value).[2]

The centrality of linguistic description becomes evident here, for as noted, Assignments are distinguishable strictly on linguistic grounds; "Cicero"-Assignments are not "Tully"-Assignments just because "[Cicero]" and "[Tully]" are different expressions. Now surely that "[Cicero]" and "[Tully]" are different expressions could hardly be called into question, but other cases are not as clearcut. So suppose we turn the tables, so that we have what appears to be the same expression, yet with more than one value—for instance, "Aristotle," taken as referring to a philosopher, and "Aristotle," taken as referring to a shipping magnate. What criteria are we going to have to distinguish *them*? If we stick to a naive criterion—if words sound (look) the same, they are the same, and if they sound (look) different, they are different—then we face a difficulty, for we would have Assignments that differ only in their values, but that would not differ linguistically. Assignments would fail to be *functional*; they would not return just one value for each distinct expression as argument. So we had better get clear about what is at stake here, for the generality of the thesis we have recently outlined will depend on prior decisions we make about the criteria for recognizing the presence of distinct expressions.

One criterion for distinguishing names with multiple bearers is suggested by Saul Kripke. In the preface to *Naming and Necessity* (1980), Kripke briefly addresses the issue, saying that names with multiple bearers are homonyms, and suggesting that, as in the case of homonyms generally, we should say that "uses of phonetically the same sounds to name distinct objects count as distinct names" (p. 8). This is a little rough; we take him to mean that uses of phonetically the same sounds to name distinct objects count as *uses of* distinct names. Uses are not themselves names. We can refine this even further, transposing Kripke's way of speaking into ours: uses of expressions containing the same name to refer to distinct objects count as uses of distinct expressions. While there is only one *name* "Aristotle"—one *phonetic type* "Aristotle," one "spelling" or "shape" "A⌒r⌒i⌒s⌒t⌒o⌒t⌒l⌒e"—there are many distinct syntactic expression-types that contain the name "Aristotle." We wish to be able to say that the philosopher and the shipping magnate *have the same name*. And, to pick up the analogy with homonyms, we wish also to say that sides of rivers and financial institutions have the same name. And so we can, but now the word "name" is stripped down to a matter of phonetics, and loses a considerable amount of philosophical baggage, but, at least here, there is nothing wrong with traveling light, for names themselves carry no referential burden. This burden falls rather on the syntactic expressions containing names; again, it is *expressions* that refer, not names. While we would not say that the philosopher and the shipping magnate have different names, we would nevertheless say that they each can be referred to by different expressions containing that name.

At this point, we may avail ourselves of a notational practice that will serve us throughout of placing indices within the brackets when syntactic identity is at issue, using this to distinguish, for instance, the expression "[$_1$ Aristotle]" from the distinct expression "[$_2$ Aristotle]." To grasp the representational content of our notation, think of logic, wherein among the things that would be specified would be a stock of variables, $x, y, z,$ etc. One would give the variables in this way because it would be perfectly clear by virtue of their *formal shape* when there are many occurrences of the same variable, as opposed to occurrences of different variables. "$\exists x \ (P(x) \wedge Q(x))$" is a different formula from "$\exists x \ (P(x) \wedge Q(y))$" in that the latter contains a free variable, where the former does not. Now, if one is being careful, it would not be appropriate to use $x, y, z,$ etc. to notate the variables, since this would limit the number of variables available. Rather, one would notate the variables as $x_1, x_2, x_3, \ldots$, since this would ensure unrestricted resources—no matter how many variables one had used, there would always be further unused variables. Such resources would be available, however, while still being able to distinguish variables on the same grounds as before, since the numerical subscripts—the indices—will provide a precise formal characterization of same and different variables in terms of their shape, without any limitations on the resources with which we annotate such differentiations.

Given this, the natural syntactic interpretation of indices is that coindexed expression-tokens (in a discourse) are occurrences of the same expression-type, but that noncoindexed expression-tokens are not. So occurrences of "[$_1$ Aristotle]" and "[$_2$ Aristotle]" are occurrences of distinct expression-types, for each of which there is a distinct Assignment; they are, reverting to our metaphor, distinct linguistic tools, which may be used by speakers to refer to distinct people. This is how they will be used by rational speakers who believe (even mistakenly) that there are two people so-named; they will utter tokens of one to refer to the philosopher, and tokens of the other to refer to the shipping magnate. They do not, on our view, use one tool "[Aristotle]" on some occasions to refer to the philosopher and on others to the shipping magnate.

The point we are making here is that the functionality of Assignments is guaranteed by the organization of grammar, in particular by the linguistic verity that lexical names are to be distinguished from their various syntactic expressions. The relation of the lexicon to the syntax is one-many, along two dimensions. A name, *qua* lexical item, may in principle occur in m-many syntactic expression-types, each of which may have n-many token occurrences (although there may be limitations on the value of *n* for any given syntactic structure; see section III of this chapter). Consequently, for any pair of expressions in a sentence, there are only two options in principle; either they are tokens of the same expression-type or not. Correspondingly, the notation recognizes only two conditions: coindexing, representing expression identity, and noncoindexing, representing expression nonidentity. These are also the only two options. We can thus *recognize* which option obtains in a given representation wholly by observing the pattern of indices in the syntactic structures of a discourse: sameness of index—that occurrences of the same expression are represented, difference of index—that occurrences of different expressions are represented. In this regard, our notation optimally encodes all the information about the projection from the lexicon to the syntax needed to decide the matter of identity. But one thing we do not need to know to make this decision is whether they are expressions containing the same name or not. Expression-identity does not depend on name-identity; the latter is necessary, but not sufficient for the former.[3] Expressions may be distinct regardless of whether they contain the same name or different names. Appropriately, the notation abstracts away from this irrelevancy.

Not only is expression-identity independent of name-identity, but, it is important to grasp, it is also independent of referential identity: "Cicero"-expressions and "Tully"-expressions may or may not corefer. From the point of view of grammar, there are no restrictions placed on this—distinct expressions may or may not refer to the same object—although speakers, for any given use, will make a particular choice one way or the other. This is to be sharply distinguished from when there are occurrences of the same expression (which of course will contain the same name). In this case speakers have no options, for all tokens of a given expression will corefer, *as a matter of grammar*. Again, thinking about logic can perhaps make the point clearer.

Suppose we have a formula of first-order logic sufficiently complex to contain multiple occurrences of two distinct variables; given the orthographic conventions for shape individuating variables, we indicate them by the letters *x* and *y* (*modulo* the remarks above). Given a standard semantics, in evaluating this formula there will be assignments of values to these variables, an assignment to *x* and an assignment to *y*. And given the logical mechanisms of assignments, the assignment to *x* will assign the same value to each and every occurrence of x. If this were not so, we would not be within our rights to say that each occurrence of x was an occurrence of the same variable, and we certainly would be subject to a charge of notational sloppiness. (Similarly for the assignment to y.)[4] The values assigned to x and y, however, may or may not be the same; nothing in the mechanisms of the assignments fixes this one way or the other, and it ultimately does not matter for the evaluation of the formula which it is. Or to take another example, which perhaps demonstrates the point in even greater relief, there are clearly two occurrences of "2" in "2 + 2 = 4," each of which refers to the same number; it takes no further calculation to determine this. On the other hand, there is only one occurrence of "2" in "6/3 + 2 = 4," and the fact that "2" and "6/3" refer to the same number does not follow from their being occurrences of the same numeral.

Natural language is much like logic in this regard, if we liken expressions (*not* names) to variables. Just as all occurrences of a given variable are assigned the same value, so too are all the occurrences of a given expression. So suppose we have an English sentence (or set of sentences, i.e., a discourse) sufficiently complex to contain multiple occurrences of the distinct expressions "Frege" and "Russell." In this sentence, each and every repetition of "Frege" refers to one and the same person, and similarly, each and every repetition of "Russell" refers to one and the same person. This is fixed by the grammar of English; all tokens of a given expression-type have the same value. What is not, however, fixed by the rules of grammar is whether "Frege" and "Russell" corefer or not. This is rather a matter of fact; "Frege" and "Russell" do not corefer, but "Cicero" and "Tully" do. Moreover, speakers may have beliefs about such matters of fact. They may just as much have true beliefs here as false; they *may* believe that "Frege" and "Russell" are coreferential, but that "Cicero" and "Tully" are not. But regardless of which it is, speakers have a choice between believing of two expression-tokens that they are coreferential or not only when they are occurrences of distinct expression-types. If, to the contrary, speakers believe they are confronted by tokens of the same expression, they do not have any such latitude; rather they must believe the occurrences all have the same value. They are compelled by the grammar to do so; factual beliefs do not enter into the picture, nor for that matter do speakers' intentions. Speakers cannot knowingly intend to use tokens of the same expression-type to refer to different things. That occurrences of the same expression-type corefer is inherent in the design of language.

There is something that is important to stress here: what we have said about distinct expressions containing distinct names applies equally well to distinct expressions of the *same* name. So when looked at from a purely *grammatical* perspective, distinct "Aristotle"-expressions may or may not be coreferential, just as distinct "Cicero"- and "Tully"-expressions may or may not be coreferential, for what is at stake is identity of expressions, *not* identity of names. Whether they are coreferential, and whether speakers believe they are, thus takes on the same importance either way; in particular, the question of the relation between sentences of the form ⌜A believes that $f(a)$⌝ and sentences of the form ⌜A believes that $f(b)$⌝, for *a* and *b* formally distinct *expressions,* arises regardless of whether *a* and *b* contain the same name or different ones. Our account of substitution in attributions of propositional attitudes (and, as we will see, the informativeness of identity statements), will proceed independently of which it is. At this level of description, the issues that arise from saying "Max believes Cicero was a poet" and "Max believes Tully was not a poet" arise equally well with "Peter believes Paderewski has musical talent" and "Peter believes Paderewski doesn't have musical talent," assuming an analysis under which we have occurrences of two distinct expressions, each of which contains the name "Paderewski." To this extent, the cases are of a piece.

The latter case just mentioned will be familiar to readers from Kripke's discussion in his paper "A Puzzle about Belief" (1979). As Kripke poses the puzzle, our normal methods of belief attribution apparently allow us to attribute to a single agent both a belief and its negation without implying that the agent has inconsistent beliefs—in the case at hand, both that Paderewski has musical talent and that he does not. In so describing the circumstances, Kripke presumes that the sort of linguistic distinctions that could be called on to distinguish "Cicero" from "Tully" are effaced, but without these, no question arises of the substitution of one distinct linguistic item for another. This is an important moral for Kripke, for it is central to his point of view that whatever issues arise regarding substitutivity of coreferential terms in propositional-attitude contexts, they are independent of any particular theory of the semantic content of proper names, and so do not favor one theory (e.g., the Fregean theory) over another, (e.g., the Millian theory). More generally, given that the content of a proper name is part of the content of the proposition expressed by a sentence, it follows that the success or failure of substitutivity is likewise independent of particular theories of propositions, for instance, of either a Fregean or Russellian ilk. From Kripke's standpoint, then, the roots of the puzzles about propositional attitudes have nothing to do with the linguistic meanings of words; rather, they arise from a breakdown in conditions that govern the *use* of language to attribute propositional attitudes. The culprit he has in mind is the Disquotation Principle, by which we can infer from a person's assent to "*p*" to his belief that *p*. For Kripke's purposes in developing the puzzles—to fend off the claim that a Fregean theory of names is preferable to a Millian theory because the former can account for failures of substitutivity—identifying this source is enough.

We are quite sympathetic with a number of Kripke's key points. For instance, we agree with Kripke that the issues brought up by the belief puzzles are independent of any particular thesis about the meaning of proper names, and, while it may very well be the case that senselike conceptual information, while not narrowly semantic, nonetheless underlies aspects of our use of proper names—we will take no stand on this one way or the other—we also agree that such information is *not* directly implicated in accounting for the puzzles, or for substitutivity more generally. (We are skeptical of any such involvement, not least because we would be trading away the clarity of formal linguistic conditions for conditions on conceptual identity that are notoriously difficult to state with precision.) Kripke's discussion, however, is not without its limitations, both in breadth and depth, that mask the extent of the puzzles, as well as their overall significance for understanding the correlation of language, meaning, and speakers' beliefs about such. The reasons for this will become apparent as we proceed, especially in chapters 3 and 4. Presently, however, our concerns take us back to the beginning point, to the way that Kripke describes the puzzle, and the linguistic assumption on which it is based.

Kripke's way of putting the puzzle assumes that the occurrences of "Paderewski" in "Peter believes Paderewski has musical talent" and "Peter believes Paderewski doesn't have musical talent" are occurrences of the same expression; in our notational lingo, they would be coindexed.

But then there would really be a conundrum, for, as we have maintained, speakers are compelled to believe of coindexed expressions that they corefer. But why are we bound by this description? We have been straining to show that this is not the only analytic option; there is another possibility, namely, that there are occurrences of *distinct* expression-types, each containing the name "Paderewski." These occurrences would not be coindexed. The description of the sentences that generate the puzzle would then involve the use of two distinct syntactic expressions that just happen to have the same phonological content. We should not be deceived by looks. The occurrences of "Paderewski" may look like occurrences of same expression, but they are not; relevant linguistic distinctions are in fact *not* effaced. Although they are dressed up in the same phonological garments, so to speak, they are nevertheless just as much tokens of distinct syntactic expressions as are "Cicero" and "Tully," or "Hesperus" and "Phosphorus," and so too can be distinguishing constituents of distinct Assignments. Any such Assignments may be part of a logical form; in the case of belief attributions this means that the attributions are *de dicto*. Analyzed this way, in all cases, including the Paderewski puzzle, disquotation may proceed, but not substitution. (We address the precise reason for this in chapter 2.) If the occurrences of "Paderewski" are not occurrences of the same expression-type, then it does not follow, as a matter of logical form, that inconsistent beliefs have been attributed to the agent, for it is left open grammatically whether such occurrences corefer or not.

There is considerably more to say about the Paderewski puzzle; we will return to it repeatedly in the chapters to follow, and it will be the central topic of chapter 4. But at least one effect of exploring this puzzle is apparent already, namely, we cannot rely on our untutored intuitive linguistic notions to provide an accurate indication of underlying linguistic reality. In most cases, our intuitive criterion—if words sound (look) the same, they are the same, and if they sound (look) different, they are different—is unproblematic, giving clear grounds for judgment in our everyday encounters with language. Accepting it would certainly prejudice us to believe that expressions of distinct names do not corefer, and that it is only expressions of the same name that do. But these merely are prejudices, for we cannot unreflectively extrapolate from observable phonological identity to occurrences of the same expression-type. At this juncture our naive linguistic intuition fails us, for the immediate inference from strings being tokens of a given name, with a particular phonological spelling, to their also being tokens of a given *syntactic* expression of that name is not in general valid. The breakdown point is quite clear. The inference will fail just where we have names that look the same; this just is not enough information to judge whether we are encountering occurrences of the same or different expressions (given that the relation of names to expressions that contain them is one-many). The Paderewski puzzle thus forces us to get clear about all this. For this clarity we appeal to linguistic theory; it is the source to which we turn to determine whether speakers have grounds for taking occurrences of a given phonological string to constitute tokens of the same syntactic expression or not. We cannot expect our commonsense observations to bear much weight in deciding about the identity of linguistic expressions; to hold otherwise would be to prejudice our judgment prior to analysis.

Recognizing syntactic identity, and thus distinguishing Assignments, is a capacity that speakers pervasively deploy throughout the back-and-forth of conversations. So, in a model of conversation, we would assume that if a hearer properly understands what a speaker says, he or she will come to represent the sentences the speaker utters as the speaker does. If there is such a formal match in the representations of production and perception, the speaker and hearer will be on the same conversational wavelength, since across their representations the expressions of names will be coindexed, and hence coreferential. In turn, the hearer may use the expressions in question in other sentences that he or she utters, and by doing so a chain of coreference will be carried on. Things, however, do not always go so smoothly. The hearer may misperceive the speaker, even though the conversation has been conducted with all due linguistic diligence. But the bounds of misperception in the case at hand are very limited; indeed, there is only one way that there can be a mismatch: instead of coindexing between the expressions in the speaker's and hearer's representations, there will be at least a pair of expressions that are not coindexed. If there is such a discrepancy, the net result will be that the discourse—that is, set of sentences—represented by the participants will not be the same. Such misperception may occur for various reasons. For instance, it may be because the participants think, unbeknownst to each other, that different people are being talked about, or one may think that one person is being talked about consistently throughout a conversation, while the other thinks there are two (or more). In such cases, the speaker and hearer will be at some level at cross-purposes, since the hearer did not properly understand the speaker, and confusion may ensue.

To take an example, suppose that Max and Sally attend recitals together, and are fans of a particular pianist. Suppose further that a pianist, as far as they know a different one, rents an apartment in their building, and that they find the music emanating from his flat quite pleasing. Now, Max says to Sally: "He is a fine pianist," referring through the use of the pronoun to the pianist they see in concert. Sally, however, thinks that he is referring to the pianist in their building, plausibly enough, since he made the utterance while passing by his door. What Max said, and wanted Sally to understand, was the sentence "He$_1$ is a fine pianist." What Sally heard, however, was not this sentence; if she had, the pronoun in her representation would be coreferential with that in Max's. Rather, in her representation there is a different pronoun; the sentence she believes she heard is "He$_2$ is a fine pianist," which does not linguistically imply coreference vis-à-vis Max's representation. Although it may take some time for it to become apparent to Max and Sally, their subsequent discussion will be at cross-purposes, since Sally has not understood what Max said; she took him to have said something he did not say. Notice that they are at cross-purposes regardless of whether the pianist in the recital hall and the one in the apartment are one and the same—regardless, that is, of whether there is in fact coreference. Either circumstance is consistent with what is said and understood, since noncoindexing is no bar to coreference, even if it implicates, in a given context, noncoreference, and hence, as in the case above, not comprehending what is said.

In the introduction, we remarked that our goal in this book would be to explore two sorts of *de lingua* beliefs, beliefs speakers have about the semantic values of linguistic expressions, and the beliefs they have about their syntactic identity. We can now see how intimately connected these two sorts of beliefs are, for individuating beliefs of the former sort, beliefs of Assignments, depend, for a given speaker, on his or her beliefs of the latter sort, about the individuation of expressions, as this is delimited by their grammatical knowledge. Accordingly, we have traversed the most ground with the question of the identity of Assignments, and for good reason, for how such identity is adjudicated has direct consequences for how our language can be employed, especially in attributing propositional attitudes and, as we will see, in making informative identity statements. But while these cases are of perennial interest for their philosophical contentiousness, and so will be our analytic focus, our account is founded on aspects of our knowledge and beliefs about language that are integral to our everyday usage; indeed, our knowledge and beliefs about referential connections in discourse are employed with virtually every sentence we utter. Thus, the reason it is so important to get the identity criteria for linguistic expressions right is that our knowledge of the referential behavior of expressions depends on it. In order to know under which circumstance two arbitrary expression-tokens corefer, we must first be able to tell expressions apart, as well as recognize when the same expression is repeated, for sometimes it is tokens of distinct expressions that corefer, while at other times it is tokens of the same expression. Which it is is of the utmost importance, for the cases depend on different sources of knowledge; the former is a matter of factual knowledge, the latter of grammatical knowledge. How we comprehend the *anaphoric* connections that pervade our language use is thus antecedent to our comprehension of the philosophically contentious cases. And so too will it be in our presentation; we turn directly, in the next sections of this chapter, to the pertinent linguistic issues about anaphora and coreference. This will fully set the stage to unfold our second theme, the explanatory role played by *de lingua* beliefs, which we will explore through application to cases in the course of the chapters to follow.

1.2 Syntactic Identity and Referential Identity

Syntactic types have tokens, and it is these tokens that occur in the syntactic structures that we use when we make our utterances; what we recognize by the criterion for syntactic identity is when such tokens are tokens of the same type, and when they are not. This is our view, although there is an apparent alternative—identify tokens with the types of which they are unique exemplars. This would be tantamount to saying that there is no type-token distinction at all; each token syntactic occurrence would be distinct from all others. As a general view about syntactic identity—that there is none—this is clearly untenable. For instance, we would be at a loss to define notions as basic as syntactic derivation, for what grounds would we have for distinguishing that which is held constant and that which is changed when one syntactic structure is transformed into another? Nonetheless, there is one area of linguistic inquiry in which this view has been influential, namely, the study of anaphora, and especially in the study of pronominalization. For such theories, the pertinent issues are the conditions under which two occurrences can be coreferential or not; theories have differed in the extent that they hold that one, the other, or both are determined by linguistic rule. Thus, theories may represent just that occurrences of expressions are coreferential, just that they are noncoreferential, both or neither. For instance, some theories have employed a notation similar to ours to represent both coreference and noncoreference—that is, coindexing represents coreference and noncoindexing represents noncoreference.[5] This use of notation, however, should not be confused with ours; indeed what we take to be represented could not be this, for on this latter view, the distinction of syntactic type and token is not available for computing anaphoric relations. Proponents of this view cannot hold that two distinct tokens are coreferential because they are of the same syntactic type.

Prima facie, then, it seems that we are faced with something of a challenge by the sort of theories we have alluded to, for our account of the philosophically interesting cases, as we have outlined it above, centrally depends on there being direct consequences of syntactic identity for referential identity. But just what is it that is up for discussion? Presumably, it is how the divergent views underlie distinct perspectives on what it is for an anaphoric relation to be linguistically determined, for the parameters for understanding what it means to say of expressions that they are coreferential or not are demarcated in very different ways. It is our view that once this discussion takes place, it will be apparent that we obtain a *better* theory of anaphora if we assume that syntactic tokens have types along the lines we have indicated. This section and the next are devoted to this discussion.

So let us look at the genesis of accounts of anaphora that integrate the alternative view. These accounts can be seen as taking root from a pair of observations that are pretty hard for anyone to deny, one about speakers, the other about the languages they use. Thus, speakers use language to express their communicative intentions—they normally wish to say something by the utterances they make—and they can do so by using sentences of the language that contain linguistically open expressions (indexicals and demonstratives) whose values can only be determined relative to context. To cite a well-know example of David Kaplan's, "I am here now" (or "He was there then") makes no particular statement in and of itself, because the who, when, and where are left open by language, but this is not true of any particular utterance of this sentence by a speaker. This fact alone is sufficient to show that a theory of meaning for a natural language must not only contain a semantics, but must be supplemented with a theory of speakers' use of language, if it is to address how sentences may be employed by speakers to make the statements (or proposals, questions, orders, and so on) they intend by their utterances.

A standard way of thinking about this matter is to give a theory of meaning for natural languages in which the semantic predicate is not simply *is true*, but rather *is true, relative to a context and an occasion of use*. Seen this way, given that sentences are grammatical structures as determined by syntactic theory, and contexts are sequences of (at least) persons, places, and times, the semantics will entail that for each s in L, there is a T-sentence of the form ⌜s is true relative to c iff s^*⌝, where s^* is a "disquotation" of s that has a value from c specified for every indexical in s. The semantics for a natural language understood this way would then realize a function $\sigma(s, c) = s^*$, where s^* is closed everywhere s is open, and, presuming that properly using a natural language entails knowing this function, the semantics will then underlie the following use principle: If an utterer U says s in context c, then U utters s under the truth conditions as given by s^*. If U makes a statement with an utterance, U then believes he or she has said what he or she intends to say by uttering a truth.[6]

One of the underlying ideas here—that what is not determined by the grammar has its value specified from context, and conversely, that which is noncontextual is what is determined by virtue of language—is nothing particularly novel. Russell, for instance, expresses very much this view in the following passage from *Human Knowledge* (1948, 92), where he uses the term "egocentric" where we would use "indexical" or "demonstrative":

"This" denotes whatever, at the moment when the word is used, occupies the center of attention. With words which are not egocentric, what is constant is something about the object indicated, but "this" denotes a different object on each occasion of its use: what is constant is not the object denoted, but its relation to the particular use of the word. Whenever the word is used, the person using it is attending to something, and the word indicates this something. When a word is not egocentric, there is no need to distinguish between the different occasions when it is used, but we must make this distinction with egocentric words, since what they indicate is something having a given relation to the particular use of the word.

Turning this perspective into an actual theory is not without its complications. To a certain extent this is because of the delicacy of the balance between the contextual and the grammatical, which is sensitive to the increasing sophistication in our concepts of both context and grammar. For instance, in addition to persons, places, and times, our notions of context may be extended to include such things as events, properties, frequencies, quantities, and so on. These additions may very well lead us to areas of indexicality in language other than the referential, locative, and temporal indexicals. On the other hand, our developing conceptions of syntax may lead to results in the opposite direction, allowing us to see as grammatically determined what otherwise might appear to be indexical.[7] Determining the correct relation between these areas is an empirical matter.

This said, we can nevertheless procure a sense of what is going on relevant to our discussion by considering the pronoun in "He left." This string, while syntactically a sentence, cannot be used as is to make a statement, since it contains an open indexical term. Hence, whatever statement(s) it may be used to make is underdetermined by its linguistic form. In order for this sentence to be used to make a statement, the indexical term must be closed; some value must be fixed for it. This is the role of context—it must provide information sufficient for closure for what is open in sentences. Thus, fixing the value of the pronoun to be Oscar, the sentence "He left" will say, *relative to context,* what the sentence "Oscar left" says. Any adequate theory of meaning for natural language must entail such relations.[8]

Now consider the pronoun in "Oscar kissed his mother." One way to proceed would be to treat the pronoun in this sentence just like the pronoun in "He left," as an open indexical. The pronoun would then be evaluated relative to context; this sentence may be used to state, for instance, that Oscar kissed Max's mother or that Oscar kissed Harry's mother. It may also state that Oscar kissed Oscar's mother, Oscar being a likely candidate for the value of the pronoun, given the salience of the name "Oscar" in the immediate (linguistic) surrounds. But while prior use of a name is one of a variety of means, both linguistic and nonlinguistic, at the disposal of a speaker to bring some individual to prominence in context, it would be improper to speak of this prior use as the *antecedent* of the pronoun, for there is no claim of a privileged linguistic relation to the pronoun. It is not as if there is an ambiguity, between whether the pronoun in "Oscar kissed his mother" is anaphoric, and hence linguistically closed, or indexical, and hence linguistically open. Rather, "Oscar" and "his" are distinct occurrences, with distinct, independent interpretations that may, or may not, coincide. If, in a given context, they do, then they are coreferential, but if they do not, then they are noncoreferential. And aside from issues of relative prominence in context, this is all there is to say about the matter.

To a large extent, essentially this view of coreference entered the linguistics literature with Howard Lasnik's paper "Remarks on Coreference" (1976). Lasnik, however, did not accept this picture as is; he took exception to the implication that the relation between distinct occurrences is wholly unregulated by grammatical constraints. His reasoning was that whatever the virtues of the pragmatic theory just described, it is not fully adequate, because it would allow coreference in "He kissed Oscar's mother" just as it does (properly) in "Oscar kissed his mother." That theory, therefore, had to be supplemented with a *noncoreference* (or disjoint reference) rule that proscribed the pronoun from having the same value as the name in the former sentence. It was central to Lasnik's approach that this be a *grammatical* rule of noncoreference, and that noncoreference stand in opposition to coreference, which is always contextual, never grammatical.[9]

Gareth Evans, in his paper "Pronouns" (1980), made the important observation that assuming a grammatical noncoreference rule undermines Lasnik's theory because it is stated in terms of reference extensionally characterized. Evans developed a number of arguments in support of this observation, perhaps the most devastating being that true identity statements will be ungrammatical. Thus, for "He is Oscar" to be grammatical, the name and the pronoun must be noncoreferential, by grammatical rule; however, if the sentence is to be true, then, to the contrary, they must be coreferential. Additionally, we can observe that negative identity statements, while they will be grammatical by the rule, will be trivial. Since noncoreference would be determined by grammar, in "He isn't Oscar" the name and the pronoun would be noncoreferential by linguistic rule, so that what the sentence asserts would be part of its meaning as a matter of language.

The idea that there is a grammatical noncoreference rule faces other problems as well. One arises with cases like the following, developing an observation of James Higginbotham's. Suppose that Max sees a man leaving the room but cannot see his face. Max asks the woman next to him who that person is, and she replies "He put on Oscar's coat; you figure it out." Here the speaker tries to implicate that the person who left is Oscar, based on the tacit assumption that people put on their own coats. But if the grammar required that the name and the pronoun not corefer, then no such implication could follow.

Yet another problem is located with what is known as the "masked ball" circumstance. An attendee at a masked ball hears someone claim that Oscar is crazy. The attendee reports this by uttering "He thinks Oscar is crazy." It turns out, upon unmasking, that the person who claimed Oscar was crazy was Oscar himself. Nevertheless, what the attendee said was true, clearly not false, and certainly not ungrammatical, which it would be if the grammar required that "he" and "Oscar" be noncoreferential on this (and any other) occasion of use of this sentence.

These problems, and others like them, show clearly that there cannot be a grammatical noncoreference rule; this is simply too strong a requirement. But what alternatives are there? One that suggests itself is to maintain that speakers, in uttering certain sentences with pronouns on given occasions, merely *intend* that the pronouns are noncoreferential with some other expression(s). This shifts the locus of the linguistic regulation of noncoreference from grammar to speakers' intentions. What is grammatically determined now is that speakers, in their use of sentences containing specified structural configurations, will intend that there is noncoreference. A speaker who utters the sentence "He is Oscar" would now be taken only to utter this sentence with the intention that "he" and "Oscar" do not corefer. Taken this way, coreference is not precluded; only precluded is that coreference comports with the speaker's intentions in uttering that sentence.[10]

Is this an advance? We think not. While it would certainly no longer be the case that "He is Oscar" is ungrammatical, as Evans observes, by sincerely uttering an identity statement, a speaker's intention is just that there *is* coreference of the phrases flanking the copula. This is a consequence of the speaker intending that his statement be true. In the circumstance with Oscar's coat, the speaker knows and intends that the pronoun and the name corefer; what he wants is for his interlocutor to figure this out on his own. Or consider a weaker case, a version of the masked ball in which the speaker has no knowledge of, or any particular beliefs about, who is behind the mask, and so would not intend to be taken as committal one way or the other regarding coreference—on unmasking, the speaker would be no more surprised to learn that behind the mask is Oscar as not. Clearly, for none of these cases would it be proper to describe the speaker as intending *non*coreference. And so it does not appear that we have made much progress; essentially the same problems have resurfaced, transposed to an intentional milieu.

One might try to refine the view under consideration by imposing finer distinctions among a speaker's intentions. So, suppose we distinguish a speaker's *primary* intention of noncoreference, which is determined by grammar as described, from his *secondary* intention, which is not constrained in this manner. Then, a speaker who uses a sentence such as "He kissed Oscar's mother" will primarily intend noncoreference, by virtue of the form of this sentence, but this may be suspended; if so, then a secondary intention may be adopted. The account of the cases at hand would now go something like the following. Since the speaker does not want to communicate with respect to his primary intention, so long as the context of utterance supplies sufficient information to the hearer to avoid confusion, the speaker can make his utterance in a way that bypasses the primary intention; in some of these contexts the speaker will do so in favor of the secondary intention (e.g., the case of Oscar's coat), but not in all (e.g., the masked ball).

Perhaps.[11] But it seems to us that at this point there is a much cleaner way to get at the proper results. This would be to simply sweep away altogether the claim that there is a grammatically based noncoreference condition, either extensional or intentional. Then the grammar would not be determinative of noncoreference; there would be nothing *grammatical* that would commit a speaker of "He kissed Oscar's mother" to noncoreference, even intentionally. Of course, this may be just the way he wants his utterance to be understood, although the speaker's communicative intentions may be otherwise; he may rather wish his utterance to be understood with coreference, or even remain noncommittal as to which it is. The grammar would allow this too; in leaving it open whether there is noncoreference, obviously coreference becomes an option. Which it is, on any given occasion of use, would be happenstance, as far as the grammar is concerned; which way it goes in any given case will depend on the speaker's intentions with respect to the context of utterance. Anaphoric uses of pronouns would now only be so-called; use of "Oscar kissed his mother" this way but not "He kissed Oscar's mother" would be but a tendency, not something determined by grammatical rule. Grammatical structure may contribute to this tendency, for instance in facilitating implicatures, but in an essential way how speakers seek to make references and cross-references through their linguistic acts will be independent of the grammatical structure of the sentences they use.

This, it seems to us, is exactly the right thing to say about coreference and noncoreference for expressions that are distinct *by virtue of being tokens of distinct types*. Not everyone agrees about this, however. Most notably, Evans (1980) argues that something more needs to be said about anaphora; to say that coreference is just a tendency is too weak. He suggests that individual tokens can be externally "chained" or "linked" or "roped" together, indicating that they are in a referential dependency; that the distributional possibilities of such connections can be syntactically fixed has been most strongly emphasized by Higginbotham (1983, 1985).[12] But there is good reason to doubt this emendation. In "2 + 2 = 4," the numerals on either side of the addition sign are coreferential—a fact about the language of arithmetic. But just think of the absurdity of drawing a line or arrow between the occurrences of "2" to indicate that they refer to the same number. (Or the equal absurdity that they are coreferential because of a saliency effect.) Nevertheless, there is something to what Evans says in urging us to take seriously that there is a distinction to be drawn between what is anaphoric and what is not—in other words, that in some way there is a grammatically grounded notion of coreference. The clue to seeing this is to think of the right thing to say about "2 + 2 = 4"—not that there is external chaining mechanism, but that there is coreference to the number 2 just because there are two tokens of the numeral "2." Full stop. But this is not only the right thing to say for the language of arithmetic; it is also the right thing to say for the languages we know and use in our everyday lives. It is not something peculiar about arithmetic, but is just as true of natural languages; here too, there are tokens of expression-types. But then there is a grammatical notion of coreference, for it is *inherent* in what it means to be tokens of a syntactic type that all the tokens have the same value; all tokens of the same type necessarily corefer (although plainly there is no such grammatical stricture for tokens of different types). Where Evans goes astray is in hewing to the orthodoxy described above, namely, that there are no syntactic expression-types. But it is this dogma that we must counter if we are to perceive how syntactic structure grammatically determines anaphoric relations. Our recommendation is to do just this.

Our view is the following: coreference may be grammatically determined, but not noncoreference, and this reflects the underlying structure of syntactic expressions. It is this structure that is represented by our notation, coindexing indicating that there are tokens of the same expression, noncoindexing, of different expressions. So, we distinguish (1):

(1) Oscar$_1$ kissed his$_1$ mother.

from (2):

(2) He$_1$ kissed Oscar$_2$'s mother.

where the use of numerals provides a clear formal means of distinguishing occurrences of the same index from those of others, and hence tokens of the same expressions, as opposed to tokens of different ones. From this alone we can conclude that "[Oscar]" and the pronoun in (1) have the same reference. (Note that there is no particular conceptual problem with grammar determining coreference through identity; this is presumably the effect of the morpheme "self" in reflexive constructions, as in "Oscar saw himself.") No such conclusion as this follows for (2), however. Noncoindexing does not *mean* noncoreference; in fact it means nothing as far as reference is concerned.[13] It only means that there are tokens of distinct syntactic types, just as coindexing means just that there are tokens of the same type. Beliefs speakers have about the form of language, about whether expression tokens are of the same type, are in this way directly reflected in their semantic beliefs about coreference and noncoreference. And these beliefs will have a direct effect on how speakers can realize their communicative goals via the anaphoric use of language.

In the remainder of this chapter we are going to elucidate this view. Much of the discussion will be somewhat technical in nature, especially where it touches on underlying notions of syntactic structure and semantic interpretation. Readers who are particularly interested in the implications of our view for a theory of anaphora per se are urged to read on. But readers who have come to this juncture and are impatient to turn to how all this plays out in the philosophically interesting cases of *de dicto* belief attributions may safely move on to the subsequent chapters. The material here may be returned to later without loss of continuity.

1.3 Anaphora, Context, and Referential Intentions

By way of formally conceptualizing our view, we can think of the derivation of syntactic structures in the following way. Assume that the grammar generates an underlying set of *index trees,* ordered graphs whose nodes are occurrences of indices, represented by numerals. Index trees are *realized* relative to a morphosyntactic interpretation, specifying the categorial and word structure of the index tree, such that coindexed nodes will receive the same interpretation, noncoindexed nodes different interpretations. We call an index tree interpreted in this way a *phrase-marker*.[14] The set of *expressions* of a language is then to be identified with the set of realizations of the constituents of index trees of the language; an expression, in this sense, is a morphosyntactic interpretation of an index occurring in a phrase-marker. We write the expression "$[_{NP}$ Oscar$]_1$" to indicate the interpretation of the index "1" as a noun phrase with the terminal element "Oscar." In this regard, we can take indices as a formal features of syntactic categories, as we do with category labels.

On this conception, a phrase-marker will encode a sameness/difference array, represented by a pattern of indexical occurrences, such that coindexing will indicate occurrences of the same expression-type. In adjudicating such identity, certain sorts of shape transformations are to be tolerated. For instance, just as we say that there are two occurrences of the same numeral in "2 + 2 = 4," even though they are in different typefaces, variation in pronunciation (or spelling) from speaker to speaker does not undermine our sense that they use the same expression. (More on this in chapter 2.) We have also tolerated another sort of transformation, allowing that a given expression-type may have both pronominal and nonpronominal tokens; "[$_{NP}$ Oscar]$_1$," has its pronominal counterpart "[$_{NP}$ he]$_1$," so that "Oscar loves Sally because he is a good son" is of the same order as "Oscar loves Sally because Oscar is a good son."[15] Although to a large extent which sort of token it is will be of little matter to our concerns—just that they are tokens of a type, as indicated by invariance of index, will meet our needs—which form an expression takes will very much matter when figuring how tokens of an expression can be distributed in a syntactic structure. This is the import of *Binding Theory*, which can be couched as a set of constraints on the possible arrays of indices, and thus the possible arrays of expression-types, that can be manifest in phrase-markers. Standard formulations of Binding Theory, originating in the work of Chomsky (1981, 1986), include the following three principles:[16]

Binding Theory
(A) Reflexive pronouns are locally bound.
(B) Personal pronouns are locally free.
(C) All other NPs (including names) are globally free.

That we can have two tokens of an expression, one of them pronominal, in "Oscar saw his mother," but not in "He saw Oscar's mother," is a consequence of Binding Theory; while by virtue of Principle B, coindexing is permitted for the former

(1) Oscar$_1$ kissed his$_1$ mother.

it is proscribed for the latter by Principle C. What is thus allowed is only (2):

(2) He$_1$ kissed Oscar$_2$'s mother.

What these arrays of indexing *mean*, with respect to any morphosyntactic interpretation that allows for pronominal tokens—that is, those that respect Binding Theory—is either that there are tokens of a single expression, as in (1), or that there are tokens of distinct expressions, as in (2).[17]

With respect to a universe of objects $\mathcal{U}$, let $\mathcal{D}$ be a family of discourses, such that each $D \in \mathcal{D}$ is a triple $<S, I, C>$, where S is an (ordered) set of sentences, I the set of indices that show in S, and C a subset of $\mathcal{U}$, specified under an assignment g mapping from I to C. (Note that we let the indices stand in for expressions on this formalization.) Then, for any $D, D' \in \mathcal{D}$, differing in at most the indices that show in $S \in D$ and $S' \in D'$, D is *discourse-equivalent* to D' iff there is a bijection h from $I \in D$ to $I' \in D'$ such that whenever φ, φ' are corresponding sentences of S and S' respectively, the index i occurs in a given (syntactic) location of φ iff $h(i)$ occurs in that location in φ'.

From these definitions, a couple of things follow immediately: (1) An indexical distribution holds with respect to a discourse, conceived of as a set of sentences. Thus, the relation between coindexed expressions when they occur in a single sentence is the same as when they occur in different sentences of a discourse, vis-à-vis syntactic identity. (2) Given the definition of discourse equivalence as a bijection that respects syntactic position, discourses that differ only in the "numerical values" of the indices are equivalent. Thus, it is syntactically immaterial which numerals are employed. What matters syntactically is only the pattern of the indices in the discourse, the array of same and difference so represented, as this represents whether we have occurrences of the same expressions or not. Thus, the string "Oscar kissed his mother" is structurally ambiguous, but only between two conditions: coindexing and noncoindexing. To take it as more ambiguous than this, even infinitely ambiguous, would be to confuse a superfluous numerical property with the linguistic distinctions the notation is being used to represent.[18]

We should perhaps make an interjection here in order to stress that the points we are making about syntactic-expression identity reflect properties of general linguistic theory, and are integral to the definition of the notion of grammar itself. As such, they are *not* a matter of any particular implementation; rather, they are aspects of *any* conceptualization of linguistic theory, independently of descriptive framework, or method or mode of representation. For sure, we have a favored notation, one, as we have argued, that is optimized to the representational demands placed on it, and any other notation would equally well have to meet these demands (and so would be at least functionally equivalent). But our point is in no way narrowly notational; the existence of the distinctions we have drawn in no way depends on our preferred way of expressing the encoding of syntactic identity.

Returning to the main thread, we refer to phrase-markers that are subject to semantic interpretation as "logical forms." *LF* designates the set of such structures. With respect to the *LF* of a discourse *D*, the value assigned to any expression bearing an occurrence of index *i* will be $c(i)$, the *ith*-individual of the context *C*. If we specify contextual points as pairings of indices and values under this relation, it follows that all coindexed expressions in a discourse will "pick out" the same contextual point, necessarily, while noncoindexed expressions will always pick out different points, although the values associated with the points may be the same.[19] A simple relation thus links coindexing to coreference: if expressions are coindexed, then they are coreferential (if they are referential at all).[20] Coindexing *entails* coreference.

In the sense that we have just described, it is appropriate to speak of "grammatically determined coreference," linguistically represented by coindexing, albeit derivatively, given the representational role played by indices. (Coindexing could not directly represent coreference, because this is not a formal property of phrase-structure as such.) Moreover, we can speak of the reading so represented as an *anaphoric reading,* as opposed to a contextual reading of the sort associated with indexicals; from this standpoint, anaphoric pronouns are *closed* expressions, in the sense of not being dependent on context, as indexicals are. Anaphora seen this way is an internal relation of expressions, and not, as we remarked above, something externally marked by roping or chaining expressions together. To reiterate, the fundamental notion in which indices are pressed into service is to represent the syntactic identity of expressions. Any anaphoric relation in which coindexed expressions stand flows from this relation. Technically speaking, there is no theory of anaphora per se; rather there is a theory that deals in sameness or difference of expressions, and their attendant interpretations. "Anaphora" is a term of art.[21]

Now, in our view, by virtue of the coindexing in (1),

(1) Oscar$_1$ kissed his$_1$ mother.

it is part of that sentence's linguistic meaning that the name-expression and the pronoun corefer, and this will be so for *any* utterance of that sentence. Speakers who use a sentence with coindexing as in (1) are committed to coreference simply by virtue of the form of the sentence. By using a sentence with coindexing, speakers cannot mean to express anything but that the coindexed expressions corefer. This is not at the discretion of the speakers. Speakers who use a sentence such as (1), therefore, would intend by their utterance to make a statement in which the name and the pronoun corefer. There is no other option; coreference is forced by grammar. What other intention could comport with their utterance? Speakers who utter a sentence containing coindexing would therefore be making an utterance that would, *ipso facto,* comport with their communicative intentions.

It might be reckoned at this point that we could get by with a position weaker than this, that when speakers use a sentence with multiple occurrences of an expression, they *only* intend that they corefer; they are not compelled by grammar to that usage. Insofar as coindexing would have any import with respect to what speakers mean by their utterance, it would be just that the speakers stand in this particular intentional state toward the indicated expressions. On this view, speakers who intend to state that Oscar kissed Oscar's mother by uttering (1) are also in an intentional state with regard to relations among components of that sentence; they intend coreference between the name and the pronoun. Thus, not only would the language be compositional, but in a sense so would be our communicative intentions in using that language; there would be constituent intentions of the speakers' intention to make a statement by uttering a sentence. This sense of intended coreference would be distinct from that described in the previous paragraph, because it would not preclude that (1), for instance, could be grammatical and true if the name and the pronoun are noncoreferential.

There seems to us good reason to doubt this picture. Suppose speakers intend to communicate something, and accordingly select a sentence they sincerely believe that, when uttered, will express what they intend. For example, suppose they wish to inform you that you should move your leg, by way of a warning against an impending accident. They might say any of the following:

You should move your leg.

Run!

Come over here!

Any of these might equally well fulfill the speakers' communicative intention; the choice between them, and presumably scores of others, will result from many factors, including what the speakers wish to assert or implicate. Suppose the speakers choose the first sentence; by doing so they utter a sentence in which there is coreference, between "you" and "your." Does the presence of this property follow from the speakers' communicative intention to issue a warning? Clearly not, since a number of other sentences might have been chosen to express the same communicative intention in which coreference does not figure. Granting that the presence of coreference does not follow from the speakers' communicative intention, is it not still at least possible to say that, given their communicative intention, the speakers choose a sentence each of whose properties is intended? That is, given that they may choose from a variety of expressive tools, isn't it true that each property of the tool chosen is one that is intended?

Consider an analogy. Suppose we tell someone to utter the word "cat," and suppose that person complies. It seems correct to say of that person that he or she intended to utter the word "cat." Part of that performance is the velar closure associated with the initial stop. Did the speaker intend velar closure? Presumably not. True, one can intend to close one's velum, and saying the word "cat" is one way to carry that intention through. But, unless one knows that velar closure is associated with the initial stop of "cat," one cannot rightly be said to have intended velar closure when uttering the word "cat." The point is that there are limitations on the extent to which one's intentions distribute down to the tools one uses to express them. By firing a revolver, Max can carry out his intention to kill Oscar, but it is immaterial to his intention that the cylinder moved, or that the hammer cocked and then struck the bullet, and so on. The only relation the revolver has to Max's intention to murder Oscar is that it is the tool whereby he could transform his intentions into actions, but Max does not stand in any particular intentional relation to the way the tool *functions* so as to carry out his general homicidal intentions. One's intentions to act do not normally distribute down to the workings of the tools by which the intentions are transformed into actions. They simply work however they work, in terms of whatever "rules" govern their functioning. So too, we think, with language. If one intends to use a sentence to express some particular communicative intention, it does not follow that each property of the sentence chosen is intended by the speaker (except in the trivial sense that it follows from the requirements of grammar). Can speakers, then, intend coreference? Of course. One can, for example, comply with the instruction to utter a sentence in which there is coreference by uttering a sentence in which there is coreference. But from this it does not follow that a speaker making a "normal" utterance of "You should move your leg" in a conversation intends coreference (in the nontrivial sense) any more than a speaker intends velar closure in making a "normal" utterance of "cat."

Anaphoric coreference is determined by grammar, as a matter of linguistic rule. Speakers do not use a sentence with coindexing *because* they intend coreference, but only because such a sentence allows them to state what they want to state. Speakers' intentions do not enter into determining such coreference; intentions only enter in to the extent that stating *s* satisfies *U*'s communicative intentions (in the case above, to issue a particular warning). What fact about speakers' use of sentences with anaphoric pronouns is being missed by this nonintentional account? It obviously cannot be that speakers use such sentences because they intend coreference, because this would only beg the question. What reason is there to assume that speakers intend coreference (or noncoreference) in any sense other than the trivial sense that arises from their using sentences in accordance with the properties the grammar assigns to them?

If coindexing determines coreference, then what does noncoindexing signify, if it is neither noncoreference nor intended noncoreference as we have already argued? It is rather the absence of grammatically determined coreference—that is, where there is no coindexing, there is no grammatical indication of coreference. What the grammar says is nothing. This leaves open, as far as the grammar is concerned, whether there is coreference or noncoreference in a sentence with the indexing in (3):

(3) He$_1$ thinks Oscar$_2$ is crazy.

Speakers, however, want to say *something* by their use of language; *they* do not normally leave referential options open. Speakers normally know to what they wish to refer, and accordingly will use sentences that they believe allow for the expression of their communicative intentions. By far the most common circumstance in which speakers might choose to use a sentence in which there are noncoindexed expressions is one in which fulfillment of their communicative intentions demands that they not be taken as coreferential; so much so, that this might be taken as the standing assumption. But it is not a requirement. Such sentences can be used to express coreference, if there is good reason to do so; a speaker will not use a sentence containing noncoindexed expressions referring to the same person unless it is to the point to do so. Thus, if a sentence with noncoindexed expressions is stated by the speaker with just its normal implicatures, it will be taken that there is noncoreference.

Suppose *A* walks up to *B* and utters out of the blue "He admires Oscar." In the sentence *A* has used to make this utterance, the subject and object expressions will not be coindexed (indeed, must not be, as per Binding Theory). With the utterance, *A* will have implicated that the name and the pronoun do not corefer. How do we know this is an implicature? Suppose that *A* continues on by uttering "In fact, he is Oscar, that arrogant SOB." *A* is not taken as having said anything contradictory, only as canceling the implicature that the name and pronoun do not corefer. (Perhaps the most common "out of the blue" cases arise when linguists discuss the anaphoric status of sentences like (3).) Now suppose that Max is not Oscar, and *A* walks up to *B* who is standing next to Max, points at Max and utters "He admires Oscar." Through the ostension, the pronoun becomes publicly grounded, its reference unmistakably known to all. This utterance now *entails* noncoreference.[22] If *A* had continued as before, it would at least have been assumed that *A* had spoken falsely, since entailments cannot be canceled in the manner of implicatures. This strengthening to an entailment also holds for the second sentence in (4) (uttered in the same context as the first sentence):

(4)   Max$_1$ left. He$_1$ admires Oscar$_2$.

Here coreference of the pronoun and the NP "Max" is grammatically determined. Since anaphora is a matter of grammar, the pronoun refers to Max and not Oscar, and this is just as much publicly grounded as it would be if the pronoun were accompanied by a demonstration as above.

The noncoreference implicature, observe, is an implicature that appears to have characteristics of both conventional and conversational implicature. On the one hand, it falls in with conventional implicature in its relation to grammatical structure. On the other hand, it can be canceled like a conversational implicature. There are various ways it can be canceled; we observed one above. Another arises from the fact that speakers do not always know who the person they are speaking of is. In such situations, such as one version of the masked ball, it comports with their communicative intentions to precisely leave coreference or noncoreference as an open matter. But while (3), uttered in this situation, will be true if the person behind the mask is Oscar, so that the pronoun and the name corefer, it remains the case that the speaker has declined to make a statement in which coreference is part of the assertion made— that is, by utterance of "Oscar thinks he is crazy." He has declined precisely because he is not in an intentional state appropriate to support the use of a sentence in which coreference is grammatically determined. For instance, he may have not been sufficiently certain it was Oscar declaiming on his mental health, or he may have had no beliefs whatsoever that it was Oscar or, for that matter, any other person. Because of this lack of knowledge, the normal implicature of noncoreference will not arise (and, indeed, if he lacks this knowledge, the speaker, while making a statement, since he does successfully refer by his use of the pronoun in (3), will not know what statement he makes at the moment of utterance). It may turn out, however, that the speaker of (3) sincerely and firmly believed that the masked person was not Oscar. He would then speak in a way that would give rise to the normal implicature of noncoreference. While in these circumstances the speaker's utterance of (3) is grammatically impeccable and indeed true, it is nevertheless of a different status than an utterance made by a speaker who wishes to leave open of whom he speaks, since the implicature has turned out to be false, based as it is on mistaken beliefs. In this case, there is a sense in which we can regard coreference as "accidental" on the part of the speaker; he did not "mean" to implicate this, but yet it is so. On the other hand, where the speaker has no relevant beliefs regarding the identity of the masked person, coreference would not be accidental, because there is no failing implicature.

Now what of the case of Oscar's coat? Here, the speaker's goal by uttering "He put on Oscar's coat; you figure it out" is to give the first premise of an inference that will lead to "That person was Oscar" as the answer to the question "Who was that person?" If the speaker had made the utterance so that it carried the normal implicature of noncoreference, then, in conjunction with the (unsaid) premise that people put on their own coats, it would lead only to the conclusion that that person was *not* Oscar, and that would only obliquely, and unsatisfactorily, answer the questioner. This would lead the hearer to assume that the normal implicature was not in place, and that the speaker wished to implicate that there is coreference, which would be grammatically consistent with the sentence uttered. This would lead to the proper conclusion. Notice that the speaker would not be well served in his communicative intentions if he had uttered "Oscar put on his (own) coat; you figure it out," in which the pronoun can be anaphoric (i.e., coindexed with the name), since then what he wishes to be inferred would follow trivially, leaving the hearer to wonder why he did not simply give a direct answer to the question.

Implicature cancellation is also at play in (5), an example from Gareth Evans:

(5) If everyone admires Oscar, then he admires Oscar.

It is a consequence of the antecedent clause that the pronoun "he" can refer to anybody; from the antecedent it follows that no one can be excluded from those who admire Oscar. The noncoreference implicature must therefore be canceled in the consequent, since it would say that there is someone who could not be referred to, namely Oscar. Example (6), on the other hand, appears to contrast with (5), in that the noncoreference implicature is in effect, short of an overt demonstration of Oscar by the speaker:

(6) If Max admires Oscar, then he admires Oscar.

But suppose that the speaker and hearer share the tacit premise that Max is the pickiest person there is; if he admires someone, then everyone does. Then as with (5) the noncoreference implicature will be canceled, since all (relevant) values must be available as values of the pronoun.

What we see then is that there are two options for the use of sentences with coreference: either use a sentence in which it is grammatically determined, or cancel implicatures of a sentence in which it is not so determined. The sentences that are used in these ways are formally distinct; with the former it is sentences with coindexing that are used, with the latter, it is sentences without. In sentences without coindexing, unless it is canceled, the noncoreference implicature will stand in the presence of noncoindexing, by far the most common circumstance. A noncoreference implicature arises because the speaker uses a sentence with noncoindexing; if it were coreference that comported with his communicative intentions, then he would have used a sentence in which coreference is grammatically indicated by coindexing. A hearer will reason that since the speaker did not choose to use a sentence in which anaphora is expressed (that is, with coindexing), then it ought to be noncoreference that comports with his communicative intentions, given that the speaker knows of whom he speaks.[23]

Underlying the current discussion is an implicit *ceteris paribus* clause; we assumed that the linguistic context was otherwise neutral with respect to the options, and that of these options, coreference in the face of noncoindexing is possible only if there is cancellation of an implicature. Linguistic context is not always so neutral, however, and can force the issue. The most important case where it does is identity statements, where the meaning of the verb makes a difference. Thus, given the meaning of "be," true identity statements—for example, "Cicero is Tully"—entail that the expressions flanking "be" corefer. This entailment supersedes any implicature of noncoreference, since, again, implicatures, but not entailments, can be canceled. Coreference in this case is the norm.

Now, if a speaker believes that "Cicero" and "Tully" are linguistically distinct names, then when they occur syntactically, their expressions will be distinct. From this alone it follows that "Cicero is Tully" must be of the form ⌜$a = b$⌝—that is, "Cicero$_1$ is Tully$_2$," (since no token of one expression can be coindexed with tokens of a distinct expression). But nothing more follows; in particular, nothing follows grammatically—*by virtue of what is represented by the indexing*—about whether these expressions corefer or not, although only if they do will "Cicero is Tully" be true, again given the meaning of "be." Something more does follow, however, for identity statements in which there are occurrences not of distinct expressions, but of the same one, those of the form ⌜$a = a$⌝—that is, "Cicero$_1$ is Cicero$_1$." Now identity of reference does follow by virtue of what is represented by the indices, for it is a grammatical requirement that coindexed expressions be coreferential. Coreference is part of the meaning of this sentence as a matter of linguistic rule, independently of the contribution of "be." In this sense, "Cicero is Cicero" analytically expresses a trivial self-identity, unlike "Cicero is Tully."

As has long been recognized, it is only identity statements of this latter form—that is, those of the form ⌜$a = b$⌝—that can be used informatively so as to relieve ignorance; for this purpose, those of the form ⌜$a = a$⌝ are of no practical use.[24] Nevertheless, such sentences are not altogether useless. They come in handy for example when one wants to illustrate an instance of the law of self-identity. So, consider the logic teacher who says (7):

(7) If everyone is himself, then Oscar is Oscar.

as a way of rendering of (8):

(8) $\forall x \, (x = x) \rightarrow a = a$

Here, "Oscar is Oscar" is being used as an *exemplar*; what matters is that it is a sentence of a certain form, where the repetition of "Oscar" in (7) tracks the repetition of *a* in (8).[25] To illustrate the law of self-identity is a typical use of such identity statements. (even in contexts in which it is appropriate to make the example with respect to a particular person), a use that falls under a more general sort of use of language that takes advantage of grammatical resources to "speak" logic, mathematics, or some other theoretical discourse. It is the use we make of language when we say, in English, "Two plus two equals two times two," or "Two is the largest prime factor of two," where there are multiple tokens of the numeral "two," each necessarily with the same reference. It is also the use we make as linguists when we report our judgment about anaphora in the sentence "Oscar saw his mother" by saying that it means that Oscar saw Oscar's mother, where we replace a pronominal token with a nonpronominal token of the same expression. So, if "Oscar" and "his" are coindexed, so too are the occurrences of "Oscar" in the report. In this formal way of talking, the distribution of expression-tokens need not be constrained by Binding Theory.[26] So just as we can say "If every number is greater than two, then two is greater than two," we can also say "If everyone admires Oscar, then Oscar admires Oscar." And just as we can say "Two equals two," so too can we say "Cicero is Cicero."

Thus, viewed solely from the perspective of the relation of syntactic expression-types and expression-tokens, there are two, and only two, types of identity statements, those of the form ⌜$a = a$⌝, and those of the form ⌜$a = b$⌝. This distinction, keep in mind, is not just that between the strings "Cicero is Cicero" and "Cicero is Tully." Because it is possible not only to have distinct expressions of different names, but also distinct expressions of the same name, it can be that "Cicero is Cicero" is of the latter form. Our notation makes this clear; alongside "Cicero$_1$ is Cicero$_1$," and "Cicero$_1$ is Tully$_2$," we also have "Cicero$_1$ is Cicero$_2$," all of which are true in the same material conditions (since, as a matter of fact, Cicero *is* Tully), although each is associated with quite distinct conditions of use. The uses that can be made of the last sort of identity statement will be of considerable interest to us in what follows, especially when we turn in detail, in chapters 3 and 4, to elaborating the aforementioned Paderewski puzzle. For now, however, we only note their existence, given the formal syntactic relation of names and expressions.

In the chapters to follow, how we understand coreference will play a pivotal role, and so we have spent considerable effort here to make clear how we understand this notion. Our emphasis has been to distinguish coreference as determined by the grammar, from that which is not, and we have seen that speakers' dispositions toward the use of one are quite different than toward the other. We have traced the distinction in question back to a formal linguistic distinction, to whether syntactic expression-tokens are of the same type or not, and we have introduced a notation to indicate which it is—coindexed tokens are of the same type, but noncoindexed expressions are not. But bear this in mind: coindexing does not represent coreference, any more than noncoindexing represents noncoreference. What they represent are syntactic properties, not semantic ones. Which syntactic property it is, however, does have a direct semantic consequence. If there is coindexing, then the *only* interpretation available is identity of reference; language is such that it allows no latitude here. But if there is not coindexing, then an additional interpretation is possible, in which reference is distinct. This, as we have seen, is the favored option, although not obligatory, because coreference is possible in some contextual circumstances, and at least in one, identity statements, required. Which interpretation will prevail, however, is a matter left open by the grammar; with respect to the identity structure of expressions alone it cannot be determined which it will be. That such matters are open in this case, but closed in the former, will play a key role in the applications of our theory, to which we now turn.

Notes

1. Looking ahead, this last observation will be central. It is what we will mean when we say that the content of our linguistic beliefs can be part of the content of what we say by our utterances. Our main thesis, that Assignments may be constituents of the logical forms of attributions, and that, because of this, they may play an explanatory role, incorporates this observation; see chapter 2.

2. Continuing the anticipation of note 1, of the two manners of difference of Assignments, it is the second that is of primary interest, for given that "[Cicero]"

and "[Tully]" are coreferential, the question immediately arises under what circumstances one can be substituted for the other. The fact is that the belief that Cicero was a senator and the belief that Tully was a senator are distinguishable. We say that a person may hold one but not the other. To what difference in the content of these beliefs can we impute this? Our diagnosis, at least for the central cases, stems from our main thesis, that Assignments, usually part of the background of language use, can come to the fore when we attribute beliefs. In the context of such attributions, we can also attribute the Assignments under which the beliefs are held; to use a familiar terminology, Assignments may become part of the propositional content of a sentence. But now our point is simply this: to say that someone holds a belief under the "[Cicero]"-Assignment is not to say that they hold a belief under the distinct "[Tully]"-Assignment. See the discussion in chapter 2.

3. This remark pertains just to expressions containing names, and not, for instance, to those containing pronouns.

4. We leave aside here cases in which conventions of scope override orthographic convention; we have distinct variables in "$P(x) \wedge \exists x\ Q(x)$," even though the same letter is employed.

5. For an explicit statement, see Chomsky and Lasnik 1995, 96.

6. We give a strong form of the use principle in the text, but since, for instance, it may be appropriate to speak irrelevantly or falsely in the service of giving rise to conversational implicature, the principle would need to be weakened, so as to allow utterers to "make as if to say." See Grice 1989 and Neale 1992 for discussion of this point.

7. For an example, see Stanley 2000.

8. The semantics could entail this in a number of ways. For instance, there could be an objectual fixation of reference, giving some sort of Russellian propositions; see Kaplan 1989. An alternative would be a substitutional approach, in which an expression that names the referent metalinguistically replaces the pronoun; see Evans 1977.

9. Technically, the usual way of stating the rule is that an expression that contains a name (that is, one that is neither a personal nor a reflexive pronoun) cannot be coreferential with any NPs that c-command it; cf. Principle C of Binding Theory below. Also, bear in mind that the comments in the text only apply to personal pronouns, and not to reflexive pronouns, for which coreference is (at least usually) grammatically determined.

10. Lasnik (1976, note 5) contemplates making an emendation along these lines, so that there is a rule of intended noncoreference. It is not clear, however, that the resulting rule would any longer be a purely grammatical one; intention is a notion neither of syntax nor of semantics. Once intentions are brought into the picture we leave the domain of grammar per se, and enter that of a theory of use.

11. One problem with the proposal is that the implicature that the speaker primarily intends noncoreference would appear to be conventional. But standardly these are not subject to cancellation.

12. Higginbotham (1983, 1985) does this by giving analogues of Binding Theory (see below) to govern the restrictions on referential links. For critical discussion, see Fiengo and May 1994, chaps. 1 and 2.

13. A particularly clear example of this mistake is found in Chomsky and Lasnik 1995, 96; they state that "if the index of α is distinct from the index of β, then α and β are noncoreferential."

14. Our thought here harkens back to ideas expressed by Chomsky in *Aspects of the Theory of Syntax* (especially chap. 3), where the phrase-structure grammar specifies a class of possible structural realizations of "is a" relations, which are then syntactically specified by satisfying the selectional restrictions associated with items in the lexicon.

15. Among the variances permitted are the alternations in point of view inherent in the use of pronouns of different persons; so long as the index remains constant, we can view first-, second-, and third-person pronouns as occurrences of the same expression (in a discourse). In *Indices and Identity*, we employ this observation in unraveling the "phone-booth" puzzle due to Mark Richard (1983) in ways that presage portions of the discussion in the present volume; see Fiengo and May 1994, sec 1.2. The general effect we are alluding to here is dubbed "vehicle change" in *Indices and Identity*.

16. An expression is *locally bound* iff within the minimal clause or noun phrase dominating it, there is some coindexed c-commanding expression; it is *locally free* iff it is not locally bound. It is *globally free* iff it is not c-commanded by a coindexed phrase is any dominating category. We purposely leave vague the notion "anaphorically local domain," glossing it for the purposes at hand as the minimal dominating noun phrase or clause. The precise formulation of such domains has been widely discussed in the literature. For some representative discussion, see the contributions in Koster and Reuland 1991.

17. As far as we can see, all approaches to Binding Theory can be cast in the form of a theory that regulates the distribution of expressions, although couched in our terms there is an issue whether it is to be cast as fixing the well-formedness of arrays of indexical occurrences directly over the index trees themselves, or as part of the morphosyntactic realization of the trees. Most current thinking would place it in the latter role, given that the binding rules are stated in terms of morphological and syntactic predicates. For our current purposes, however, we allow ourselves the presumption that all relevant issues of formalization of Binding Theory have been resolved, because all cases we will consider will be uncontroversially consistent with all versions of Binding Theory of which we are aware.

18. Essentially the same point has been emphasized by Davidson (1974, 147, 154) in discussing aspects of decision theory:

> When we represent the facts of preference, utility and subjective probability by assigning numbers, only some of the properties of numbers are used to capture the empirically justified pattern. Other properties of the numbers used may therefore be chosen arbitrarily. . . . If there is an indeterminacy, it is because when all the evidence is in, alternative ways of stating the facts remain open. An analogy from decision theory has

already been noted: if the numbers 1, 2 and 3 capture the meaningful relations in subjective value between three alternatives, then the numbers −17, −2 and +13 do as well. Indeterminancy of this kind cannot be of genuine concern.

19. For discussion of the interpretive relation of indices and context, see Fiengo and May 1994, chap. 2.

20. The rider is all-important, because this entailment has apparent failures, as Geach in *Reference and Generality* (1962) has instructed; "A man loves Sally because he is a good son" is not the same as "A man loves Sally because a man is a good son," since the latter, but not the former, is compatible with Oscar loving Sally because Max is a good son. This is not to say, however, that the pronoun in this case is not anaphoric, only that the indexical identity that underlies anaphora is not manifest in the structure as depicted. It is not manifest because the relevant coindexing holds not between "he" and "a man," but between "he" and a *variable* bound by "a man" in this sentence's logical form. The pronoun is another occurrence of this variable, and in this sense anaphoric; but the syntactic identity that makes this so does not entail coreference in the sense that this term is applicable to names and pronouns anaphoric to them. Thus, we can clearly speak of coindexing as representing or determining anaphora, by virtue of syntactic identity, but not of coindexing as representing or determining coreference (or, for that matter, variable binding).

21. There are at least two other uses of pronouns that we categorize as anaphoric, in the sense that their interpretation is a matter of linguistic rule, which we will not otherwise discuss here. One is Evans's eponymous E-type pronouns (Evans 1977, 1980), as these are found in the context of Geach's (1962) "donkey" anaphora; cf. "Everyone who owns a donkey beats it." To these, there are two broad classes of approaches: (1) the pronoun is identified with a variable, with concomitant adjustment of the quantificational structure of the antecedent (Haïk 1984; Heim 1982; Kamp 1984); (2) the pronoun is identified with a description that is recovered from its antecedent as it occurs in its linguistic surroundings (Evans 1977 and Neale 1990 in somewhat different versions). The second type is what Geach (1976) called "pure pronouns of laziness," where a pronoun has an antecedent that itself contains a pronoun. Geach remarks that these are a "repetition or near-repetition of an antecedent for which a pronoun goes proxy," but that they do not "repeat or continue the reference of the antecedent as its original occurrence"(p. 27). An example of a pure pronoun of laziness is in the sentence "Max, who sometimes ignores his boss, has more sense than Oscar, who always gives in to him," where the pronoun "him" serves as a proxy for "his boss"—that is, Oscar's boss. We have analyzed the basic effect here, which falls under the phenomenon of sloppy identity, in Fiengo and May 1994, chaps. 3–5.

22. This distinction between implicature and entailment corresponds to a distinction between whether different assignments corresponding to different indices is just assumed in context, subject to revision in the course of the discourse, or whether this is fixed in context. For more extensive discussion of the relation of indices and context, see Fiengo and May 1994, chap. 2.

23. Notice that such implicatures are based on the structure of the sentence a speaker actually uses. The possible meanings of any other sentences of the language will be immaterial; the hearer need not have any access whatsoever to the identity of any particular sentence that the speaker did not say. This is unlike the theory of Reinhart 1983; on her proposal, "He saw Oscar" is understood with noncoreference because of the existence "Oscar saw himself." But suppose there was a language just like English except that the latter sentence was ungrammatical (or otherwise unavailable in the language, say because there were no reflexive pronouns). On Reinhart's theory, since there is no alternative to which the speaker has access in such a language, the natural way to understand "He saw Oscar" would be with coreference. But this does not seem right, because nothing about this sentence is any different in the two languages. (We assume no difference in Binding Theory, and hence in indexing, between the languages.) Since it is the same sentence in both languages, the uses to which it could be put by speakers of each would appear to be precisely the same, so that in either case the noncoreference implicature should arise with normal use. For extended critical discussion of Reinhart's proposal, see Fiengo and May 1994, 12–14; 1996, 127–129.

24. In chapter 3 we will have more to say about this. Our view is that even sentences of the form ⌜$a = b$⌝ *simpliciter* cannot be used informatively, although they figure in sentences that can be.

25. To be clear, we are assuming that the occurrences of "Oscar" as they appear in (7) are coindexed. It might be thought that this would be superfluous for this case, since "Oscar" is being used as a logically proper name (individual constant) that independently has a value that is invariant over occurrences. But this would ignore that it is *English* that is being used to express logic, and so we need to represent that we have a sentence that expresses (8), and not (i):

(i) $\forall x \, (x = x) \to a = b$

That is, what indicates to us that (7) is not comparable to "If everyone is himself, then Oscar is Max"? What indicates it is the coindexing. For us, there is no category of "logically proper name" per se, although expressions of English can be used in this way, given the available linguistic resources.

26. Given what we have said in the text, the only aspect of Binding Theory that is superfluous is Principle C. If our technical talk allows pronouns, then the point can be extended to Principle B, given that "If everyone admires Oscar, then Oscar admires him" can be used to the same effect as the example given in the text. If reflexives are allowed, as they seem to be, given examples like "Two plus two equals two times itself," then Principle A still appears to be in force. We can have "If everyone believes Oscar admires Max, then Oscar believes Oscar admires Max," yet "If everyone believes Oscar admires Max, then Oscar believes himself admires Max" is quite ungrammatical.

2
Names and Expressions

Natural languages allow that distinct expressions may refer to the same individual, but it would be wrong to think that it is never important which one of these is chosen. Sometimes it is of the essence. A sentence containing one expression may differ in truth value from a sentence containing another expression cofererent to it, even if the sentences differ in no other way. Analysis of puzzling facts such as this led Frege to propose that associated with an expression, or sign, is not only its reference, but also its mode of presentation; distinct expressions, he held, may have the same referent but different modes of presentation. He then argued that failures of substitution are only apparent, arising when expressions refer not to their usual referents but to their modes of presentation. More recent explanations for substitution failure continue to appeal to modes of presentation; on one account, an agent may believe a proposition under one mode of presentation, but disbelieve the same proposition under another mode of presentation. Of course, the term "mode of presentation" is used here in a way different from Frege's, but there is a functional similarity. One may think of a "mode of presentation" as that in a theory serving to explain why coreferential expressions are not everywhere intersubstitutible (following, in essence, the usage of Schiffer 1990). Using the term this way, the identity of the modes of presentation may vary from theory to theory.

It is apparent that, if an account of substitution failure based on distinct but coreferring expressions having different modes of presentation is to be successful, it will be necessary at some point to provide a criterion of mode identity—given distinct expressions with the same referent, what features of them are distinct such that they could play the mode-of-presentation role? Frege's answer was that the expressions have distinct senses, and that senses play the mode-of-presentation role. Given the nature of his program, this was not unreasonable. But other answers can be given. For example, if we wish to find distinct features of distinct but coreferential expressions, it is clear that among the candidates to consider will be the features that distinguish the two expressions in the first place. If, in particular, there are formal syntactic criteria by virtue of which expressions are distinguished, those formal distinctions themselves might play the mode-of-presentation role. While it is often thought that there are insuperable problems with such an approach,[1] we feel that such an answer deserves a hearing. There is, however, an important prerequisite to this undertaking. If an account of *how* syntactic expressions serve the mode-of-presentation role is to be forthcoming, we must first have a formal theory of syntactic-expression identity for natural language. For reasons that will become clear, such a theory must, among other things, formally distinguish syntactic expressions from names. This latter task is one that must be faced in any event, as a chapter in the theory of syntax; it will be our point of departure. We will then be in a position to consider the fitness of linguistic expressions, so conceived, for the mode-of-presentation role.

2.1 Distinguishing Names and Expressions

In a representational sense, the distinction between syntactic expressions and names has been explicit in the syntactic literature for many years. *Names* are lexical items, members of a "lexicon," a list that also contains the other words of the language. They appear as terminal symbols in syntactic structures (phrase-markers), which also contain nonterminal symbols, or *nodes*. These nonterminal symbols, inclusive of their terminal, lexical, contents, are the *syntactic expressions*. When names, the sort of words we will focus on throughout, appear in syntactic structures, they are dominated by the *node* NP. Thus, given that "Max" is a name, there are syntactic expressions of the form "[$_{NP}$ Max]." The distinction between words and expressions arises in natural language in part because in natural language, the form of a word, its phonological "spelling," does not in itself reveal the syntactic category of the word, and the ordering of a string of words does not in itself reveal the syntactic analysis of the string. In natural languages, category membership reveals these things in a way that phonological spelling alone cannot.

There are certain important differences between the terminal and nonterminal symbols to be noted. The nonterminal symbols—nodes such as NP, VP, and the like—are members of a very small universal inventory. The theory of natural-language syntax, at least ideally, is sufficient to determine their identity, and the linear and hierarchical relationships that may hold among them. With respect to these matters, the theory of syntax is very narrowly defined. The terminal vocabulary is very different in these respects. If we survey the lexicons of individual speakers, even those who would be said to share a language, we find significant variation in the inventory of entries. It would be very rare for two individuals to fully share a lexicon; an individual has some words in his or her lexicon and not others. This being so, if we are to determine the identity conditions for words, and, in particular, names, we should determine the identity conditions on words *as they appear in the lexicon of an individual*. We will find that the *beliefs* of individuals will be criterial in the statement of those identity conditions on words: two occurrences of words are occurrences of the same word for an individual if and only if that individual believes they are the same.

What criteria, then, does a speaker use to determine whether he or she is confronting two occurrences of the same word, or occurrences of distinct words? It seems clear that pronunciation can be criterial: a speaker may believe that there are two occurrences of distinct words, and not two occurrences of the same word if the speaker believes that there is distinctness of pronunciation between the two occurrences. But what sort of distinctness of pronunciation counts? Consider the sorts of distinctions one finds between the voice quality of two individuals: suppose one is young and the other old, or one is female and the other male. Although their pronunciations will be acoustically distinct, and easily discriminable, people do not consider a word said in a male voice to be a different word from one said in a female voice. In general, the sorts of acoustic considerations not considered linguistically relevant in the broad phonetic transcriptions of phonologists are not criterial for the layperson in the individuation of words.

Nevertheless, there are circumstances under which the layperson allows that one word may be pronounced quite differently, where the differences in pronunciation are linguistically relevant. A speaker who grows up speaking one dialect of English, and then moves to an area in which an unfamiliar dialect of English is spoken, will learn a set of correspondences (e.g., when they say "Noo Yawk" they mean "New York") and then might come to be fluent in both dialects. If so, he or she will come to know not only how each name is pronounced in the two dialects, but also how some new name, previously unfamiliar, should be pronounced in the two dialects. In this case, there is difference in pronunciation of a linguistically significant sort, but the speaker will not consider the distinctness criterial; the difference in pronunciation will be considered to be within dialectal variation. Of course, the speaker might not be aware of the dialectal variation just referred to: the speaker might then take "New York" and "Noo Yawk" to be different words. We will return to this matter below. For now, we may draw the conclusion that phonological distinctness, when it is believed to fall outside the range of dialectal variation, may be individuative of words. And, if it can be assumed that expressions that contain distinct words are occurrences of distinct expressions, then phonological distinctness may be individuative of syntactic expressions as well.

But what of the converse proposition: Does phonological identity underwrite expression identity? If two expression-tokens are phonologically identical, does it follow that they are tokens of the same expression-type? Certainly if the tokens are categorially distinct (e.g., the noun "Ford" and the verb "ford") the answer will be no, but what if they are categorially the same? One response would be to claim that there are ambiguous or indeterminate expression-types (for example, "Max"), and that context serves to fix their reference, on any given occasion of use. From that standpoint, there is, and can only be, one syntactic *expression-type* "Max," the value of its tokens being determined in a manner analogous to the valuation of indexicals. This approach presumes that the individuation of syntactic expressions is not itself fine-grained enough to distinguish noncoreferent occurrences whose phonological spelling is the same. But there is no good reason to believe this, and there is an alternative, which, it seems to us, is ultimately more compelling. First, consider the name "Max," understood to be defined solely with respect to its phonological spelling. There are, of course, many people named "Max," and it is natural to say that these people have the same name. It is also natural to say that some speakers but not others have the name "Max" in their lexicons, and when they do, they have only one entry of this name, phonological spelling being unique. For these reasons it makes sense to say that there is one *name*-type "Max." But tokens of the name "Max" may be deployed in many distinct syntactic expressions, themselves tokens of distinct expression-types, and, when they are, those syntactic expressions refer to distinct individuals named "Max." On this way of looking at things, there is no value associated with the name "Max" *qua* lexical item. In fact, on this account, names do not refer at all; reference accrues to syntactic expressions. While we commonly say that names refer (or are used to refer), this usage would be understood as informal.

There are two major assumptions behind the story just told. One is the distinction between names and the syntactic expressions that contain them. The other is that natural-language syntax is *formal*. We take it that for an account of language, including natural language, to be formal, it must be possible to determine, on examination of occurrences of its symbols, whether they are occurrences of the same symbol. No account not satisfying this requirement can be considered formal, although different kinds of accounts can impose the formality requirement in different ways. In the story just told, the symbols with respect to which natural languages are formal are the syntactic expressions, not the names that they may contain. This is the moral we draw from the problem of names with multiple bearers: if natural language is to be completely susceptible to a formal account, something other than sameness or difference of phonological spelling must be considered.

At this point, we need a notation that appropriately reflects this formality of natural language, one that precisely displays in syntactic structures the array of occurrences of expressions. We favor the indexical notation developed in our *Indices and Identity*, which provides the minimal characterization needed: if NPs are occurrences of the same expression, they are coindexed; if they are occurrences of different expressions, they are not coindexed. Thus, there may be any number of occurrences of the expression-type "$[_{NP_1}$ Max]" in a discourse (set of syntactic structures), all of which, if they refer at all, must refer to the same individual. Occurrences of an expression-type corefer if they refer at all; all occurrences in a given discourse will be coindexed, and hence coreferential as a matter of representation. Each occurrence of "$[_{NP_1}$ Max]," however, will be an occurrence of a different expression-type from any occurrence of "$[_{NP_2}$ Max]," and occurrences of different expression-types may or may not refer to the same individual. This is not determined representationally; it is left open whether noncoindexed expression occurrences corefer or not.[2]

As we have observed, two expression occurrences may be spelled differently and yet be considered by a speaker to be occurrences of the same expression-type. This was the case of dialectal variation. We can also have it that two expression occurrences may be spelled alike and yet be considered to be occurrences of distinct expression-types. This was the case of names with multiple bearers. A certain "autonomy" of syntactic expression is derived from such a view: identity of spelling appears to be detached from identity of syntactic expression. But can we also have it that there can be two distinct syntactic expressions that contain the same name and also have the same value? Yes, according to the condition we have given—although, it will turn out, no speaker would believe this to be so. This seeming paradox, we believe, is at the heart of Saul Kripke's referential puzzles, which we will discuss in more detail below.

2.2 Beliefs Concerning Language

On this way of viewing syntactic expressions, the circumstances under which a speaker will believe that two expressions are translations of each other will be various. There is the case of distinct expressions that refer to the same thing and the case of occurrences of the same expression that are pronounced differently. The question is to determine the conditions under which one expression may be substituted for another. The notion of translation we wish to consider is a broad one; it embraces not only translation in the familiar sense, but anaphora as well. There is, therefore, no implication that translation is between distinct languages.

Translation
Let us call a statement of the form (1), which expresses a symmetrical relation between expressions, a *translation statement*:

(1) ⌜"X" translates "Y"⌝

where "X" and "Y" are schematic letters for expressions. Now the term "translation" has technical and nontechnical uses, and criteria for successful translation depend on what properties of the expressions to be related the translator is anxious to preserve. Those criteria, of course, are various. In our usage of the term, a Translation Statement is about linguistic equivalences, the sorts of linguistic equivalences that the ordinary person is aware of or has opinions about. Roughly put, a person will believe that two expressions are translations of each other, in our sense, if the person believes that the two expressions are covalued. The notion is actually not quite that simple, and we will have occasion to return to this topic below.

Translation Statements express relations between two expressions (not lexical items), and those expressions may be coindexed or not. Thus, for indexed NPs, Translation Statements may be of the form (2) or (3):

(2) "NP_i" translates "NP_i"

(3) "NP_i" translates "NP_j"

The two forms have very different epistemic status. Grounds for believing Translation Statements of the form (2) are quite different from the grounds for believing Translation Statements of the form (3). This becomes clear when one considers cases.

Consider (2) first. We observed above that a speaker will believe that expression occurrences are occurrences of the same expression-types only if he or she believes that any difference in their phonological spelling is due to linguistic variation. But there is a systematic exception to this found in every language, designated elements for which pronunciation is not criterial in the individuation of syntactic expressions. These elements are the pronouns. Two NPs may be occurrences of the same syntactic expression even though one may contain the name "John" and the other the pronoun "he"; Binding Theory proceeds on this assumption.[3] Thus we have Translation Statements such as (4):[4]

(4) "[$_1$ John]" translates "[$_1$ he]"

The grounds for believing a Translation Statement such as (4) are purely linguistic in nature. Coindexed NPs are covalued, and, if covaluation is a sufficient license for translation, knowledge of the truth of (4) is grammatical in origin. The point is general: if two NPs are coindexed, they are translations of each other. Uniform substitution of another index in (4) will also yield a translation.[5] In that sense, translation of coindexed expressions holds irrespective of the values of the expressions. Given knowledge of various properties associated with an expression, and knowledge of English morphology, one knows the pronominal form of that expression.

Consider now a slightly different case. Some speakers believe that (5) is true, regional phonetic differences being for them no barrier to identity of expressions.

(5) "[₁ New York]" translates "[₁ Noo Yawk]"

Anyone conversant with the regional dialects of English would know that these are two different dialectal pronunciations of one English expression, and if they are conversant in this way, they will believe (5). But suppose someone does not know this. They might hear occurrences of "New York" and occurrences of "Noo Yawk" and not realize that they are different pronunciations of the same expression. Depending on circumstances, they might conclude that "New York" and "Noo Yawk" are names of different cities, or they might conclude that they are distinct names of the same city, in that they are no more instances of the same expression than "Cicero" and "Tully" are. If they come to the former conclusion, they will not believe (5), indeed they will not believe that "New York" and "Noo Yawk" are translations of each other at all. If they conclude the second, they will believe (6):

(6) "[₁ New York]" translates "[₂ Noo Yawk]"

Notice that the grounds for believing (6) would be quite different from the grounds for believing (5). A speaker will come to believe (6) on the basis of hearing the same city called by two names; the speaker lacks the linguistic knowledge that the two names are dialectal variants of the same expression, and assumes that they are distinct expressions.

But now consider (7) and (8):

(7) "[₁ London]" translates "[₁ Rondon]"

(8) "[₁ London]" translates "[₁ Londres]"

If a speaker knows that "London" and "Rondon" are the English and Japanese pronunciations of the same expression, the speaker will believe (7). Similarly for the French example. But the speaker might not know this; the speaker might believe that the pairs are translations but translations of different expressions. In that case, he or she would believe (9) and (10).

(9) "[₁ London]" translates "[₂ Rondon]"

(10) "[₁ London]" translates "[₂ Londres]"

Of course, the speaker might believe that "Rondon" and "Londres" are names of cities that are distinct from London and not translations at all.

The interlanguage circumstance just considered is in no way different from the dialectal one, and that is how it should be. There are, it should be mentioned, no linguistic criteria that define the boundaries between what we call dialects of the same language and what we call different languages. These sorts of distinctions are sociopolitical, not linguistic. More to the point, speakers do not appear to respect those boundaries either; they have beliefs about the individuation of expressions that transcend the distinction between difference of dialect and difference of language, however that distinction is made.

To summarize, we have the following inventory. Translation Statements may hold between coindexed expressions. There are two cases of this kind to be distinguished. The "pronominalization" example constitutes a belief licensed by the machinery of grammar itself: the belief is analytic relative to grammar. The cognate examples constitute beliefs speakers have concerning the phonetic variation a single expression may display. Translation Statements may also hold between noncoindexed expressions, and these are learned case by case.

In many instances, substitution *salva veritate* holds between expressions that are translations of each other. As we have seen, when translation relates coindexed expressions, this follows relatively trivially from knowledge of grammar. But when Translation Statements relate distinct expressions, matters become much more complex. So, suppose that we have (11) (setting aside the remote possibility that a speaker might somehow take "Cicero" and "Tully" to be dialectal phonetic variants):

(11) "[₁ Cicero]" translates "[₂ Tully]"

Given (11), we are licensed to move from (12) to (13);

(12) [₁ Cicero] is [₂ Tully]

(13) [₁ Cicero] is [₁ Cicero]

Since these are both true in all and only the worlds in which Cicero exists, the substitution is unproblematic. There is also no problem associated with moving by substitution from (14) to (15); provided that the final NPs in both are understood in the same way, both attribute to John a (trivial) belief of the self-identity of Cicero:

(14) John believes that Cicero is Tully.

(15) John believes that Cicero is Cicero.

Yet the move from (12) to (13) and (14) to (15) is not so simple; there is Frege's intuition that (12) but not (13) can represent an extension of knowledge, and that (15) might be true and (14) false. Once we have developed a notion of "Assignment," we will be in a position to consider this problem.

Assignments

By asserting "Cicero was a Roman," speakers commit themselves to certain beliefs. In particular, if they are to speak sincerely, they normally commit themselves to the belief that Cicero was a Roman; if they did not believe this, they would not have spoken sincerely. It is immaterial to the sincerity of the speakers' beliefs that it might turn out, through further research into classical antiquity, that Cicero actually was not Roman at all, but rather Greek. Speakers are committed to speaking what they *believe* to be the truth; they may be sincere, but incorrect. Another belief that speakers of "Cicero was a Roman" commit themselves to is the belief that "Cicero" refers to Cicero. The speakers might not be able to pick out Cicero by any definite description, and might in fact not be able to distinguish Cicero from Caesar by any means at their disposal. But for the sentence to be said sincerely, the speakers must believe that "Cicero" refers to Cicero, whomever they might take Cicero to be.

Some of these beliefs might go wrong. The speakers might have stood in the Roman Senate, and, indicating Catiline, asserted "Cicero is a great orator." By saying that, the speakers may, through charity on the part of the hearers, be taken to mean that Catiline is a great orator although confused as to Catiline's name, or, in different circumstances, be taken to mean that Cicero is a great orator, but confused as to the identity of Cicero. In either case, sincere speakers believe that they demonstrated the appropriate person and that "Cicero" refers to Cicero.

Let us now focus on attributing the belief that Cicero was a Roman. If the speakers believe that Crassus believed that Cicero was a Roman, they may say "Crassus believed that Cicero was a Roman." For this sentence to be true, it need not be the case that Crassus believed that "Cicero" refers to Cicero. In fact, he may have never encountered the name "Cicero," and, if asked, he might have denied that he had ever before had the belief that "Cicero" refers to Cicero. Nevertheless, putting aside a kind of charitable attribution we will consider momentarily, for the sentence to be true, it must be Cicero that Crassus believed to be a Roman. To see this, consider the circumstance in which the speakers believe that Crassus knew the name "Cicero" but that Crassus was confused about the identity of Cicero himself. He mistook Caesar for Cicero; when he encountered Caesar, he took him to be Cicero, and he never encountered Cicero himself. Suppose further that the speakers (and the hearers) are not confused in this regard. It seems clear that the speakers cannot say "Crassus believed that Cicero was a Roman" to attribute the belief that Cicero was a Roman in this circumstance, at least not, as was mentioned, without assuming a certain charitable interpretation. Nor can they say "Crassus believed that Cicero was a Roman" to attribute the belief that Caesar was a Roman. Although Crassus believed that "Cicero" refers to Cicero, and would have said as much, he named the wrong man "Cicero"; again, for the attribution to be correct, it must be Cicero that Crassus believed to be a Roman.

In the cases just considered, it was assumed that the speakers were intending to be taken literally, and on that assumption, it was correct to say that, knowing Crassus's confusion, the speakers cannot attribute the belief to him that Cicero was a Roman. For the hearers would naturally take the attributed belief to be about Cicero, not Caesar, and the wrong belief would be attributed. To change the example slightly, if Crassus took Plato for Cicero, and the speakers asserted that Crassus believed Cicero was a Greek, the hearers would naturally conclude that Crassus was mistaken as to the nationality of Cicero, not that Crassus had misidentified the unmentioned Plato as Cicero. Again, the speakers would have failed to attribute the correct belief to Crassus. But suppose that both the speakers and the hearers are aware, and the speakers believe that the hearers are aware, that Crassus took Plato for Cicero. Then it would seem that the speakers can say that Crassus believed Cicero was a Greek. An arch form of charity is at play here; the speakers are using the term "Cicero" as they believe the agent uses it (incorrectly, as it happens) and, since they believe that the hearers are willing to go along with this, the correct belief can be attributed. We would emphasize that this example must be distinguished from the cases just considered, since here it is a requirement that the speakers believe that the hearers are aware of the agent's confusion. No such requirement holds in the normal case. Thus this exception proves the rule. There will be more to say about this case below.

Apart from the case just considered, the speakers use the name "Cicero," believing that "Cicero" has the value Cicero. They also believe they are correct as to who Cicero is. If the speakers believe that the agent is wrong as to whom "Cicero" refers to, they cannot use the name "Cicero" to attribute the belief that Cicero was a Roman to the agent. Thus, when speakers use an expression containing a name, they do so in accordance with a semantic belief about its reference. We can characterize what the speakers believe by a sentence of the form

(16) $\ulcorner$"$[_{NP_i} X]$" has the value $NP_i\urcorner$

where X is a schematic letter covering the syntactic contents of NP_i. We refer to sentences of the form (16) as *Assignments*. For each NP_i in a discourse, an NP_i-Assignment states that there is a pairing of NP_i with a value; thus, what speakers believe when they use an expression is an Assignment that mentions that expression. We can state the principle that governs such beliefs as follows:

The Assignment Principle: To be sincere, if a speaker uses a sentence containing an occurrence of the expression NP_i, the speaker believes an NP_i-assignment.

The Assignment Principle, at least to the extent that it is correct, follows from two things: the desire on the part of the speakers to speak truthfully, and the fact that it is a condition on the truth of sentences that the expressions have the appropriate values. Thus, the speakers know that for an utterance of "Cicero is a Roman" to be true, it must be the case that Cicero exists, that "Cicero" has the value Cicero, and that Cicero was a Roman. Sincere speakers uttering this sentence believe that their expressions have the appropriate values; the speakers say things that they believe to be true about the values that they believe their expressions have. As already emphasized, one or another of these beliefs may be wrong, but that does not affect the sincerity of the speakers, nor the fact that their behavior conforms to the Assignment Principle.

When speakers make assertions, the Assignments believed by the speakers need not be part of the logical form of the sentences that the speakers utter. They may be, rather, elements of the context that the speakers assume. Assignments, however, are not always just the background to assertions; they may stand as part of the truth conditions of the assertion itself, in which case they give rise to apparent exceptions to the Assignment Principle, to which we now turn.

2.3 Belief Ascription and Attributed Assignments

As mentioned above, if speakers believe that expressions are translations of each other, it will be immaterial, at least sometimes, which expression is used. In that case, the speakers believe that the Assignments associated with the expressions are *equivalent,* in that they assign the same value to different expressions.[6] But there are circumstances under which it is material which of a set of equivalent expressions is used. The speakers, for example, may wish to speak of the terms under which an agent holds a belief. In that case, the speakers may specify the particular Assignment that they believe the agent would assent to. The speakers may, that is to say, attribute Assignments. Let us consider the beliefs of speakers and the ways they may be reported in more detail.

The first thing to establish is that it is possible to attribute Assignments. This occurs in example (17):

(17) John believes "Cicero" has the value Cicero.

Here the attribution of an Assignment is overt. But, in our view, there are also tacit occurrences. Consider (18):

(18) John believes Cicero was a Roman.

In (18), the belief is overtly attributed to John that Cicero was a Roman. But there is a way of saying (18) in which what is attributed in (17) is also attributed. Furthermore, this extra attribution is optional, so there are actually two logical forms for this sentence, one that includes a tacit Assignment, and one that does not:

(19) a. John believes [[Cicero$_1$ was a Roman] and ["Cicero$_1$" has the value Cicero$_1$]]

  b. John believes [Cicero$_1$ was a Roman]

While for either of these to be true it must be the case that John believes Cicero was a Roman, for (19a) to be true, John must believe that Cicero was a Roman and referred to by the "Cicero"-expression. If he fails to believe that Cicero was either or both of these, then (19a) is false. Thus, (19a) is false if John believes that Cicero was a Roman, but not that he is referred to be the "Cicero"-expression, or, if he does not believe that Cicero was a Roman, but does believe that he is referred to by the "Cicero"-expression, or if he believes neither. There are two points of syntax that should be emphasized. First, the presence of the syntactic indices in (19a) indicates that we have, in the attribution, two occurrences of the expression "Cicero" (excluding the occurrence within quotation marks). This is crucial to deriving the proper truth conditions for (19a), since it fixes that these two occurrences of "Cicero" be covalued: for (19a) to be true, John must believe that the "Cicero"-expression refers to a person who was a Roman. Second, in (19a), *one* belief is attributed, that one belief being expressed as the conjunction of two sentences. Thus the belief attributed in (19a) is to be distinguished from the conjoined attribution of beliefs, which could be expressed by a structure such as that in (20):[7]

(20) John believes [Cicero was a Roman] and John believes ["Cicero" has the value Cicero]

This distinction is crucial; the truth conditions associated with (20) allow that John might believe, quite independently, that Cicero was a Roman, and that Cicero is referred to by the "Cicero"-expression, never having considered the two beliefs together. But the truth conditions associated with the structure in (19a) exclude that possibility; in (19a), John is said to have a single belief, which, as it happens, is expressed as the conjunction of two sentences. And for him to have *that* belief it must be the case that he believe that one person was a Roman and referred to by the "Cicero"-expression. In what follows, structures of the form in (19a) will be our focus, never that in (20).[8]

It is natural to call attributions containing Assignments *de dicto;* their logical forms explicitly contain the expressions with respect to which the beliefs are held. For, by choosing to utter (18) under the logical form (19a), which includes a tacit Assignment, rather than (19b), which does not, speakers commit themselves to a claim about the terms under which the agent holds a belief, and provide information as to what the agent believes over and above that given by the overt, primary attribution. For the attribution to be correct, it must be the case that the agent would agree that Cicero was a Roman referred to by the "Cicero"-expression. Recall, however, that the Assignment Principle requires that sincere speakers, when using a sentence containing an expression NP_i, must believe an Assignment. When Assignments are attributed, however, the domain of the principle changes. Since the Assignment resides within the scope of the attribution, the Assignment is attributed to the agent, by the speakers. Under this circumstance, the requirement is that sincere speakers, by attributing to an agent belief of an Assignment, must believe that the agent believes the Assignment. It is the speakers who are *using* the expression "Cicero" of course, but they are using it so as to attribute the "Cicero"-Assignment to the agent. They are using it as they believe the agent would. But why would speakers choose to use an expression as the agent would, especially if they believe that they and the agent use the expression to refer to the same thing? Certainly the most familiar reason, and the one that has been traditionally most emphasized, is that there is some *other* attribution, containing some *other* equivalent Assignment, that the agent does *not* believe. If that constitutes the reason for the inclusion, then it stands as an *implicature* of an attribution containing an Assignment that there is some other incorrect attribution, an attribution containing an Assignment that the agent does not believe. To choose to include an Assignment will, in this case, implicate that to have chosen a distinct Assignment would have been incorrect.

To take an example, for (19a), with the included expression being "Cicero," the excluded expression can be "Tully," but not, for instance, "Caesar," at least given speakers with the normal beliefs. The speakers must hold that the included and excluded expressions refer to same thing, that their Assignments are equivalent. Under the circumstance envisaged, this means that there is an implicature that the agent does not believe another attribution—say one containing a "Tully"-Assignment—equivalent to the "Cicero"-Assignment. Now, if an Assignment is included in a belief attribution, it must be the Assignment of an expression that is included in the overt belief attributed. This is for the usual conditions of relevance. Given that the relevancy requirement is just as much in force with respect to the excluded Assignments as with respect to the included, what the speakers may implicate relative to (19a) is that an attribution such as that in (21), which is a logical form of "John believes Tully was a Roman," would be incorrect:

(21) John believes [[Tully was a Roman] and ["Tully" has the value Tully]]

Observe that neither (19a) nor (21) entails the other. Example (19a) involves reference to the "Cicero"-expression and (21) involves reference to the "Tully"-expression. Because these are distinct expressions, one cannot move by substitution from (19a) to (21) or vice versa; substitution within the quotes is prohibited. Of course, if one adds the premise that John believes that "Cicero" translates "Tully" and the premise that he has brought his "Cicero" belief and his "Tully" belief together, and the premise that John is logical, and perhaps other premises as well, the entailment from one to the other would go through. But there is no direct route from (19a) to (21) just by substitution. In any event, if the speakers believe that John does not believe that "Cicero" translates "Tully," which could be either because he believes that "Cicero" and "Tully" are expressions that refer to distinct individuals or because he does not know the expression "Tully," they may correctly say (18) with the *de dicto* logical form (19a).[9]

But this is not the only reason speakers might have for attributing an Assignment. Consider again the case of the confused Crassus, described above. The point there was that if the speakers believe that the hearers are aware of Crassus's confusion (that, as we would say, "Cicero" is a name of Plato), they may say that Crassus believes that Cicero was a Greek. By a form of charity on the part of the speakers, they may attribute the belief that Plato was a Greek, and by a form of charity on the part of the hearers, they will be so understood. But in what does that charity consist? On the part of the speakers, it consists in using the expression "Cicero" as they believe that the agent does, and on the part of the hearers it consists in taking it that way. The charity is arch, in that it does not correct a mistake but preserves it. Nevertheless, the point is that the attribution contains an Assignment distinct from that which the speakers believe. Thus this unusual case provides another reason for attributing an Assignment.

One thing we are suggesting by our account is that there is a fundamentally *contrastive* element to the classical instances of *de dicto* belief ascription. There are, however, limiting cases. Imagine a religion in which "God" is the one and only name allowed for the deity. And imagine that one only comes to know that name through the process of initiation. By assumption, there is no other Assignment equivalent to the "God"-Assignment that a person might know. Yet one might say of Max that he knows that God is great and attribute the "God"-Assignment to Max, meaning to entail that he has acquired the "God"-Assignment and thus that he has been initiated. If one wished to speak of contrast here, the contrast would be between believing an Assignment and not believing one. But it might also be said that in this circumstance the normal contrastive implicature is suspended: if the speakers believe that the hearers believe that the deity has only one name, the implicature must be different in nature. We allow that there may well be other circumstances in which the attribution of Assignments would be warranted. Nevertheless, the contrastive nature of the most interesting cases of *de dicto* belief is, we believe, correctly captured.

We have discussed (19a), the *de dicto* logical form of (18) at some length but, as we mentioned, there is also (19b), in which no Assignment is attributed to the agent. Since no Assignment is attributed, it is an implicature of (19b) that it is not relevant under what terms John holds the belief that Cicero was a Roman. The speakers may choose any Assignment that is equivalent to: ""Cicero" has the value Cicero," without committing themselves to any claim about which among equivalent Assignments the agent might or might not hold; in this regard, (19b) is a non–*de dicto* attribution. Understood non–*de dicto*, to say (18) is the same as to say (22):

(22) John believes Tully was a Roman.

The irrelevance of the terms of attribution extends to cases in which the agent is a monolingual speaker of a language other than English. Example (19b) is true just in case "Cicero was a Roman" is a translation of a sentence in John's language that John believes.

As we use the terms, *de dicto* and non–*de dicto* name types of attributions; both sorts of attribution are "semantically innocent." The distinction between them depends in part on beliefs about whether or not expressions are translations of one another. But whether agents believe that two expressions are translations of each other is independent of whether they believe that the reference of the expressions exists. Thus, the ambiguity that we find with (18) is just as much found with (23), which contains a so-called empty name:

(23) John believes Santa Claus is an elf.

Example (23) will have two logical forms, (24a) and (24b):

(24) a. John believes [[[$_1$Santa Claus] is an elf] and ["[$_1$Santa Claus]" has the value Santa Claus]]
b. John believes [[$_1$Santa Claus] is an elf]

The first will be said when, for example, the speaker wishes to have it as an implicature that there is some other attribution containing an Assignment mentioning a name unfamiliar to John ("Kris Kringle," for example), which John does not believe. The second will be said when the terms of John's belief are not relevant. The difference between these logical forms will reveal itself, as before, when translation possibilities are considered. Suppose the speaker believes the Translation Statement (25):

(25) "[$_1$ Santa Claus]" translates "[$_2$ Kris Kringle]"

Example (24b) may then be translated as (26):

(26) John believes [$_2$Kris Kringle] is an elf.

But (24a) cannot be translated this way. One cannot, in particular, get to (27), since substitution within the quotes is prohibited:

(27) John believes [[[$_2$Kris Kringle] is an elf] and ["[$_2$ Kris Kringle]" has the value Kris Kringle$_2$]].

What we see, then, is that sentences such as (23) are ambiguous between *de dicto* and non–*de dicto* readings, and in exactly the same way that sentences that do not contain empty names are, admitting of the same possibilities of translation and attribution. This holds regardless of one's views about the reference of empty names; the distinction between *de dicto* and non–*de dicto* attributions is independent of this.[10]

Translation of Attributed Assignments: The Translated *De Dicto* Puzzle
It should be understood that attributed Assignments can as much be "translated" as other attributed beliefs. Consider Sextus, a new member of the Roman Senate. He had heard the name "*Cicero*" (pronounced, in the nominative case, "Kikero") and the name "*Tullius*"

(again the nominative case of the name rendered now in English as "Tully"), but he was not aware that Cicero was Tully (he was not aware that, as he would have said, "*Cicero Tullius est*").[11] Suppose Sextus believed that Cicero was a Roman, but did not believe that Tully was. The following would be the logical form of the relevant ascription, as we would say it now in English:

(28)   Sextus believed Cicero was a Roman and "Cicero" had the value Cicero.

It is clear that Sextus had no contact with the English sentence ""Cicero" has the value Cicero," but of course he did have contact with its (rough) Latin translation: ""*Cicero*" *Ciceronis nomen est*." It is a condition of the puzzle as we have presented it that the conjoined Latin sentence attributed to Sextus be translatable as a conjoined English sentence attributed to Sextus. These are presented in (29) and (30):

(29)   Sextus believed that Cicero was a Roman and "Cicero" had the value Cicero.

(30)   Sextus believed that *Cicero Romanus erat et* "*Cicero*" *Ciceronis nomen erat*.

Consider the second clauses of the pair. For translation to go through, it will be required that ""*Cicero*"" and ""Cicero,"" (the names of the expressions "*Cicero*" and "Cicero") be translations of each other. Similarly it will be required that ""*Tullius*"" and ""Tully"" (the names of the expressions "*Tullius*" and "Tully") be translations of each other; these will appear in the attributed Assignments that Sextus, by implicature, is said not to believe. But the *de dicto* translation relation we require must have it that ""*Tullius*"" (the name of the expression "*Tullius*") and ""Cicero"" (the name of the expression "Cicero") *not* be translations of each other.

Let us take it that translation, in this case, requires identity of value. It will be required, then, that "*Cicero*" and "Cicero" be believed to be occurrences of the same expression, just as it is required that *Cicero* and Cicero be believed to be the same person. We are not imagining that there are two *kinds* of translation here; there is just one kind of translation, proceeding at two different levels. ""Cicero"" has as its value the expression "Cicero" and ""*Cicero*"" has as its value the expression

"*Cicero,*" whereas "Cicero" has as its value Cicero and "*Cicero*" has as its value *Cicero*. In the first instance, the translation relation will require that the expressions "Cicero" and "*Cicero*" be believed to be identical, while in the second case the translation relation will require that Cicero and *Cicero* be believed to be identical.

In what sense may the expressions "Cicero" in English and "*Cicero*" in Latin be believed to be identical? We argued above that speakers may believe varying pronunciations of the same name not to be criterial in distinguishing expressions. This is such a case. On this way of viewing things, there is one "Cicero" expression, which, through its lifetime, has changed phonetic shape. Just as a person retains the same name while changing physical constitution from infancy to adulthood, so too does a word retain its identity as an expression while changing its phonetic constitution. (The point can be found in Kaplan 1990.) All of this being true, the translated *de dicto* attribution goes through, assuming, of course, that the speaker believes that "Cicero" and "*Cicero*" are cognates.

To summarize, our claim has been that when speakers attribute a belief, they may or may not commit themselves to the terms under which the agent holds the belief. Thus, for us, the primary distinction to be drawn among belief ascriptions is between *de dicto* and non–*de dicto* belief ascriptions. This distinction is linguistically represented by the presence or absence of attributed Assignments. *De dicto* belief ascriptions are represented in logical forms involving (1) the overt belief ascribed, and (2) attributed Assignments to one or more the syntactic expressions, dicta, out of which the overt ascription is formed. On the other hand, non–*de dicto* belief ascriptions will involve nothing other than the overt belief ascribed. In their logical forms, there will be no attributed Assignments associated with NPs, and, in that circumstance, any equivalent translation may be substituted for them.

2.4 Singularity

We have now considered two kinds of belief about language that speakers have. The first, governed by the Assignment Principle, has it that the sincere use of expressions requires that speakers believe the Assignments associated with them. In the normal course of conversation (that is, where all participants are presumed to be sincere), each speaker will believe that all others speak in accordance with this principle, by virtue of believing that his or her interlocutors are competent speakers of the language. The Assignments each speaker believes may vary, of course, reflecting the variance between speakers in the names in their lexicons. The second sort of belief we have considered are beliefs that expressions are translations of each other. These too may vary from speaker to speaker; one speaker may believe of a pair of expressions that they are translations of each other and another may believe of the same pair of expressions that they are not. Moreover, speakers believe that other speakers have beliefs of this sort, and again speakers may vary on whether or not they believe someone believes that expressions are translations.

There is one other belief, which all speakers share, that we must recognize in order to complete our understanding of how speakers may deploy expressions in their language. To gain an intuitive grasp of its content, consider once more the case of Cicero. It is clear that speakers may believe a "Cicero"-Assignment, and that they may also believe a "Tully"-Assignment, and that they may or may not know that Cicero and Tully are one and the same. But under what conditions may speakers believe the Assignment: ""[$_1$Cicero]" has the value Cicero$_1$," and the Assignment: ""[$_2$Cicero]" has the value Cicero$_2$"? The answer we wish to give is that speakers may believe Assignments for two distinct but cospelled expressions of names just in case they believe that the Assignments are *not* covalued. That is, with respect to any discourse and context, if speakers believe two "Cicero"-Assignments, they believe that there are two people named "Cicero," while if they believe that there is only one person named "Cicero," they will believe only one "Cicero"-Assignment. We will call this principle *Singularity*. It may be stated as follows:

Singularity: If cospelled expressions are covalued, they are coindexed.

It is understood that there is great speaker-to-speaker variability with respect to Assignments believed, and, as has been emphasized, that speakers believe an Assignment is no guarantee that they correctly use the expression the Assignment evaluates, for they may mistake the identities of the people to whom they refer. Nevertheless the Assignments speakers believe are not completely unstructured. They are subject, as a class, to Singularity.

Assignments, when attributed in the context of *de dicto* attributions, must also accord with Singularity, but in this case it with respect to the agent's, not the speakers', beliefs. To see the effect of this, we turn to a pair of puzzles well known since their introduction by Kripke (1979). In the first of these, it is supposed that a speaker believes that John believes, for whatever reason, that there are two people named "Paderewski," but that the speaker believes there is only one such person. Against this background, the speaker may say (31) and (32) without contradiction:[12]

(31) John believes that Paderewski is a genius.

(32) John doesn't believe that Paderewski is a genius.

Why are (31) and (32) not contradictory? Their logical forms will be as follows:

(33) John believes that Paderewski$_1$ is a genius and "Paderewski$_1$" has the value Paderewski$_1$.

(34) John doesn't believe that Paderewski$_2$ is a genius and "Paderewski$_2$" has the value Paderewski$_2$.

The logical forms of the *that*-clauses in (31) and (32) are indexically distinguished in (33) and (34). Therefore, (31) and (32) say nothing inconsistent about John, since the beliefs attributed to John are distinguished. This is in accordance with the standard intuition concerning this puzzle, which has it that the speaker and agent are both perfectly logical. One of them, perhaps even both, are, of course wrong about the facts, but this makes no difference. What matters for the puzzle is that the speaker's and agent's beliefs diverge as described. Since the Assignments in (33) and (34) are attributed, only the agent must believe them, and since the agent believes them in accordance with Singularity, it is he who is said to believe that there are two people named "Paderewski." It is not a consequence of (33) and (34) that the speaker holds this belief.

Since it is explicit in (33) and (34) that the agent believes two "Paderewski"-Assignments, the *de dicto* nature of this puzzle, first emphasized by Kripke, is captured.[13] The logical forms (33) and (34), however, are not the only ones that (31) and (32) could have; they could also have logical forms with no attributed Assignments. These logical forms would also be consistent, but would not comport with the conditions of the puzzle. For it would now follow from the Assignment Principle that the *speaker* believes that there are two "Paderewski"-Assignments, and from Singularity that the speaker believes that there are two people named "Paderewski." Of course, in a different scenario, the speaker could believe that there are two Paderewskis, and if he did, he could make the first-person ascriptions: "I believe Paderewski$_1$ is a genius" and "I do not believe Paderewski$_2$ is a genius"; given Singularity, it follows from these self-ascriptions that he believes there are two people named "Paderewski." He may be right or wrong about this, but if there is just one Paderewski, then these first-person ascriptions are comparable to those in the third person with respect to the puzzle scenario. But there is a difference between the cases. Since the speaker is the agent of the belief in the first-person ascriptions, there is no disparity in beliefs between speaker and agent of the sort that gives rise to the *de dicto* character of third-person ascriptions. Thus, in this case, the puzzle has a non–*de dicto* nature, characterized by logical forms from which Assignments are withheld.[14]

Singularity specifies of cospelled expressions that if they are covalued they are occurrences of the same expression. We have just contrasted the effects of Singularity as it applies to Assignments attributed to an agent with its effects when it applies to the Assignments of the speaker. The contrast arises when the speaker and agent disagree as to the number of people named "Paderewski." The possible effects of variation between speaker and agent with respect to beliefs concerning translation are not addressed in this scenario. But translation will present similar kinds of problems, since different occurrences of an expression that are not cospelled may be translations of each other and covalued. As we pointed out in the translated *de dicto* puzzle, a speaker may believe that the English word "Cicero" and the Latin word "*Cicero*" are phonetic variants of the same expression, and thus, trivially, translations of each other. But what are the effects when speakers and agents have different translational beliefs? To answer this, we turn to the second of Kripke's puzzles.

To set the stage, Pierre, a monolingual French speaker, has read about London and has come to believe that London (or, as he would have said, "Londres") is beautiful. He then moves to London and learns English. Becoming familiar with the city, he comes not to believe that London is beautiful. He has, of course, made no logical error, nor has he changed his mind; he is simply unaware that London is Londres. Now imagine a speaker, who believes that "London" and "Londres" are occurrences of the same expression, reporting Pierre's beliefs by uttering (35) and (36):

(35) Pierre believes that Londres is beautiful.

(36) Pierre does not believe that London is beautiful.

If "London" and "Londres" are taken as the *speaker* takes them, as occurrences of the same expression, then the speaker will have spoken inconsistently. She will not have spoken this way, however, if, in common with the "Paderewski" scenario, (35) and (36) have logical forms containing attributed Assignments:

(37) Pierre believes that Londres$_1$ is beautiful and "Londres$_1$" has the value Londres$_1$.

(38) Pierre does not believe that London$_2$ is beautiful and "London$_2$" has the value London$_2$.

Recall that there are two things that Pierre is unaware of. One is that London is Londres, that they are the same place. The other is that "London" and "Londres" are phonetic variants of the same expression. If he believed the second, the first would follow trivially (although if he believed the first, he might not believe the second: he might know that London is Londres but not believe that "London" and "Londres" are cognate, and therefore variants of the same expression (cf. "John" and "Ian")). It is clear, then, that the expressions mentioned in the Assignments in (37) and (38) cannot be coindexed, since, if they were, and Pierre brought all of his beliefs together, he could conclude just from them alone that London is Londres. But the conditions of the puzzle are such that he must not be able to conclude that just by dint of logic. Pierre would report that London and Londres are different cities, from which it can be inferred that he could not hold that "London" and "Londres" are variant expressions referring to the same city.

In the "Paderewski" scenario, given the beliefs of the speaker, Singularity required that the speaker believe one "Paderewski"-Assignment, and, given the beliefs of the agent, Singularity required that the agent believe two "Paderewski"-Assignments. In the present case, because "London" and "Londres" are not cospelled, Singularity allows that the speaker believe both a "London"-Assignment and a "Londres"-Assignment, and that the speaker believe that "London" and "Londres" are not only translations of each other, but occurrences of the same expression. Of course, the speaker in the "Paderewski" scenario believes that "Paderewski" and "Paderewski" are not only translations of each other but occurrences of the same expression, since he believes that there is only one "Paderewski" expression and every expression is a translation of itself. In this respect, the "Paderewski" and "Londres" scenarios are similar. Note, however, that from the fact that "London" and "Londres" are believed to be occurrences of distinct expressions it does not follow that they are believed to have different values; they might be held to be like "Cicero" and "Tully." But from the fact that "Paderewski$_1$" and "Paderewski$_2$" are believed to be occurrences of distinct expressions it *does* follow, by Singularity, that they are believed to have different values. Thus, in contrast to the "Paderewski" scenario, it does not *follow* from (37) and (38) that Pierre believes that there are two cities; all that follows is that Pierre does not believe that "London" and "Londres" are occurrences of the same expression (and thus translations). But, given the assumption that Pierre is logical, this is enough. For if Pierre believed that "London" and "Londres" were distinct but covalued expressions, he could hardly hold that Londres is beautiful and London not. What the reports of Pierre's beliefs about London and John's beliefs about Paderewski have in common, then, is that each pair contains equivalent Assignments to distinct expressions. Where they diverge, however, is just at the point at which Singularity comes into play.

2.5 Identity Puzzles

In essence, the Assignment Principle and Singularity, as aspects of speakers' linguistic competence, are conditions on *expressibility* in language. They determine, in part, how speakers may deploy expressions, given their beliefs about their reference. Such beliefs are directly reflected in the identities each sort of speaker would assert. Any speaker who has the name "Paderewski" in his or her lexicon could assert (39),

(39) Paderewski$_1$ is Padereswki$_1$.

but speakers who believe there are two people with the name in question could assert something else consonant with their beliefs, the nonidentity in (40):

(40) Paderewski$_1$ is not Padereswki$_2$.

Speakers who believe there is only one person named "Paderewski" of course would not assert (40), because it entails something that, given the Assignment Principle and Singularity, they believe to be false—that there are two people named "Paderewski." But that they would not assert this does not bar them from attributing it to someone else, provided that they do so *de dicto*. Thus, they may say (41), with the logical form in (42):

(41) John believes Paderewski isn't Paderewski.

(42) John believes [Paderewski$_1$ isn't Paderewski$_2$ and "Paderewski$_1$" has the value Paderewski$_1$ and "Paderewski$_2$" has the value Paderewski$_2$]

The puzzle as to how (41) can report a consistent belief thus echoes the puzzle that has been under discussion in the previous section.

In this case, as with all the puzzle cases considered, it is immaterial whether it is the speaker or hearer (or neither) who is factually correct. Rather, it is the conflict in their beliefs that is significant, and that conflict might go in different directions. So suppose that a speaker, who believes that there are *two* people named "Paderewski," wishes to tell a hearer, who believes the same, that someone else believes they are one and the same. The speaker could accomplish this by just attributing the opposite of (41)—that is, by saying (43):

(43) John believes Paderewski is Paderewski.

What are we to take the logical form of (43) to be? If the embedded sentence is indexed as in (39), then (43) would attribute a true but trivial belief to John. As we have described it, however, this is not what the speaker of (43) wishes to say. Rather, he or she wishes to say to the hearer that the agent, incorrectly in their view, identifies two people that they distinguish. That (43) may be used to say this follows from its having the following logical form:

(44) John believes Paderewski$_1$ is Paderewski$_2$.

Examining (44), since there are no Assignments attributed, we may conclude from the Assignment Principle and Singularity that the "Paderewski"-expressions it contains are used in accordance with the speaker's belief that they are not covalued. Nothing, however, follows by virtue of their occurrence about the *agent's* beliefs about Assignments. Rather, what the agent believes is *entailed* by the attribution. From (44), it follows that what is distinguished by the speaker through the use of distinct "Paderewski"-expressions is equated by the agent, and from this can be derived, given the dictates of the Assignment Principle and Singularity, that, if the agent knows the name "Paderewski," then he or she believes only one "Paderewski"-Assignment, not two.

In thus reversing the beliefs of the speaker and the beliefs the speaker wishes to attribute, we observe a shift from *de dicto* to non–*de dicto* attribution. Indeed, in this context, if the attribution were to be *de dicto,* so that the embedded clause of the logical form of (43) would be:

(45) [Paderewski$_1$ is Paderewski$_2$], and "Paderewski$_1$" has the value Paderewski$_1$ and "Paderewski$_2$" has the value Paderewski$_2$.

the inconsistency would be attributed to John that he believes that there are two people with the name "Paderewski" (given the attributed Assignments), and that he believes that only one person is named "Paderewski" (given the truth of the primary attribution). We should note something about the logical form (45), however. Its inconsistency is not inherent; it only becomes so when placed in overtly attributed contexts. Outside such contexts it may be asserted. So suppose we have a speaker who, as in the initial scenario, believes there is just one person named "Paderewski," and an addressee, John, who believes there are two, an addressee, that is, who would be prepared to assert (42). In that circumstance, to straighten the addressee out, the speaker may deny (40) by uttering (46).

(46) But John, Paderewski is Paderewski.

The speaker would not achieve this goal, however, if she were taken to have said "Paderewski$_1$ is Paderewski$_2$," since this would only entail something about her own Assignments, something in fact false, that she believes there are two people named "Paderewski." Rather, the logical form of (46) must be as in the attribution in (45), in which, since there are attributed Assignments, it follows that it must be someone other than the speaker who holds this belief. The only possibility in this context is the addressee. Thus, by an utterance of (46) in denial of (40), the addressee is asked to believe that two of *his* Assignments are equivalent. The speaker's assertion to the addressee is, in effect, *your* "Paderewski"-expressions corefer. Taken this way, an utterance of (46) would be cause for the addressee to alter his beliefs; it would act as a corrective to what are, from the speaker's point of the view, the mistaken beliefs of the addressee.

It would appear from this case that *de dicto* interpretation of NPs is in no way restricted to their occurrence in *that*-clauses. This observation is stengthened when we shift out attention to the puzzle of London and Londres, where to straighten Pierre out, a speaker may address him and say "Londres is London." Analyzing this in a parallel fashion, the relevant logical form would then be:

(47) Londres$_1$ is London$_2$ and "Londres$_1$" has the value Londres$_1$ and "London$_2$" has the value London$_2$.

The speaker in saying (47) is attributing Assignments to the addressee Pierre, who is thereby invited to believe that the values named in his two Assignments are the same.[15] The parallelism between this case and the "Paderewski" case is not, however, complete. So, consider Pierre's situation. He does not know that Londres is London and he does not know that "London" and "Londres" are occurrences of the same expression. Consider the ignorance of John. He does not know that there is one Paderewski and he does not know that there is one "Paderewski" expression. To relieve Pierre's ignorance, it is enough to say *de dicto* that London is Londres. To relieve John's ignorance, it is enough to say *de dicto* that Paderewski is Paderewski. In John's case, given Singularity, he must revise his Assignments; there will be one "Paderewski"-Assignment instead of two. In Pierre's case, he must revise his Assignments in such a way that the "Londres"-Assignment and the "London"-Assignment have the same value. But he need not conclude that the "Londres"-Assignment and the "London"-Assignment are Assignments of coindexed expressions, since he must also become apprised of the fact that "London" and "Londres" are variants of the same expression. One could apprise him of this explicitly, of course, but, short of that, Pierre could hold, in the face of being told that London is Londres, that "London" and "Londres" are no more variants of the same expression than "Cicero" and "Tully" are. It is at this point that the treatment of the "Paderewski" and "Londres" puzzles diverge.

This divergence can be observed further, reverting to the reverse scenario introduced above, in which the hearer believes there is one person named "Paderewski"; the speaker believes there are two. The speaker then tries to straighten the hearer out by uttering: "Paderewski is not

Paderewski." It is clear that the speaker's utterance will not alone suffice to meet this goal. For consider the form of the speaker's utterance. It cannot contain attributed Assignments, since the speaker believes that the addressee believes Singularity and therefore will have only one "Paderewski"-Assignment. Thus the logical form of the speaker's utterance will be as in (48):

(48) Paderewski$_1$ is not Paderewski$_2$.

How is the hearer to take (48)? He might reason as follows: If the speaker is not uttering a contradiction of the form (49) (and why would any speaker do that?), the speaker's sentence must have the form (48).

(49) Paderewski$_1$ is not Paderewski$_1$.

But, if the sentence has the form (48), Singularity, which the speaker must believe, dictates that the speaker believes that there are two "Paderewski"-expressions. The hearer could then conclude that the *speaker* believes that there are two people named "Paderewski," but he would not be enlightened by an utterance of (48) about anything he himself holds about Paderewski. The speaker, unlike in the case just discussed, would not be denying anything the hearer holds to be the case, and the hearer will be left in the dark by (48) as to what two people the speaker is distinguishing.

But what of Pierre, in a comparable reverse scenario, where we suppose he believes that there is one city with the two names "London" and "Londres," and also believes that "London" and "Londres" are variants of the same expression? Pierre believes (50):

(50) "[$_1$ London]" translates "[$_1$ Londres]"

To inform Pierre that he is incorrect, the speaker may utter:

(51) London$_1$ is not Londres$_2$.

But this utterance, in contrast to the formally identical (48), succeeds to the desired end. Why should this be?

By believing (50), Pierre believes that the expressions "London" and "Londres" are variants of the same expression, and that, since they are, they are covalued. But he does not hold that this belief is analytic. He knows that he might be wrong that the two names are translations. Thus, when the speaker says (51), he may bring together his translational belief and the assertion of the speaker and find them to be in conflict, and, if he decides to believe the speaker, he will accept (51) as corrective. Matters are quite different in the case of John. He believes that (52) is true:

(52)   Paderewski$_1$ is Paderewski$_1$.

But (52) really is analytic, and is not therefore, a candidate for revision.

We may now raise an important point concerning (37) and (38), repeated here.

(37)   Pierre believes that Londres$_1$ is beautiful and "Londres$_1$" has the value Londres$_1$.

(38)   Pierre does not believe that London$_2$ is beautiful and "London$_2$" has the value London$_2$.

Supposing that the speaker believes the translation statement (50), he will consider (53) a translation of (37), since he considers "London" and "Londres" to be variants of the same expression:

(53)   Pierre believes that London$_1$ is beautiful and "[$_1$London]" has the value London$_1$.

Therefore, in principle, the speaker can correctly describe Pierre's problem by uttering (38) and (53). There would have to be some sort of preparation for this, however; since the distinction between the two "London"-expressions is inaudible, a hearer would not otherwise be able to distinguish them. Now suppose someone—we have Kripke in mind—were to ask the following question:

(54)   Does Pierre, or does he not, believe that London is pretty?

The hearer of (54), if he understands it as a *de dicto* attribution, would have to know which question is being asked; on one indexing of the question the appropriate answer is (38), while on the other indexing the appropriate answer is (53). On the other hand, if it understood as a non–*de dicto* attribution, then Kripke is assuredly right that the question cannot be answered as asked, since it is unambiguous, the speaker believing, unlike Pierre, that there is only one place London, and given the Assignment Principle and Singularity, that there is only one expression "London."[16]

2.6   Concluding Remarks

Our goal in this chapter has been to present a theory that incorporates the view that syntactic expressions of natural language play the role of modes of presentation. By attributing an Assignment to an agent, a speaker says that the agent holds a belief with respect to a certain mode; but to attribute that belief under a different but equivalent Assignment is to attribute with respect to a different mode, and is not to attribute the same belief. On our way of conceiving of "substitution," the central consideration thus becomes the individuation of syntactic expressions and the conditions that govern their deployment in speakers' utterances.

A speaker may have firm grounds for attributing semantic beliefs to an agent; in the case of *de dicto* attributions, a speaker may know, for example, that the agent uses one expression and not another to refer to an object. The speaker can know such things about an agent while knowing nothing about the qualities the agent associates with the objects the agent refers to. A person may come to the conclusion that there are two people with the same name, and then deploy two cospelled expressions to refer to those people. But what the grounds would be for her coming to the conclusion that there are two different people, or how she thinks of them, is a different matter altogether. However an agent may conceive of an individual, and whatever role this may play in how one associates a name with a value, such conceptions are not modes of presentation in our theory.[17]

The virtue of taking expressions as modes of presentation is that there are precise criteria by which the modes may be individuated.[18] The analogy of syntactic expressions to modes of presentation as classically conceived is not complete, however. As Frege had it, the modes of presentation were senses of expressions, but this created difficulties. In particular, he had to face the fact that the sense of an expression may vary widely from speaker to speaker. Given his theory of indirect reference, this had the consequence that it would be at best unlikely that one could ever attribute the same belief to two persons. Ultimately, Frege was forced to concede, in "The Thought" ([1918] 1977, 12), that "we must really stipulate that for every proper name there shall be just one associated manner of presentation of the object so designated." That requirement played the role of Singularity in Frege's theory. But Frege had no right to this requirement, which flew in the face of the facts. Of course Frege had early on decided that expressions themselves could not serve the role of modes of presentation, the result being his misidentification of

Singularity as a condition on senses—not, as it should be, a condition on syntactic expressions. Our version of Singularity is much more natural. In the case of shared belief, if speakers believe that there is a person named "Cicero," then they believe that there is one "Cicero"-expression that refers to him. Furthermore, that "Cicero"-expression may serve as a mode of presentation of Cicero in a belief attributed to them. Admittedly, they might not put their belief in exactly these terms. They might say that Cicero has a name and that that name is "Cicero." But they will agree that Cicero has only one name "Cicero." That is the essence of Singularity, as we conceive of it.

To conclude, then, the analysis we have presented seems to us to confirm the distinction between names and expressions we have drawn, as well as the utility of that distinction in explaining belief attribution. We have argued that speakers' beliefs concerning Assignments, as well as their beliefs concerning the beliefs of others concerning Assignments, may be syntactically represented in the logical forms of sentences. This lies at the heart of the *de dicto*/non–*de dicto* distinction we have advocated. The role of syntax in these matters is thus greater, in our opinion, than has generally been recognized. As Kripke emphasized, there is nothing paradoxical in the various puzzles we have discussed; there are perfectly straightforward descriptions that accommodate all the facts. The problem, of course, is to discover the terms in which the description should be stated. The syntactically based description presented here, we have argued, does that well.

Appendix: The Propositional Status of Assignments

A large part of our knowledge of language is unconscious; we know its character only indirectly. But there are some aspects of our knowledge of language that are conscious, or at least can be made so. We know, and can be conscious of the fact, that the expression "pewter" refers to a certain metal, and that "Aaron Burr" refers to Aaron Burr. In the case of words like "pewter," we can even worry, when confronted with a metal object, whether "pewter" is the right expression to use when referring to it. This kind of worry, which we often feel, provides direct evidence that we can have conscious awareness of the relationship between an expression and what it refers to. The case of the expression "pewter" is in some ways different from the case of the expression "Aaron Burr," but, parallel to the case of "pewter," we can wonder who the name "Aaron Burr" refers to, or if, somehow, we were confronted by Aaron Burr, we might wonder what his name was. These are conscious worries concerning the relationship between expressions and their referents, worries concerning Assignments.

But very often we are not conscious of the Assignments we know. When we say "Aaron Burr shot Alexander Hamilton," we typically do not entertain the occurrent beliefs that "Aaron Burr" refers to Aaron Burr and that "Alexander Hamilton" refers to Alexander Hamilton. Nor do we typically entertain the occurrent belief that "shot" denotes shooting. Expressions may be used to refer, but their use is not typically guided by occurrent conscious knowledge of the Assignments that state what their referents are. Assignments, which play an important role in explaining our referential behavior, stand to the side. Using expressions to refer is typically "second nature."

Normally, when we converse, we tacitly believe that we and our interlocutors are operating with the same set of Assignments. We can, however, discover that this is not so, and then the conflicting Assignments become the subject of conscious examination. We may find that while one believes that a certain expression "*A*" refers to *X*, the other believes that "*A*" refers to *Y*. Or we may find that one believes that *X* is referred to by "*A*," while the other believes that *X* is referred to by "*B*." And then we become conscious of our Assignments, and overtly ascribe Assignments to each other. Of course, among the things we believe, Assignments are not unusual in this respect. Very frequently, in the course of conversation, we discover that we do not share beliefs. The beliefs need not have been the subject of conversation, and need not have been consciously held by either party. Even so, we may discover ourselves to be in conflict, and beliefs that were not previously conscious become the subject of conversation.

In the body of this chapter we argued that not only can we overtly ascribe Assignments to each other, but we can do this covertly as well. In this respect, Assignments are certainly unusual. Normally, when we ascribe a belief to another person, we actually utter a *that*-clause that refers to the belief. Reference is overt. But we can ascribe Assignments without uttering them. The *de dicto* reading of "John believes that Cicero was an orator" depends, in our account, on ascribing to John the beliefs that Cicero was an orator and that "Cicero" refers to him as a complex. The former ascription is overt, the latter covert. When we say that an agent has a belief, we can do so in such a way as to make it crucial in what terms the belief is held. The covert ascription of Assignments is the means by which we do this.

Assignments are beliefs concerning language; they are *de lingua* beliefs about linguistic *expressions*. To talk about Assignments, or ascribe them, we have used sentences of the form ⌜(that) "[A]" refers to A,⌝ or ⌜(that) "[A]" refers to B,⌝ forms that express propositions that contain relationships between expressions and their values. About these propositions, a number of questions present themselves, circling around how expressions and their values are tied to each other. Is it arbitrary that "Cicero" refers to Cicero? Is it trivial that "Cicero" refers to Cicero? Can Assignments be informative? Is it contingent that "Cicero" refers to Cicero, or it is necessary that this is so? These questions are important within the confines of the analysis we develop in this book. It is particularly important that Assignments have the appropriate metaphysical status, a point of particular importance in the next chapter. But these questions have more general importance as well. Assignments stand at the heart of our semantic knowledge. If we wish to know the kind of knowledge that knowledge of language is, we must, among other things, know what kind of knowledge Assignments represent. In furtherance of both goals, let us take up these questions.

Are Assignments Arbitrary?
Theorists with very different perspectives have said that signs are arbitrary. Frege said it, but so did Saussure. The claim can be taken in different ways, however, depending on how one takes the term "sign," and how one takes the term "arbitrary." If what is meant is that we might have had different names, that we perhaps *do* have different names in different possible worlds, then it is a claim that is perfectly true, and no concern of ours. But this is not to be confused with a quite different claim that does concern us. If included with the extension of "signs" are the syntactic expressions that contain names, it is the claim that such expressions might be given their values in any old way. But taking the claim as written, as being about *expressions,* we can see that it must be wrong, for the following reasons.

To qualify as a speaker of a language, a certain buy-in is required; we must enter into a certain sort of social contract, agreeing to use the words of the language in certain specified ways so as to fit into a society of language users. Such agreement is part of acquiring a language, and once the contract is signed, a speaker's usage is in no way arbitrary; to the contrary, it will be in conformance with the covenants of the contract. This all goes for Assignments. In the language of the society into which we enter the contract, Assignments are one way and not some other, and, as the contract reads, the connections between expressions and their values are certainly not arbitrary; it matters which way they go. In the English contract, the one we have all agreed to, "[Frege]" refers to Frege, and "[Russell]" refers to Russell. That is how the social contract reads in this world. It is not the case in this world that "[Frege]" refers to Russell and "[Russell]" refers to Frege. So Assignments for expressions that contain names are hardly arbitrary once the world is specified.

The same goes for common nouns. Dogs are called "chiens" in French, and there is a possible language in which cats are called "dogs" and dogs are called "cats." But that is not the way things are in English in this world. So while it is right to say that given any human vocable there might be a language such that expressions containing that vocable refer to dogs, it is not right to say that you can use any human vocable in any language to refer to dogs. It does not follow from the fact that something *could* have been called differently that speakers may *refer* to that thing as they please. And again the reason involves the social dimension. If you have agreed to the English social contract, expressions containing "dog" refer to dogs, and expressions containing "cat" do not. So Assignments for expressions that contain common nouns are hardly arbitrary once the language is specified. In the normal practice of speakers, there is really no need for them to consider the arbitrariness of the signs they use; for all intents and purposes, from the perspective of the language user, there is no arbitrariness at all.

Now Frege held, in the opening paragraphs of "On Sense and Reference" ([1892] 1970, 50), that the signs "a" and "b" cannot be under discussion in "$a = b$," since those signs are arbitrary. "Nobody can be forbidden to use any arbitrarily producible event or object as a sign for something," he tells us. Frege is making two points. The first point is expressed in the sentence quoted, that one can use any sign for something that one wants. The second point is that, because this is so, because signs are arbitrary *in this sense,* it cannot be the case that signs are under discussion in "$a = b$." Now the first point is perfectly fine if addressed to someone who is in the business of language design, perhaps setting up a formal language for reasoning about some domain. If you want to have, in your language, a constant term to refer to an item, Xerxes, say, then nobody can forbid you to use any arbitrary sign you want to refer to Xerxes. But suppose that you are not in the business of setting up such a language, but are rather in the business of saying something to your friend about Xerxes. And suppose that you are an English speaker and that your friend is too. Then you are certainly not free to use any arbitrary sign you want to refer to Xerxes. If you say "Xerxes was cruel" you will be understood as attributing cruelty to Xerxes, but if you say "Frammis was cruel" you certainly will not be understood that way. Of course you could have an understanding with your friend that you will use "Frammis" instead of "Xerxes" whenever you wish to refer to Xerxes—in other words, you could *establish* that sort of code—but that would be to amend the social contract that you were both assuming, which had it that "Xerxes" refers to Xerxes and that "Frammis" does not.

That is the point that Frege missed. Thus, if we focus on how languages are actually used, it cannot be argued that identity sentences in English, German, or any other natural language are not about the signs they contain because those signs are arbitrary. And that is because, in languages in general, signs are not arbitrary. They are fixed by social conventions, and flouting those conventions risks not being understood. So Frege's second point collapses; still left hanging is Frege's conclusion, which now can only be called a claim. And that claim is that in "$a = b$" the signs "a" and "b" are not under discussion, where now we are considering natural-language occurrences of sentences of that form. As far as what Frege argues, then, it might or might not be the case that signs are under discussion in sentences of the form "$a = b$." In the next chapter we present our case that in some occurrences of identity statements, signs are mentioned, and that in other cases this is not so—that they may be *de dicto* or non–*de dicto*. In any event, signs are not arbitrarily used; the Assignments we believe are examples of codicils in an agreed-to contract. They are socially binding, nonarbitrary, and we treat them as such.

Are Assignments Trivial?
Is ""[Frege]" refers to Frege" trivial? If we are incautious, it might seem that it is, but this would be mistaken. If trivial means incapable of conveying information not previously known, then it is hard to see how ""[Frege]" refers to Frege" could be, since the information it conveys is no different than what is conveyed by "[Frege] refers to Gottlob," and that does not seem trivial at all. Since each of these pairs the same expression with the same value, and since this is a relation that we may be in the position of not knowing obtains, a nontrivial proposition is expressed, regardless of the form it takes.

But though apparently not trivial, surely ""[Frege]" refers to Frege," when said to someone, fails to be very *helpful*. Certainly, if people have never heard of Frege, or of "Frege," if they know nothing of the man or his name, then being told ""[Frege]" refers to Frege" is no better than being told ""[Grefe]" refers to Grefe." For those people, there is no connection to anything they know of. And matters do not improve much if they are knowledgeable in one of these ways or the other (inclusively). Consider the cases: (i) If the hearers know the name, but not the man, then ""[Frege]" refers to Frege" is no better than ""[Frege]" refers to somebody." But unless the hearers had imagined that expressions containing the name "Frege" might not refer at all, the hearers were already assuming that "[Frege]" refers to somebody. (ii) If the hearers do not know the name, but know Frege, saying ""[Frege]" refers to Frege" still will not be helpful, since precisely what the hearers cannot do is to identify Frege by name. They will not know who is being talked about, at least not through hearing that utterance alone. All they will learn is that someone is named "Frege." (iii) As for those that know the man and the name, there are two groups. There are those that have already connected the man with his name, and they will gain nothing from being told ""[Frege]" refers to Frege." And, as for those that know the man and the name but have not connected them, being told ""[Frege]" refers to Frege" does not alone serve to connect them.

Saying ""[Frege]" refers to Frege" thus seems a pretty useless endeavor no matter who you are talking to, at least if not supplemented by deixis, or some other way of independently making it clear who is being talked about. But it is a far cry from uselessness to triviality, and these should not be confused. ""[Frege]" refers to Frege" may not be a very effective way of communicating this particular relation, but it is no more trivial, *qua* proposition, than ""[Frege]" refers to Gottlob."

Are Assignments Informative?
If Assignments have nontrivial content, as we have argued, then there should be some information that a speaker can acquire by virtue of having grasped that content; otherwise, they would be uninformative, to go along with the lack of utility we have just surveyed. Certainly, if we suppose that one knows the name "Aristotle," knows who Aristotle was, and knows that "Aristotle" refers to him, then the statement ""Aristotle" refers to Aristotle" seems true, but nonetheless uninformative to us because of what we already know. But suppose we take some of this knowledge away; does ""Aristotle" refers to Aristotle" still strike us as uninformative?

By way of answering this, consider the statement ""And" refers to and." But before doing so, we need to make an emendation in order to dispense with the irrelevant and misleading conventions of current written English to capitalize proper names and initial words of sentences. What we wish to consider is the statement that we write: ""and" refers to and." Now, *if we already know that "and" is a name,* then it seems right to say that ""and" refers to and" is true, at least if and exists and "and" is and's name. Again, it is not trivial that "and" refers to and; if and also has the name "but," then ""and" refers to and" is no more trivial than ""and" refers to but."

But suppose that we do not know whether "and" is a name. What then? Is the statement still uninformative? Suppose it turns out that "and" is not a name but a conjunction. Does the conjunction "and" refer to and? And what would it mean to say that it did? What is troubling here is that the word "and" is being used in a syntactic position that it is uncomfortable occupying; the word "and" cannot appear in the positions in which expressions containing names can appear, and expressions containing names cannot appear in positions in which "and" can appear. If "and" is a conjunction, then it is a (syntactic) category mistake to say ""and" refers to and." For that reason, although many things have been said about the logical connectives, no one has ventured to say that "and" (or "$\wedge$" or "&") refers to and (or $\wedge$ or &).

The moral to draw from this is that the seeming truth and uninformativeness of statements of the form ""X" refers to X" crucially derive from the prior assumption that "*X*" is a name. But nothing in the statement ""*X*" refers to *X*" says that "*X*" is a name. So if we restrict ourselves just to the content of statements of the form ""*X*" refers to *X*" (and are careful not to smuggle in assumptions that are not contained in the propositional content of statements of that form, at least as traditionally conceived), then it becomes clear that they are by no means uninformative; they can in fact be false, or perhaps nonsensical, depending on one's analysis of category mistakes, and other such violations that might arise. One could guard against this possibility by stipulating that certain conditions be antecedently met; we could insist that only if "*X*" is a name, and *X* exists, does "*X*" refer to *X*. The point, however, is that there is nothing about the statement ""*X*" refers to *X*" *itself* that tells us that these conditions are satisfied, for any given value of "*X*."

There is an inference, however, that can be made; given the existence of linguistic category mistakes, from the simple assumption that a sentence is syntactically well formed we can infer both that "*X*" is a name, and that *X* exists. To see this, observe that the two-place predicate "____refers to ____" imposes grammatical requirements, including, importantly, requirements of a syntactic sort, on the expressions that surround it. Putting aside the locution in which we say people refer, the first must be the name of an expression and the second must be something namable. Noun Phrases (NPs) are the syntactic constituents of sentences in natural languages that contain names and refer to things that are namable. Conjunctions are not. So it follows that we bring to the appreciation of sentences such as ""Aristotle" refers to Aristotle," the grammatical knowledge that, if ""Aristotle" refers to Aristotle" *is* grammatical, it must be that ""Aristotle"" refers to a name and "Aristotle" refers to something namable. So if we are to evaluate the statement ""and" refers to and," we have a choice as to whether it is grammatical or not. If it is, then "and" is a new and unfamiliar name, and and is a new and unfamiliar object. If it is not, then, "and" might be the familiar conjunction, in which case the statement makes no sense. Here is the important point. Suppose we are told that ""Glemp" refers to Glemp." And suppose we assume, as we virtually always do, that what we have been told, mysterious though it might be, is at least grammatical. That assumption allows us to infer a lot. We can infer that the speaker believes that the name "Glemp" exists. We can infer that the speaker believes that Glemp exists, and we can infer that the speaker believes that the name "Glemp" refers to Glemp. All this we can infer while for all the world having no idea who in fact Glemp is; rather, these are inferences that are underwritten solely by our grammatical, more specifically, syntactic, knowledge.

That we can draw these inferences is another way to see the nontrivialness of Assignments, since they may serve to inform people of the existence of names and their links to individuals; Assignments are neither trivial nor inherently uninformative. But, as discussed, if a proposition such as that "Glemp" refers to Glemp is expressed as ""Glemp" refers to Glemp," it will be virtually useless. Expressed this way, such statements fail, in and of themselves, to inform someone who they are *about*; nothing follows from them that is, traditionally speaking, part of their propositional content. It is a hard question, one not addressed here, how speakers come to know the relationship between expressions and the objects they are acquainted with. There are many paths and many cases to consider. But it is clear that what we say about Assignments applies more generally. To take the case of definite descriptions, if one knows the meanings of all of the words in a language, and certain compositional rules, one thereby knows the meanings of all of the definite descriptions in that language. But that does not guarantee that one will know what those definite descriptions denote. We know the meaning of the definite description "the oldest woman in Dallas," but probably none of us knows who that definite description denotes. But definite descriptions are such that, since we know what they mean, we know what properties a person would have to have to rightly be called "the oldest woman in Dallas." Frege thought that the same should be said about names, while Kripke argued that he was wrong to think that. But whichever way it is, nevertheless few statements in and of themselves, without appeal to prior knowledge on the part of the hearer, have the capacity to acquaint the hearer with the topic under discussion and to say something about that thing. As we have seen, much that we are informed of when hearing statements of the form ""X" refers to X" derives from our knowledge of syntax. And that knowledge is not trivial. But syntax alone, though much more important than has been realized, is not sufficient to acquaint us with the objects under discussion.

Are Assignments Contingent or Necessary?
We have established so far that Assignments, when expressed in certain ways, while almost useless, are neither arbitrary, trivial, nor uninformative. But how do they stand metaphysically? Are they necessary or contingent?

In answering this question, we initially must be clear about the following, that within the semantics of each language, there is an Assignment *function* from the expressions in that language to their values. Let us reflect this fact directly in the statement of Assignments, so that "*g*("[Aristotle]") = Aristotle" expresses one application of that function. This application makes reference to the expression "[Aristotle]" and to the person Aristotle, and states that the latter is the value of the former, truthfully, we presume, although others may be false, for instance, "*g*("[Aristotle]") = Plato." Assuming then that "*g*("[Aristotle]") = Aristotle" is true, the question now is whether it is contingently true or necessary.

The expression "[Aristotle]" in our example is an expression of English, and the Assignment itself is a clause in the semantics of English. "*g*("[Aristotle]") = Aristotle" expresses a piece of the semantics of English. It is true if the expression "[Aristotle]" exists, and if Aristotle exists, and if the latter is the value of the former. But what does it mean to say that "[Aristotle]" is an expression of English? As the term "language" is used here, difference between Assignment functions entails distinctness of language. It is not allowed that one language have more than one Assignment function. To be sure, speakers know different people and have different expressions to refer to them. And we say, in our rough but reasonable way, that such speakers may nevertheless speak the same language. But the important point for language use is whether the participants *consider* themselves, for current purposes, to be speaking the same language with the same Assignment function, and of course we often *do* consider ourselves to be operating with the same Assignment function. When we suspect that we might differ in this way, we take the appropriate precautions, a point we touched on before. But in the not-very-idealized way of speaking in which the Assignment function (in part) determines the language, we may say that, in all circumstances in which the language is spoken, the Assignment function will be the same. For convenience, let us use the term "English" to designate a language in this sense, and let us further suppose that we speak this language in common.

So the expression "[Aristotle]" exists in all worlds in which English is spoken. But it is also true that it exists *only* in the worlds in which English is spoken. "[Aristotle]" is an expression of English, and English only; it is not an expression of French, or any other language. It is true that the vocabulary of French contains a word *like* our word "Aristotle" (a word that is pronounced slightly differently), and, for certain purposes, the French word and the English word stand as tokens of the same type (see the discussion in chapter 2). But the English expression "[Aristotle]" does not appear among the Assignments of French, or any other language. Therefore there will be no languages, and no possible worlds, in which "g("Aristotle")= X" is true, where "X" refers to someone other than Aristotle. Given that "g("[Aristotle]") = Aristotle" is true, it is true in all and only the worlds in which English is spoken and Aristotle exists. And since the worlds in which English is spoken are exactly the worlds in which the expression "Aristotle" exists, the Assignment "g("[Aristotle]") = Aristotle" will be true in all possible worlds in which "[Aristotle]" exists and Aristotle exists. Given the existence of the items referred to, "g("[Aristotle]") = Aristotle" is necessary. Of course this result is completely general; an Assignment to a term in a language is true in all worlds in which both the language is spoken and the referent of the term exists. The function g expresses a necessary relation between a term and its referent.

Of course, when we say, in English, ""[Aristotle]" refers to Aristotle," we first mention an expression of English and then use one. And if what we really have is ""[Aristotle]" refers to [Aristotle]," we have mentioned and used the same expression of English. Oddly, to evaluate the truth of ""[Aristotle]" refers to [Aristotle]," we must, in order to determine the value of the last expression, use a piece of the semantics of English that states that which the sentence we are analyzing asserts. In asserting a metalinguistic truth, we grammatically rely on the same metalinguistic truth. This is another source for the belief, already discounted, that Assignments are trivial. But when we come to cases such as ""[Frege]" refers to Gottlob" we use a metalinguistic truth about the expression "[Gottlob]" to evaluate a metalinguistic statement concerning the value of the expression "[Frege]." And there is no feeling of triviality at all. But these observations do not touch the question whether Assignments are necessary or contingent; as is well known, necessary truths may be given trivial expression or nontrivial expression.

Lastly, it should be clear that it is quite another matter from the one addressed here to ask whether the same person in different possible worlds might bear different names, or whether the same name might have different bearers in different possible worlds. The argument just given relies crucially on distinguishing names from expressions. Expressions are bits of syntax, not bits of sound, and are the unique property of the languages that contain them. Once one sees that, the necessity of true Assignments becomes clear, as befits propositions that express identities.

So Assignments are nonarbitrary, nontrivial, informative in certain ways, although for certain purposes of little practical use. But not all. They are useful in circumstances in which the form of words speakers choose makes a difference in what they say; not only are they useful, they are essential to and characteristic of the *de dicto* use of language. *De dicto* use, we should emphasize, is not limited to attributions of belief and other propositional attitudes. It is to be found wherever sentences are used in an *explicit* context of Assignments, as we have it, with Assignments as constituents of their logical forms. Often it will be of no matter whether this context is explicit or not; to that extent there will be no discernible difference between the use of a sentence *de dicto* or non–*de dicto*. But sometimes it does. Propositional attitudes is one example. Others include identity statements, the topic of the next chapter. In that context, that Assignments are necessary, if true, will be of no small importance.

Notes

1. We have in mind puzzles such as the Paderewski puzzle, initially discussed by Kripke (1979). In this chapter, we discuss this case, and the related Londres puzzle, in section 2.5.

2. Notationally, what we have is not unlike what is done in logic, where, for instance, the variables that occur in formulas are distinguished as "x_1," "x_2," "x_3," etc. Any number of each variable may occur in a given proof, and while all occurrences of a variable will have a uniform assignment, occurrences of different variables may or may not be assigned the same values. And comparably to logic, where we would not normally have a different proof under a uniform permutation of the variables, so too do we need an invariance principle for discourse, so that they do not differ when different numerals are employed to display the same pattern of expression occurrences.

3. See the discussion in chapter 1, section 2.3.

4. In our *Indices and Identity,* we constructed a theory of anaphora based on this conception, reserving the term "vehicle change" for this relation. Included among vehicle changes are point-of-view translations—for example, translation between "I" and "you" or "he," with indices kept constant. This has important consequences for invariance of logical form; full discussion lies beyond the scope of our present concerns, however.

5. Such substitution may yield an equivalent Translation Statement, if the statements are relative to equivalent discourses (roughly, discourses that differ only in the numerical values of the indices employed). Otherwise, the Translation Statements will be of distinct expressions.

6. A bit more precisely, we say that Assignments are *equivalent* if and only if they pair expressions with the same value. It now follows that an Assignment is equivalent with itself, as well as to covalued Assignments to distinct expressions.

7. As it happens, English can be structurally misleading in this regard, in ways that French, for example, is not: the English complementizer *that* may often be deleted, so that even if one has a sentence of the form "John believes that S and S'" it might be of the structure "John believes [*that* [S and S']]" or "John believes [*that* [S]] and [*that* [S']]." In the first, a *single* belief, expressed as a conjoined sentence, is attributed; in the second, *two* beliefs are attributed, this latter form being, in effect, a reduced form of (20).

8. A logical form such as (19a), in the terms of our account, is not itself subject to further analysis, in that there is no new information to be gained by appending an attributed Assignment to an attributed Assignment. Suppose that we were to analyze a logical form containing an attributed Assignment in this way. There are two possibilities, depending on which term the attribution applies to:

(i) a. John believes "Cicero" has the value Cicero and "Cicero" has the value Cicero.
   b. John believes "Cicero" has the value Cicero and ""Cicero"" has the value "Cicero."

In neither of these logical forms does the Assignment attributed add anything to what is otherwise provided by the primary attribution. In the former, it is simply redundant. In the latter, the information expressed by the Assignment is known trivially, by virtue of knowing the language and the quotation-mark convention. Example (19a), as it stands, is completely analyzed.

9. One might object on factual grounds that, given our requirement that in the *de dicto* case, the agent must hold his or her belief under a particular Assignment, our analysis of substitution failure is insufficiently general. There is the intuition that it is true to say of Lois that she believes that Superman flies but not that she believes that Clark Kent flies even if she has never heard the names "Superman" and "Clark Kent." Nothing that we have said would prevent this substitution. However, as pointed out by Saul (1997), there is also the intuition that intersubstitution of these names is problematic even in what would seem to be transparent contexts—for example, "Superman has more luck with women

than Clark Kent." This suggests that, whatever one's analysis of these "dual-identity" cases, it may well be correct to claim that substitution failure derives from more than one source and that there is no general theory of substitution failure. *De dicto* attribution would constitute one limitation on substitution; whatever the principles are behind the dual-identity cases would constitute another. We wish to thank Stephen Schiffer for first bringing these considerations to our attention.

10. It might be argued that rather than analyzing *de dicto* attribution as containing both a use and a mention of an expression, we could gain essentially the same results by allowing that a single expression plays dual semantic roles. (See Loar 1972 for a suggestion along these lines.) The argument derives from Quine's (1953) well-known example:

(i) Giorgione was so-called because of his size.

On Quine's view, substitution failure of "Barbarelli" for "Giorgione" in producing (ii) from (i) shows that the occurrence of "Giorgione" makes a dual contribution: Giorgione himself and the expression "Giorgione."

(ii) Barbarelli was so-called because of his size.

If the occurrence of "Barbarelli" also makes a dual contribution—Barbarelli (=Giorgione), and the expression "Barbarelli"—the falsehood of (ii) is then explained. There is reason to doubt, however, that this argument supports the dual-role conclusion, since it neglects the role played by "so." Syntactically, "so" is a pronoun, which as it occurs in (i) is incorporated into the verb; see (iii) from which it derives, which suffices to exclude (iv):

(iii) Giorgione was called so because of his size.
(iv) *Giorgione was so-called "Giorgione" because of his size/*Giorgione was so-called so because of his size.

This suggests that (i) is syntactically parallel to (v), with "so" taking as its value a name of the person referred to by the subject of the sentence.

(v) Giorgione was called "Giorgione" because of his size.

Substitution cannot carry us from (i) to (ii) simply because the antecedent of "so" is thereby changed; the result would be comparable to "Barbarelli was called 'Barbarelli' because of his size." Substitution is possible, however, if the antecedent of "so" is not the subject—for instance, if it is in another sentence. If so, it is immaterial whether "Barbarelli" or "Giorgione" is the subject:

(vi) I was surprised to learn that Barbarelli was the Venetian painter Giorgione. I was not surprised that Barbarelli/Giorgione was so-called because of his size.

The role of anaphora in substitution is further shown by the true examples (vii) and (viii):

(vii) Giorgione was named for his size.
(viii) Giorgione was so-named for his size.

Unlike with "called," "so" is optional with "named," and substitution in (vii) yields the true (ix), while comparable substitution in (viii) yields (x), which is false with "Barbarelli" as the antecedent of "so."

(ix) Barbarelli was named for his size.
(x) Barbarelli was so-named for his size.

On the dual-role account, it would have to be a special property of the predicate "was so-called because of his size" (or perhaps just "so-called") that requires that its subject make a dual contribution. Certainly not all predicates are constrained in this way. What property would that be? The minimal contrast between (ix) and (x) tells the tale: it is the presence of the "so" that makes the difference. If we are correct, then there is no expression that makes a dual contribution; it is "so" that provides the second contribution.

11. Since the English/Latin distinction is central to our point in this section, we will use italics when citing Latin examples; English will continue to appear in roman type.

12. In presenting this puzzle, the story is often embellished by saying, for instance, that the agent believes that there are two people, one a statesman, the other a pianist. Putting matters this way, however, makes it appear as if the agent's having distinct descriptions is somehow part of the puzzle. This is incorrect. All that is required to generate this version of the puzzle is that the agent believe there are two people with the same name in contrast to the beliefs of the speaker—in other words, that the agent believe two "Paderewski"-Assignments.

13. Taken *de dicto*, a speaker uttering (31) and (32) says that the agent has one belief, but does not have another, distinct belief; when (31) is paired with "John believes Paderewski is not a genius," the speaker says that the agent has two distinct beliefs. This follows for the latter case by the same analysis as for the former—that is, by their having logical forms in which Assignments are attributed.

14. Normally, first-person reports in the present tense will be non–*de dicto*; they will only be *de dicto* to the extent that the speaker/agent wishes to contrast his own beliefs relative to Assignments that he believes to be equivalent. It is perhaps difficult to imagine a circumstance in which, given a belief, he would want to say he has it relative to a "Cicero"-Assignment, but not relative to a "Tully"-Assignment, given, of course, that he believes that they are equivalent Assignments. Otherwise, he would have no grounds for contrasting them, so there would be no need for him to commit himself to a belief with respect to a specified Assignment.

15. There are two other logical forms, both non–*de dicto*, which are in principle possible for "Londres is London." One is "$Londres_1$ is $London_1$." While for the speaker, this is a translational triviality, since Pierre believes that Londres is not London, he cannot believe that "Londres" and "London" are variant expressions for the same city. So it is hard to see how this could be the logical form. The second is "$Londres_1$ is $London_2$." But the speaker would utter this only if he did not believe "Londres" and "London" are cognates, and then we would only have a variant of the standard "Cicero"/"Tully" case.

16. On Kripke's view, all of the belief puzzle cases, including the standard cases of substitution failure of distinct but coreferring names (e.g., "Cicero" and "Tully"), arise from what he sees as paradoxical properties of belief reporting.

Crucially for him, this includes cases that he believes cannot be analyzed as arising from failures of substitution—for example, the Paderewski puzzle, in which he maintains there is no distinction comparable to that between "Cicero" and "Tully." Our disagreement with Kripke lies here; what we are saying is that Kripke's discussion is predicated on a misanalysis of the notion of linguistic expression. Once this is in place, the puzzle cases, understood *de dicto,* become uniform with the standard cases of substitution failure, but in a way, we note, compatible with a Millian theory of names. "Cicero" can be substituted for "Tully," for they corefer, but ""Cicero"" cannot be substituted for ""Tully,"" because what they refer to are plainly not identical; they are two different expressions (leaving aside aberrant beliefs about translation). Similarly, "Paderewski$_1$," can be substituted for "Paderewski$_2$," but not ""Paderewski$_1$"" for ""Paderewski$_2$,"" for they too refer to different expressions.

17. Given these remarks, it should be clear that we would not liken indices to footnote markers, where the footnotes themselves describe how an agent conceives of an individual, which seems to be what is envisaged in Bilgrami 1992.

18. Thus meeting a challenge set by Schiffer (1990, 257) that words cannot play the role of modes of presentation "until we are given the intended method of word individuation" without "appeal to word meanings."

3

Identity Statements

3.1 Two Intuitions about Identity Statements

It is common wisdom that primary among the things that one would want from an analysis of identity statements such as "Hesperus is Phosphorus" or "Cicero is Tully" is an account of their *informativeness*.[1] But there is a problem that any such account will encounter, one that has been appreciated at least since Frege. We may put it in this familiar way. If the content of the proposition expressed by an identity statement is just the referents of the terms flanking the identity sign and equivalence, then statements of the form ⌜α = β⌝, if true, have the same propositional content as statements of the form ⌜α = α⌝. "Hesperus is Phosphorus" and "Hesperus is Hesperus" would each have the same propositional content. But if the propositional content is identified with the information conveyed, how can it then be that these two statements differ in "cognitive value," as they must, given that "Hesperus is Hesperus" is a logical triviality, something that "Hesperus is Phosphorus" is not? How can it be that the information these statements convey differs when the propositions they express do not?[2]

In his writings, Frege advanced two quite distinct views of identity statements. The first is presented in section 8 of *Begriffsschrift*; the second is presented chiefly in the *Grundgesetze der Arithmetik* (see §§7, 20, 50, and 138), and in "On Sense and Reference." These two views have something in common; both deny that statements of the forms ⌜α = β⌝ and ⌜α = α⌝ express the *same* proposition. Frege's views about propositions—*judgeable contents* in the terminology of *Begriffsschrift*, and *thoughts* in latter Fregean terminology—and their constituents differed substantially in the two theories, however. In *Begriffsschrift,* Frege held that the content of identity statements is that the expressions flanking the identity sign have the same conceptual content (reference).[3] But then, to say of two distinct expressions that they corefer is clearly to say something different than that one expression corefers with itself. On this analysis, the identity symbol is analyzed as "identity of content" (symbolized as "≡"); see note 3. In contrast, in the latter theory of *Grundgesetze* and "On Sense and Reference," Frege maintains that the identity symbol is a sign of objectual identity; it denotes the concept that maps each object uniquely onto itself. This goes along with his introduction of the general distinction between sense and reference, because this relieves the burden on the reference of expressions to distinguish the propositions expressed by ⌜$\alpha = \beta$⌝ and ⌜$\alpha = \alpha$⌝. Since senses are part of the thought expressed, the identity sign can be taken to refer to objectual identity.

One way to conceptualize Frege's two theories is that they each capture distinct intuitions we have about identity statements: the *Begriffsschrift* theory captures the intuition that identity statements say of two expressions that they have the same reference, while the "On Sense and Reference" theory is that "be" is construed as objectual identity. While it will be our view that an analysis of identity statements should incorporate both of these intuitions, it was Frege's view that they were incompatible, and he ultimately jettisoned the former and maintained the latter. But he did not think that taking this step solved the problem of informativeness. To the contrary, Frege was aware that no theory stated solely in terms of the designata of expressions and objectual identity could do this, since all that a true statement of the form ⌜$\alpha = \beta$⌝ would express is that an object is self-identical, and this is not anything, in and of itself, that is informative, and nothing different from what ⌜$\alpha = \alpha$⌝ expresses. This semantic characteristic of identity statements, that when true they are about only one thing, appears to be at odds with their apparent logical structure as *relational* sentences;[4] grammatically, "be" occurs as a two-place predicate, and shows, with appropriate choice of items, the sort of grammatical properties usually associated with transitive clauses (e.g., case assignment in "He is him"). This tension did not go unnoticed; Frege begins "On Sense and Reference" by asking whether identity is a relation, and Russell, in *The Principles of Mathematics* (1937, 63), remarks that "The question whether identity is or is not a relation, and even whether there is such a concept at all, is not easy to answer. For, it may be said, identity cannot be a relation, since, when it is truly asserted, we have only one term, whereas two terms are required for a relation." The reason for concern with the relational character of identity statements was Frege's (and Russell's) insight that there must be *some* difference associated with the terms related by the identity predicate in order for identity statements to be informative; informativeness, they observed, springs, somewhat paradoxically, from difference, *not* from identity. Their common worry was that whatever this difference is, it is not to be found in the referent, given the conditions for the truth of identity statements.[5]

It is in overcoming this worry that the genius of the theory of "On Sense and Reference" lies, because Frege was able to reconcile in an entirely natural fashion taking "be" as objectual identity with the relational structure of identity statements. The initial building blocks of this analysis were already in place in *Begriffsschrift*, with the notion of mode of determination (*Bestimmungsweise*) found there.[6] But in *Begriffsschrift*, Frege only acknowledged this essence of what he later labeled *Sinn* for names, but not for sentences; the determination of reference was no part of the content expressed by a sentence. It is only when Frege comes to recognize that the sense/reference distinction could be applied to whole sentences that the senses associated with expressions can become constituents of propositions; thoughts become compositions of senses. Since the sense of "Hesperus" is not the same as that of "Phosphorus," "Hesperus is Phosphorus" and "Hesperus is Hesperus" express different thoughts (with different "cognitive values"); hence they may convey different information, the result sought by Frege. "A difference can arise," Frege says, "only if the difference between the signs corresponds to a difference in the mode of presentation of that which is designated," the sense being "wherein the mode of presentation is contained."[7] Thus, Frege recognizes the distinction between the thought (I):

A and *B* determine (present) the same reference.   (I)

and the thought (II):

A and *A* determine (present) the same reference.   (II)

where "*A*" and "*B*" stand for distinct senses. In (I) the object in question is presented in two distinct ways,[8] while in (II) the object is presented in but one way (albeit twice over). It is for this reason, Frege tells us, that the former can be informative, but not the latter. Moreover, because of the way (I) and (II) differ, statements that express thoughts as given in (II) must be analytic. Propositions (I) and (II) are not merely different propositions, they are also different *sorts* of propositions.

Cases (I) and (II) do not exhaust the cases, however. Suppose one stipulated that, in a language otherwise like English, there are names—let's use "Max" and "Oscar"—that have the same sense. If people *fully* grasped the sense of each of these names, they would then grasp that they are the same, and would realize that "Max is Oscar" expresses a thought of the form (II), allowing them to conclude that there is one man with two names. Furthermore, if those people then attended to the sense of "Max is Max," which also expresses a thought of the form (II), they would be in a position to realize that it is the same as the sense of "Max is Oscar." This, however, does not describe the normal course of events; according to Frege, it would be rather rare. He remarks that "when we use the word 'integral', are we always conscious of everything appertaining to its sense? I believe this is only very seldom the case. . . . If we tried to call everything to mind appertaining to the sense of this word, we should make no headway. Our minds are simply not comprehensive enough" (Frege [1914] 1979, 209). If we cannot become conscious of every aspect of the sense of a given word, then we also cannot become completely certain whether the sense of a word is the same as that of some other. Of course, if people grasp the sense of an expression "*a*," then they have also grasped a sense that is the sense of any other expression that expresses that sense. But from this it does not follow, even if they have grasped this sense *as* the sense of "*a*," that they will recognize it *as* the sense expressed by any other expression. People may know the sense of "*a*" and also know the sense of a distinct expression "*b*," but from this it does not follow that they would know that the two are the same, for they might never have been brought together in their minds.

Given this, suppose we have a person, who, although her language contains the synonymous names "Max" and "Oscar," does not know that Max is Oscar, and has never noticed that "Max" and "Oscar" express the same sense. This person would know the sense of "Max" and know the sense of "Oscar," but might not know that one sense is the sense of them both. In such a circumstance, this person might believe, through no error of logic, that there are two people, one named "Max" and one named "Oscar," not one. But then the question comes, how can it be that "Max is Oscar" is informative, in contrast to "Max is Max," if informativeness depends solely on sense, not on linguistic form? Observationally, the circumstance here seems no different from that of "Hesperus is Hesperus" and "Hesperus is Phosphorus"; it appears, in the case stipulated, that we have a contrast in informativeness between sentences that express the same thought.[9]

If Frege held that it is only difference in sense between expressions flanking the identity sign that allows for informativeness, it now appears that such a difference is not required. What options would be available at this point? We could deny that "Max" and "Oscar" could ever have the same sense, and hence dismiss the case at the outset. But to hold that distinct expressions do not share a sense would be at pains of denying that there are ever synonyms; we could just as well have given the above argument using the expressions "bellies" and "tummies" for someone who did not realize that they are synonymous.[10] But holding that no two distinct expressions can be synonymous would be an embarrassing piece of legislation, for now any possibility of synonymy would depend on expression identity. There would have to be a rule making the question whether two expressions have the same sense depend on whether they are tokens of the same type. In that way, expression-meaning would depend on expression-identity; the sense of an expression would depend on its form. But expression-identity is arbitrary, depending on contingent facts concerning particular languages, and is not the sort of thing that should have any force with respect to matters of sense. Thus this path is not open to Frege. But there is little else for him to do. Frege explicitly allows that distinct expressions may have the same sense; as he says in "On Sense and Reference" ([1892] 1970, 58), "The same sense has different expressions in different languages or even in the same language."[11] This allows that there might be no difference in the thought expressed by statements of the form $\ulcorner \alpha = \beta \urcorner$ and $\ulcorner \alpha = \alpha \urcorner$. But then, if statements of the form $\ulcorner \alpha = \beta \urcorner$ and $\ulcorner \alpha = \alpha \urcorner$ may differ in informativeness, while expressing the same thought (the thought (II)), it follows that informativeness is not just a matter of the thought or proposition expressed; something else must figure into informativeness. But if informativeness can be independent of sense, on what does it depend?

One move that naturally presents itself by way of an answer to this question is to reinstate a metalinguistic slant to the analysis, and recommendations to this effect are to be found in the literature. For instance, Howard Wettstein (1991a, 156; also see 1991b) suggests that "the explanation of the fact that 'Cicero' and 'Tully' may play different cognitive roles . . . would involve simply pointing out that competence with two names does not put one in a position to know whether or not the names corefer," while John Perry (1988, 241) asks, "What does . . . a competent speaker come to believe, when he accepts an utterance of "Cicero = Tully" as true? He or she surely learns that "Cicero" and "Tully" stand for the same thing, for this is required for the utterance to satisfy its truth conditions." Taken this way, the informativeness of "Cicero is Tully" turns, in some way or other, on there being two distinct expressions, as opposed to "Cicero is Cicero." This information about sameness and difference of linguistic forms, however, is *not*, on this view, to be taken as part of the proposition expressed by an identity statement; it is *extrapropositional*.[12] That it is makes sense in the context of a "senseless" analysis of identity statements, one that rejects that expressions are associated with Fregean senses; by divorcing information content from propositional content, the latter can be taken to be simply that an object is self-identical, for any identity statement whatsoever. Informativeness, on the other hand, arises from the sort of observation just cited—because expressions corefer, nothing thereby follows that speakers must believe that they do. Speakers are no more equipped to know that "Cicero is Tully" is true than to know that if "Cicero was a Roman" is true then so too is "Tully was Roman," for nothing in knowing a language inherently endows a speaker with information whether formally distinct expressions corefer or not. Interconnections of this sort must be learned; it is something about which one must be "informed." No such information can be conveyed, however, by statements of the form $\ulcorner \alpha = \alpha \urcorner$.[13]

But this sort of account carries a certain burden, for it still must show how identity statements can be used to *tell* someone that names are coreferential, so that they come to be informed. This is not to be achieved by virtue of the propositions they express; rather it must be that their use somehow implicates the relevant information. It is this implicature, grounded not in the meaning of identity statements but rather in the linguistic forms used to express that meaning, that is to account for how a true identity statement of the form $\ulcorner \alpha = \beta \urcorner$ can fill gaps in a speaker's beliefs. But, even if this burden can be met, divorcing meaningfulness from informativeness along the lines just described implies the rejection of a very fundamental principle central to Frege's thinking, that the informativeness of identity statements (any sentences, for that matter) results from the content of the propositions they express. Our claim will be that whatever the virtues of this principle might be, its rejection is not required in order to maintain an account of informativeness in which linguistic content plays a central role. For suppose that what is expressed by "$a = b$" includes the information that "a" refers to the same individual that "b" refers to. Frege's principle will now be respected; the relevant information will no longer be extrapropositional. Moreover, because the relevant linguistic information is now part of the proposition expressed by an identity statement, and will be directly conveyed by its use, relief will be provided from the burden of accounting for how someone could be informed by accepting an identity statement. Such relief would be general, applicable just as much to "Cicero is Tully" (for Frege, the case of distinct senses), as to our example "Max is Oscar." These cases are indistinguishable, not only in the sort of proposition they express, but also in their informativeness; they differ in both these regards, however, from "Cicero is Cicero" or "Max is Max."

For reasons that will become clear as we proceed, it is our view that an account along the lines just described, when suitably worked out, has much to recommend it; one immediate virtue we can cite is that it incorporates our two intuitions about identity statements, that derived from "On Sense and Reference" and *Grundgesetze* about objectual identity, and that from *Begriffsschrift* about expressions. But in accepting this view, we recognize that we part company with Frege in an important way, detaching ourselves from sense as Frege understood the notion. On his own terms, the Frege of "On Sense and Reference" was quite right to reject the metalinguistic aspects of the theory of *Begriffsschrift;* given his goals, linguistically particular information had no place, for the point was to abstract away from "arbitrary" characteristics of languages by which thoughts are conveyed. An account that would even be in part informative about the language itself, saying that two expressions are signs for the same thing, would to that extent not convey the right sort of information; it would not be what Frege would deem proper knowledge about the thing itself.[14] As he remarks in "On Sense and Reference"

([1892] 1970, 56), because an object can be *determined* in more than one way, "statements of the form $a = b$ often contain very valuable extensions of our knowledge and cannot always be established *a priori*." But in order for an identity statement to *cause* an extension of our nonlinguistic knowledge, it clearly need not *contain* that knowledge. Identity statements, we will argue, convey information, including the information that two names have the same reference, and that certainly cannot always be established *a priori*. The *informativeness* of identity statements is then the effect that this information can have on our epistemic states; insofar as accepting an identity statement, with the content it has, causes a change in these states, its utterance will have been an informative one.[15]

The task that faces us now is to show how we get from ⌜$\alpha = \beta$⌝ to ⌜the reference of "α" is the same as the reference of "β"⌝. Our tactic will be to show that this analysis follows from a general account of information content and its conveyance, an account in which, contrary to Frege's in *Begriffsschrift*, identity statements are not singled out for special treatment. We are not taking identity as content identity; if we were, that would be to parse ⌜the reference of "α" is the same as the reference of "β"⌝ as containing a relation *between expressions*, namely, "the reference of ___ is the same as the reference of ___," with the blanks to be filled in by terms denoting expressions. That is, we are *not* proposing an analysis of the identity sign as a relation between expressions, as did Frege in *Begriffsschrift*; rather, our view is that the identity sign denotes *objectual* identity. This implies that the terms standing to the sides of this sign in ⌜$\alpha = \beta$⌝ have their normal reference; thus our account will pose no bar to deriving the necessity of true identity statements of this form.[16] The trick for us will be to show that identity statements if true have more significance than simply as assertions of self-identity, that they also convey linguistic information to the effect that an object has two names. It will be our thesis that linguistic information can be conveyed by identity statements because the terms "*a*" and "*b*" not only have their normal reference, but may also be mentioned. These two aspects of the analysis, the objectual and the metalinguistic, will not be unconnected, for in "$a = b$," "*a*" refers to *a* and "*b*" refers to *b*, and the analysis turns on how this connection is made, as we will see.

3.2 On What It Is That Bears Reference

One characteristic invariably found in linguistic systems, be it logic or natural language, is a distinction between the lexicon and the syntax; we standardly distinguish between a listing of the vocabulary items of the language, and the occurrences of those items in sentential structures. Clearly, the criteria for identifying lexical items is not the same as that for syntactic items; we naturally say that there are two syntactic occurrences of the one lexical item "student" in an occurrence of "This student saw that student." The importance of observing this distinction comes immediately to the fore when we take the first step in giving an analysis, that of specifying the object of inquiry, by asking what can be the replacement instances of the schematic letters α and β in ⌜α is β⌝. The answer to this question, if our goal is to give a semantic analysis of identity statements, is that α and β must be *referring letters,* in that their substitutends must be terms that can be used to refer. But this still does not settle the matter, for it leaves open whether what answers to these letters are linguistic atoms, isolatable from their syntactic contexts, or parts of larger sentential molecules. In "Cicero is Tully," are we to take it that "Cicero" and "Tully" can be substituted for each other by virtue of the fact that they are coreferential words, or does their intersubstitutivity depend on their positions within the larger fabric of sentential structure? From this perspective, the issue about referring letters is thus the issue as to what sorts of linguistic objects can be used to refer: Are they items defined in lexical terms or syntactic items (an issue that arises just as much with the letters that occur in ⌜α is a Roman⌝ or ⌜α denounced β⌝ as in ⌜α is β⌝)? To put some terminology on the distinction we are drawing, let us distinguish between the lexical item or *name* "Cicero" and the syntactic *expression* of that name. We may then ask: Do names refer, or is it expressions that contain them? Let us explore this matter.[17]

Each speaker of a language, as part of knowing that language, has a vocabulary, or more precisely, a lexicon. A lexicon consists of a list of entries, organized with respect to certain linguistic criteria that individuate the entries; a particular speaker's lexicon is built in part on his or her beliefs about how those criteria individuate. Among these criteria perhaps the most primary is pronunciation, what would be encoded in a lexical entry as a phonological spelling. Speakers normally assume that if two items are pronounced differently, they are different items, up to limits of variation of dialect and language. For instance, one could imagine speakers having different beliefs as to whether "New York" and "Noo Yawk" are dialectical variants, or whether the English word "Venice" is the same word as the Italian word "Venezia." In general, speakers will not take what they believe to be *cognate* forms as reflecting distinct lexical items. By this criterion, then, there is one, and only one, lexical item "Cicero," for there is only one such pronunciation, and it is a different item from "Tully," which has a different pronunciation (at least for those who, like most of us, do not believe that they are variant pronunciations of one word).[18]

Now, in and of themselves, lexical items are just entries in a lexicon, itself a compendium of words, organized in terms of relevant properties. But, we may ask, how may such lexical items be used by speakers so as to refer? Presumably, by occurring in linguistically appropriate settings for such use. Primary among these settings are as parts of *sentences*—that is, when they occur as constituents of syntactic structures, as terminal elements of syntactic categories. When a lexical item such as "Cicero" occurs in the sentence "[$_S$ Cicero was a Roman]," we say that it is syntactically *expressed* as "[$_{NP}$ Cicero]." Speakers who utter this sentence thereby use this syntactic expression, and with such use, speakers normally believe that they can accomplish the goal of speaking about that which they intend to speak about. Speakers who wish to speak of Cicero will use the expression "[$_{NP}$ Cicero]" because they believe that "[$_{NP}$ Cicero]" refers to Cicero, and that by using this expression they may refer to Cicero.

Let us call such beliefs, which can be expressed by sentences of the form

⌜"[$_{NP}$ X]" has the value NP⌝

beliefs of *Assignments*.[19] *Names*, in this way of looking at matters, are lexical items that appear in syntactic structures for which there are Assignments. They are contained in syntactic expressions, and they are replacements for "X" in the schema above. Speakers' beliefs of Assignments are tied to their usage by the following principle:

The Assignment Principle: To be sincere, if a speaker uses a sentence containing an occurrence of an expression, the speaker believes an Assignment to that expression.

Sincere speakers who use an expression containing the name "Wittgenstein" do so in accordance with the Assignment Principle; when they utter "Wittgenstein wrote the *Tractatus*," they believe they make a truthful utterance about Wittgenstein because, in part, they believe a "Wittgenstein"-Assignment. Their belief is that the expression "[$_{NP}$ Wittgenstein]," not the name, refers to Wittgenstein, for it is by syntactic expression that speakers use names to refer. Speakers hold this belief even though they may be mistaken as to who Wittgenstein is; when uttering "Wittgenstein" they may systematically point to Russell, and insofar as the speakers' conceptual or factual knowledge can be divined, it would be Russell who would (uniquely) satisfy it. But no matter, the speakers still believe their "Wittgenstein"-expression refers to Wittgenstein, and their usage accords with this belief. Because the speakers' linguistic behavior conforms to the Assignment Principle regardless, we can confidently attribute to them the belief that "[$_{NP}$ Wittgenstein]" has the value Wittgenstein; we can say of the speakers: "They believe that "Wittgenstein" has the value Wittgenstein."[20] Making such an attribution is tantamount to saying that the speakers have the name "Wittgenstein" in their lexicon, for if they did not, they would not hold any beliefs relevant to it, and one would withhold any such attribution.[21]

Now, with respect to the Assignments speakers may be said to believe, they may believe that some of them are equivalent, in that they assign the same value. When speakers have such a belief about expressions—that is, that they are covalued—we will say that they believe them to be *translations*. Translations may be of two sorts, depending on whether the speakers believe that the difference between the expressions is within the limits of linguistic variation of dialects and languages. Speakers may believe "Venice" and "Venezia" are expressions of the same word, only affected by the forces of linguistic diachrony, but they need not believe this in order to believe that they are translations.[22] Virtually all speakers believe that the expression "Cicero" and the expression "Tully" are distinct, inherited from the phonological distinctness that distinguishes them as words.[23] But still speakers may believe that occurrences of "Cicero" and occurrences of "Tully" are translations. When speakers do, they will consistently assent to or dissent from "Cicero was a Roman" and "Tully was a Roman," and one could equally well say that those speakers believe

Cicero was a Roman or that they believe Tully was a Roman (although conversational conditions may dictate that reporting their belief one way may be more appropriate in a given situation than reporting it the other, just as a speaker may deem it to be more appropriate to use one of "Cicero was a Roman" or "Tully was a Roman" in a given communicative context).

When speakers believe that two expressions are translations of one another, they believe that a *Translation Statement* holds of them; they believe a statement of the form ⌜α translates β⌝, where substitutends for α and β are names of expression-types. There are two cases to consider:[24]

(i) ⌜"NP_i" translates "NP_i"⌝

(ii) ⌜"NP_i" translates "NP_j"⌝

(i), where α = β, is the case of linguistic identity (*modulo* the sort of linguistic variation mentioned above); (ii), where α ≠ β, is the case of linguistic distinctness.[25] If speakers believe a Translation Statement, they will believe that the related expressions are covalued, although only for statements of the form (ii) are speakers not compelled to believe this as a matter of grammar. For distinct expressions, our primary concern here, a speaker may or may not believe a Translation Statement holds of them. When she does not, a speaker may assent to one of "Cicero was a Roman" and "Tully was a Roman" but dissent from the other; but when she does, substitution of expressions is licensed in this sort of syntactic context, as well as in any other in which the expressions may occur (as it would be also by a belief in a statement of the form (I)).[26]

To see how these principles operate, consider a speaker who sincerely asserts "Cicero was a Roman." He does so because he believes, among other things, that (i) Cicero was a Roman, and (ii) "Cicero" has the value Cicero. Normally, it would not be necessary to explicitly express all this information, for a speaker would hardly take it that (ii) would add anything to the content of his assertion. Given that the Assignment Principle governs all uses of an expression by a sincere speaker, the mention of the Assignment can be consigned to background assumptions of discourse, as part of the general presumption that speakers use their words in the normal way. But it is not always the case that a speaker wants to leave this semantic information implicit; there may be good reasons for including it as part of what he says.

The primary, although not the only, context in which a speaker may want to do this is *attribution,* as, for example, with propositional attitude ascriptions, when one is speaking of what someone believes, thinks, and so on. A speaker can say that someone believes that a person referred to by "Cicero" is a Roman by attributing a complex consisting of (i) and (ii), so that by an utterance of "John believes Cicero was a Roman," what the speaker *says* is (1):

(1) John believes [[₁ Cicero] was a Roman and "[₁ Cicero]" has the value [₁Cicero]]

Why would a speaker say this? The reason is that by doing so he refrains from attributing the belief that Cicero was a Roman with respect to any translation of "Cicero." For instance, it cannot be inferred from (1) that John also believes that a person referred to by him as "Tully" was a Roman—that is, (1) does not imply (2):

(2) John believes [[₂Tully] was a Roman and "[₂Tully]" has the value [₂Tully]

This inference fails because ""[₂Tully]"" cannot be substituted for ""[₁ Cicero]."" These expressions, unlike "[₂Tully]" and "[₁ Cicero]," are not coreferential; they denote different expressions of the language, and hence cannot be translations.[27]

Let us remind ourselves of some terminology we are employing. We call forms that contain Assignments *de dicto,* because they mention the language used; those that do not contain Assignments we call *non–de dicto.* Examples (1) and (2) are *de dicto* attributions; non–*de dicto* attributions differ only in the absence of Assignments. Our result then is that belief attributions (more generally, attributions of propositional attitudes) are systematically ambiguous between *de dicto* and non–*de dicto* attributions. Substitution normally fails for *de dicto* attribution; thus, when speakers make a *de dicto* attribution, it is because they wish to refrain from saying whether the agent of the attribution believes any translations of the terms by which the belief is attributed. They are only prepared to go as far as attributing the belief in one way. On the other hand, speakers would make a non–*de dicto* attribution, one that does not attribute an Assignment, when they are neutral, uncommitted, or unconcerned about the manner in which the belief is held by the agent, for in this case, the inference from "John believes Cicero was a Roman" to

"John believes Tully was a Roman" is valid. Thus, while the conditions under which speakers would utter a belief attribution one way or the other are pragmatically grounded in the speakers' intentions, the de dicto/non–de dicto distinction itself is semantic, the difference between them being significant to truth conditions of the attributions.[28]

In conclusion, in this section we have made two main points. The first is that speakers may believe Assignments; the second is that speakers may believe that the expressions mentioned in Assignments are translations. These latter beliefs are idiosyncratic to individual speakers; every speaker who has the name "Cicero" in his lexicon believes a "Cicero"-assignment. and every speaker who has the name "Tully" in her lexicon believes a "Tully"-assignment, but not every speaker who has both of these beliefs also believes that "Tully"-expressions are translations of "Cicero"-expressions. These two sorts of beliefs are tied together by *de dicto* attribution, saying of someone other than oneself that *he* believes something with respect to an Assignment, and hence ultimately with respect to the name of someone. In this way reference to language is brought into the equation, but no longer as part of the presuppositions of the speakers' assertions, but as part of what they say about someone else. To speak *de dicto* is for speakers to attribute to others in this regard, not to themselves. One may speak *de dicto* when there is good reason to do so, when linguistic information is relevant. We have just considered one such case: *de dicto* attribution of a belief to a third party. But there is also the case of *de dicto* attribution of a belief to the addressee; in the next section, we will develop this case, focusing on identity statements.

3.3 The Logical Form of Identity Statements

When we left the discussion of identity statements at the end of section 3.1, we had given ourselves a task: to develop an analysis that could account for both the informativeness and necessity of identity statements, while still retaining Frege's intuition about the relation of the information conveyed by a sentence to what it expresses. We are now in a position to approach this task. Our point of departure is to be found in answering the question we posed at the outset of the previous section—what are valid substitution instances for the schematic letters in $\ulcorner\alpha$ is $\beta\urcorner$? As noted, there is a constraint on our answer: we want the instances of the schema to be instances that have *semantic* content. This precludes the letters ranging over names that can appear in the string of words that make up an identity statement; not being the sort of things that can be used to refer, they have no semantic content to contribute. What does have semantic content to contribute are *expressions* containing names, in the sense that we have just defined. It is these that satisfy the schematic letters, in answer to our question. The objects of our analysis, therefore, are the sort of linguistic structures that contain such expressions as constituents, and that may be used (if declarative) to make statements that may be true or false.

Let us use the term *logical form* to designate that part of the syntactic description of a sentence that determines (along with other nonlinguistic factors of context of utterance and indexicality that we set aside), the truth conditions of statements made by using that sentence. To formalize our usage somewhat, we say that there are (partial) logical forms $\ulcorner P \wedge A \urcorner$, where replacements of P and replacements of A are sentential in form. We call a replacement of P a primary clause, and a replacement of A an Assignment; a logical form must contain a primary clause, and may contain an Assignment. While any logical form that is syntactically sentential may be a primary clause, an Assignment is specified as a sentential structure of the form $\ulcorner g(\text{``}\alpha\text{''}) = \alpha \urcorner$, where g is a function from expressions to values.[29] A is an *admissible* Assignment for P iff A is an Assignment to an expression occurring in P. In the simplest case (i.e., for sentences with predicates of unary adicity), there are thus two admissible types of logical forms:[30]

$\ulcorner \xi(\alpha) \urcorner$

$\ulcorner \xi(\alpha) \wedge g(\text{``}\alpha\text{''}) = \alpha \urcorner$

The former type of logical form are what we have called *non–de dicto* logical forms; the latter are what we have called *de dicto*.

Let us identify the *informational content* of a sentence with the entailments of its logical form. A sentence, by virtue of having the logical form that it does, *has* informational content; a statement, we then say, *conveys* the informational content the sentence used to make that statement *has*. (Where no confusion will arise, we will speak (loosely) of a logical form itself conveying or having informational content.) We now observe that a *de dicto* logical form, but not a non–*de dicto* logical form, entails

$\xi(g(\text{``}\alpha\text{''}))$

To take an example, "Cicero was a Roman" has the following *de dicto* logical form:

(3) Cicero was a Roman and g("Cicero") = Cicero

from which it follows that the reference of "Cicero" was a Roman. This information, however, is not conveyed by the statement "Cicero was a Roman" if its logical form is non–*de dicto* (i.e., (4) *sans* Assignment). Thus, statements will convey different information depending on which sort of logical form they have.

Our concern with identity statements now reduces to the question of their logical forms, and the information they convey. Identity statements, like any other sentences, are ambiguous between having *de dicto* and non–*de dicto* logical forms. It then follows that the identity statement "$a = b$" with a *de dicto* logical form ("a" and "b" linguistically distinct expressions) will convey the information that the reference of "a" is the same as the reference of "b," by virtue of the presence of Assignments to "a" and "b" in their logical forms. For, if (4) represents the general form of a *de dicto* logical form for an identity statement,

(4) $a = b \wedge g("a") = a \wedge g("b") = b$

it follows trivially that $g("a") = g("b")$. To take an example, "Cicero is Tully" with the *de dicto* logical form (5)

(5) $Cicero_1$ is $Tully_2 \wedge g("Cicero_1") = Cicero \wedge g("Tully_2") = Tully_2$

entails that the reference of the expression "Cicero" is the same as the reference of the expression "Tully," for if "Cicero" refers to Cicero, and "Tully" refers to Tully, and Cicero and Tully are one and the same, then "Cicero" and "Tully" corefer. *De dicto* logical forms convey information by virtue of what they *show* or *display* that their paired non–*de dicto* counterparts do not.[31] Therefore, nothing follows just from what is shown by the non–*de dicto* logical form of "Cicero is Tully," namely,

$Cicero_1$ is $Tully_2$.

about the expressions "Cicero" and "Tully." A speaker who makes an utterance of "Cicero is Tully" does so backed by the beliefs that (i) Cicero is Tully, (ii) "Cicero" has the value Cicero, and (iii) "Tully" has the value Tully. Only if she utters a sentence with a *de dicto* logical form do the latter beliefs become part of what is said by the speaker; by virtue of the explicit occurrences of Assignments, she will convey the information that two distinct expressions corefer.[32]

Here it is worth noting that, as we have previously observed, the content of an Assignment sometimes can be stated in forms other than the "disquotational" form we have taken as canonical. So, if Cicero is Tully, then "$g(\text{"Cicero"}) = \text{Cicero}$" is no different than "$g(\text{"Cicero"}) = \text{Tully}$." However, if this Assignment were to be expressed in the latter form, it would immediately follow in conjunction with "$g(\text{"Tully"}) = \text{Tully}$" that "Cicero" and "Tully" are coreferential, that is, that $g(\text{"Cicero"}) = g(\text{"Tully"})$. But clearly this is not something that speakers know simply by virtue of knowing their language; if they did, identity statements would never be informative. On other hand, if as a rule we render Assignments as we do, there is no prejudgment as to coreference. Nothing follows from the Assignments to "Cicero" and "Tully" whether they corefer, unless they occur, as they do in (5), in the context of an explicit assertion of identity.

The question that faces us now is what the import is of this information about the expressions. The answer is that *this information is sufficient grounds for forming a belief of a Translation Statement.* Speakers who sincerely assert "Cicero is Tully" *de dicto* thereby convey to a hearer that "Cicero" and "Tully" corefer; hearers who accept this utterance will then be provided with sufficient grounds to form the belief that the expressions "Cicero" and "Tully" are translations, if they do not already believe this.[33] Now, coming to believe a Translation Statement in this way may amount to very little, in fact, to little more than just the information directly conveyed by the identity statement that one person has two names. For instance, this would be the total significance for someone who did not have the names "Cicero" and "Tully" in his lexicon prior to accepting "Cicero is Tully"; he would now have these two names in his lexicon, believe a translation statements of their expressions, and no more. But what of someone who already has these names in her lexicon, along with various prior beliefs about Cicero and Tully? For her, the impact of accepting the statement "Cicero is Tully" may extend considerably beyond this. This is because for such a person accepting an identity statement *de dicto* would provide sufficient warrant for valid substitutions. So, a person who believed that Cicero was an orator and that Tully was a poet, taken to be beliefs about different people, would on accepting "Cicero is Tully," take them to be beliefs about the same person, or if she believed that Cicero was a Roman and that Tully was a Greek, she would now revise her beliefs as best she could in order to maintain consistency. Just what effect the information conveyed by an identity statements will have for people will depend on their prior epistemic states. The ancient astronomer, when he says to his astronomical colleagues "Hesperus is Phosphorus," does so because his observations about the cosmos show that the heavenly body seen first in the evening from Earth, and that seen last in the morning, are one and the same, and most likely his colleagues will rapidly conclude, given their epistemic states, that an empirical fact has been adduced, one that constitutes a valuable extension of their knowledge. This fact itself, however, is no part of the content of the sentence uttered. What the ancient astronomer has *said* is that "Hesperus" and "Phosphorus" corefer, which, of course is not what he discovered. But his discovery can be conveyed to those who are in a position to be receptive by saying that they do. In this regard, one could think of the "informativeness" of identity statements as a measure of their causal/epistemic role for an individual—think of an identity statement as like a virus implanted into a interwoven nexus of beliefs, and assess the damage it does. But insofar as we have such a notion of informativeness for identity statements, it is derivative from the information conveyed by *de dicto* logical forms, that the expressions flanking the identity sign corefer.[34]

At this juncture we arrive at the famous puzzle of identity statements—given that "Cicero" and "Tully" are coreferential, why should substituting one for the other change the informativeness of the proposition that "Cicero is Tully" and "Cicero is Cicero" commonly express? Our solution is not Frege's. Rather, we proceed by noting by way of comparison to the logical form of "Cicero is Tully," given as (5) above, that the logical form of "Cicero is Cicero"

$Cicero_1$ is $Cicero_1 \wedge g("Cicero_1") = Cicero_1$

implies only that two occurrences of the expression "Cicero" refer to the same thing. Now as we have it, "Cicero is Tully" may be informative precisely to those who do not know that "Cicero" and "Tully" refer to the same person. Whether a speaker knows this or not is independent of their linguistic knowledge; one can lack the knowledge that "Cicero" and

"Tully" corefer without impugning their linguistic competence. In contrast, that two occurrences of the name "Cicero" corefer is information that no competent speaker of the language could be without; it is, as we have discussed, determined by the grammar speakers know when they know a language. But if every speaker knows that different occurrences of the same expression always refer to the same thing, then it will not be informative to anyone to be told that such is the case in this one instance of "Cicero is Cicero."

We see now why a speaker would utter an identity statement with a *de dicto* logical form; by utilizing beliefs people share by virtue of their sharing a language—beliefs of Assignments—a speaker may communicate a belief that they could not share on linguistic grounds alone about the relations of the prior shared beliefs—a belief of a Translation Statement. It is from this that the communicative value of identity statements arises.[35] The natural question to ask now is under what conditions a speaker would utter a sentence with a non–*de dicto* logical form, one that does not contain Assignments. After all, this is the sort of logical form we have assumed to accrue normally to assertive uses of sentences other than identity statements (and propositional attitude ascriptions). The answer is that there aren't very many circumstances at all for the use of non–*de dicto* identity statements, not at least in ordinary discourse. If one asserts "Cicero is a Roman," one does so intending to communicate a certain fact, that Cicero is a Roman. One assumes that the particular words chosen will do the job, so there is no reason to make anything of it by making Assignments part of what is said. But if "Cicero is Tully" were asserted non–*de dicto,* what would be said of substance that the hearer would not already know? All that would be conveyed is that there is a person who is self-identical. Now this is fine, if the speaker's purposes in making an utterance do not include being informative to the hearer. This might arise, for instance, in a circumstance in which the speaker and hearer both have "Cicero" and "Tully" in their lexicons, and already believe that Cicero is Tully, in which case the hearer is already informed that "Cicero" and "Tully" corefer. But beyond a desire on the part of the speaker to reaffirm their shared beliefs, most contexts of utterance of identity statements in ordinary speech call for the extra information contained in *de dicto* logical forms. This is because ordinarily we speak assertively (and sincerely) just *because* we want to speak informatively, and hence we will utter our sentences under logical forms that best achieve that goal. For identity statements, because of what "be" means, this allows for only one option, the *de dicto* option. There may be, of course, contexts that allow for noninformative, yet nontrivial uses of identity statements; we might think of identities in mathematics or logic in this way.[36] But if so, this sheds light on the differences between equalities in natural language, used by speakers of that language, and those formal systems in which there is no role for speakers and their communicative intentions. We would not then expect the distinctions we are making for natural language to necessarily obtain for such systems. Analytically, then, it is *de dicto* identity statements that are primary, if our goal is accord with the character of ordinary speech.[37]

Our account of identity statements, in maintaining both that "be" denotes objectual identity, and that they are about the expressions used, does, as promised, vindicate what we saw as the dual intuitions Frege embedded at different times in his analyses of identity statements. But in doing so we have jettisoned Frege's central assumption of a realm of objective senses, to which all speakers have equal access. On our view, the analysis of identity statements is continuous with that of other sentences of the language, including attributions of propositional attitudes; with respect to their logical forms, all expressions, including expressions that refer to expressions, have their standard sorts of denotations. We have not, however, eschewed Frege's rationale for such a domain. We hold with him that there must be something that can be shared between speakers by virtue of which identity statements garner their communicative efficacy. The constancy we find is through the language that speakers share; it is a fact about language that speakers who have a name in their lexicon can express via their utterances *de dicto* logical forms. What speakers may all share is the belief that the expressions "Cicero" and "Tully" corefer, even if they share no other beliefs about their reference.[38]

3.4 Names, Expressions, and Rigidity

While counterpart *de dicto* and non–*de dicto* logical forms convey different information, this is not information that affects the *sort* of truth expressed by an identity statement: if an identity statement is true, it will be a necessary truth, *regardless* of the type of its logical form. If "$a = b$" is necessarily true non–*de dicto*, then it is also necessarily true *de dicto*, since a *de dicto* logical form is the conjunction of the same primary clause as in the non–*de dicto* form with two other statements, the Assignments. But Assignments themselves are identities, and as we discussed in the appendix to chapter 2, are just as much necessary truths, when true, as the primary clause. Since trivially the conjunction of necessary truths is itself a necessary truth, the conjunction of a primary clause in a *de dicto* identity statement with one or more Assignments will also be a necessary truth. True identity statements express necessary truths regardless of whether they are read *de dicto* or non–*de dicto*.[39]

The conclusion just reached is straightforward enough, but it does rest on a certain assumption: not only do "*a*" and "*b*" as they occur in a *de dicto* logical form rigidly designate, but so do "g("*a*")" and "g("*b*")," for only then will (true) Assignments be necessarily true. As we have conceived *g*, it is a function from rigid designators to their values; hence "g("*a*")," for "*a*" a rigid designator, is a rigid designator, (i.e., the value *g* picks out for "*a*," an expression of our language in this world, it picks out for all possible worlds, irrespective of whether that value is called "*a*" in that world). Now, it might be thought that the requirement that the Assignment relation be a function proceeds on a yet prior assumption, commonly made, that the problem of names with multiple bearers may be safely ignored, since plainly if many individuals may have the same name, the relation from names to values is not a function. But this would be to misread the true situation, for it would not keep in mind the distinction between names and expressions as we have drawn it. Reference, on our view, is carried not by names, but by their syntactic expressions; thus, it is not names, but their expressions that rigidly designate and hence comprise the domain of the Assignment relation. Expressions containing names are more finely individuated than names themselves; since no more than one individual may be referred to by tokens of an expression, the Assignment relation, when taken to have expressions as its domain, is indeed a function. People *have* or *bear* names, and many people may have or bear a particular name; both the shipping magnate and the ancient philosopher have the same name, "Aristotle." But each would be referred to through the use of distinct expressions of that name. There is no "problem" of names with multiple bearers as such.[40]

It is of course quite common in philosophical jargon to say that *names* are rigid designators, a way of speaking that we have rejected. Nevertheless, it is worth considering the implications of such a proposal for the problem of names with multiple bearers. Kripke, in *Naming and Necessity* (1980, 7ff., and especially note 9), points out, perfectly reasonably, that to speak of the truth conditions of a sentence, the sentence must be taken to express a single proposition. But, if a sentence contains a name such as "Aristotle" that, given that names may have multiple bearers, may refer to Onassis on one occasion, and to the Greek philosopher on another, there comes the question as to which proposition is expressed. Suppose that context favors the philosopher. Once that is found to be so (by whatever means), the truth conditions of a sentence containing "Aristotle," so understood, may be stated, and the name "Aristotle," so understood, rigidly refers to the great Greek philosopher.[41] On this way of acknowledging the problem of names with multiple bearers, occurrences of the name "Aristotle" refer to different people on different occasions of use, and rigidly so once those occasions are disambiguated. A sincere and appropriately knowledgeable speaker sometimes uses the name "Aristotle" to refer to the Greek philosopher, and sometimes uses the name "Aristotle" to refer to the shipping magnate. Thus, what is to be distinguished on this theory are *occasions of use of the name*; for a given context of use, the referential intentions of a sincere and knowledgeable speaker are definitive in sorting out which occurrences of "Aristotle" are which. Let us call this the "asyntactic" theory of names with multiple bearers.

The asyntactic theory is in agreement with the syntactic account we favor in one important way; both hold that "the reference of the name α" is an improper description. There is no speaking of *the* name "Aristotle" (rigidly) designating, because there is no unique individual who is the referent of that name. Rather, we must recast such talk in terms of occasions on which the name "Aristotle" is used to refer to the philosopher, and occasions on which that very same name "Aristotle" is used to refer to the shipping magnate. Similarly, we must recast remarks such as Kripke's that, after a baby's parents call it by a certain name, "the name is spread from link to link as if by a chain," for what is this unique name that is spread from link to link? Rather, it is occasions of use of this name that would constitute, at least in part, and on at least one understanding of the causal theory of reference, the histories of those two uses of the name "Aristotle." But there would be no saying of *the* name "Aristotle" that it is spread from link to link, since that would be to confound the different uses of that name. What is proper to speak of on this theory is the reference of such and such occurrence of the name "α," since, once disambiguated, occurrences of the name rigidly designate. And so too, it would appear, would the entire description just used rigidly designate. Suppose that such and such occurrence of the name "Aristotle" refers to the philosopher Aristotle, and refers to the philosopher Aristotle in all possible worlds; then the referent of such and such occurrence of "Aristotle" must be the philosopher Aristotle in all possible worlds. If this is right, and it is hard to see how it could not be, then the expression "The referent of such and such occurrence of the name "Aristotle"" is a rigid designator.[42] The function *g*, on the asyntactic account, would now be understood as contextually dependent; it maps from pairs of contexts and names to values.

Such contextual dependencies could easily be mimicked on the syntactic theory; the proper terminology to gloss *g* would now be "the reference *of such and such occurrence* of the expression α," whose rigidity could be established by the obvious analogue to the argument just given. But it is hard to see why we would want to do so, since all the results obtained thus far are unaffected if we delete the italicized words. What we see as at play in the example is that there are two distinct syntactic expression-types (of the category NP) "[$_m$ Aristotle]" and "[$_n$ Aristotle]," all tokens of the first rigidly designating Onassis (and no one else), and all tokens of the second rigidly designating the great Greek philosopher (and no one else).[43] Sentences containing these distinct expressions have distinct logical forms, and each expresses a different unique proposition. (There is no single syntactic structure expressing different propositions on different occasions, as on the asyntactic view; this is precluded because the *name* "Aristotle," in and of itself, does not refer at all, so it does not rigidly refer.) A sincere and knowledgeable speaker never uses tokens of the expression-type "[$_m$ Aristotle]" intending to refer to anyone other than the shipping magnate, or tokens of "[$_n$ Aristotle]" to refer to anyone other than the philosopher. The practice of speakers in using tokens of such expressions to so refer, we could say, is initiated by an initial dubbing, via which an individual is provided with an expression type, tokens of which are thereafter used to rigidly designate that individual. The causal chain linking our use of "[$_n$ Aristotle]" to refer to the philosopher, and his baptism, at which the expression "[$_n$ Aristotle]" was born, consists of the uses of other tokens of "[$_n$ Aristotle]"; each link consists of a tokening of that expression-type. What expression-type a token is a token *of* is something that is discernible on formal grounds; distinct indexing *shows* distinct expressions. This distinction, however, may not also show phonologically, but only syntactically, and in such cases we may need to rely on context, conceivably including speakers' intentions, to disambiguate what syntactic structure has been uttered on a given occasion. But this is not the robust role for context required on the asyntactic view, for we need not add any additional parameters to the Assignment function to accommodate context; its role is to point out the logical form of the sentence being used, and not (at least not directly, as on the asyntactic view) the proposition it expresses.

The syntactic theory, as we see it, captures a certain intuition about rigidity, that it is a property of the language used, and not of speakers' intentions to use that language; it is not a property that speakers imbue language with by using it. But intuitions of such a nature may of course clash, and one may wish to remain adamantly attached to names being the carriers of reference, and what that entails. Doing so, however, carries a burden; a clear criterion must be provided of what are occasions of use of a name. Suppose we have a discourse, made up of some number of sentences, containing some number of occurrences of the name "Aristotle." (Discourse here is to be taken to cover both conversation and, when sufficiently temporally extended, historical chains.) How are we to group these occurrences together, such that some count as occasions of referring to the shipping magnate, and others count as occasions of referring to the philosopher (and none count as referring to both)? An immediate hypothesis that comes to mind is to isolate such "occasion-types" by grouping them by their referents; we could "index" the occurrences by their referents. That, however, would be too coarse a criterion. Suppose Max were to believe, quite mistakenly, that there are two people, one a famous pianist, the other a great statesman, each named "Paderewski." He comes by this belief not through any lack of logical acumen; he is merely uninformed about the fact that there is one and only one such person. A benevolent and knowledgeable speaker comes along and, in this context, utters (6):⁴⁴

(6) But Max, Paderewski is Paderewski.

If Max takes the point, he will have grounds for changing his beliefs, and if he does, he will come to hold, as do the rest of us in the know, that there is only one person named "Paderewski," who is both a pianist and a statesman. Hence, (6) may be uttered by the speaker so as to impart information to the hearer that will be sufficient cause for the hearer to change his beliefs about the reference of "Paderewski." But the problem is: How can we see (6) as being other than an uninformative logical tautology of the form ⌜$\alpha = \alpha$⌝, if the basis for discrimination is just the mere joint requirement of phonological and referential identity? There must be something more fine-grained going on than just this.

Kripke (1980, note 9) makes the following suggestion: "Two totally distinct 'historical chains' that by sheer accident assign phonetically the same name to the same man should probably count as creating distinct names despite the identity of the referents." Although Kripke gives this remark an unnecessarily paradoxical air—is there one name, or are there two?—his intent is clear: causal/historical chains are to be taken as an additional criterion. This, however, is circular, for such chains are defined as links of occasions of use; but it is precisely occasions of use that we are trying to individuate, such that the two occurrences of "Paderewski" in (6) are different occasions of use.⁴⁵ A different suggestion, noncircular but still consistent with names being the bearers of reference, would be to chase the problem away by bringing speakers' intentions into the mix. But this would be no advance if such intentions are themselves classified by the referents toward whom the intentions are directed; all intentions to refer to Paderewski are the same intention (abstracting from whomever is the agent of the intention). There could be different intentions, of course, if the intentions were directed toward a description of a referent, rather than the referent itself. Speakers' intentions to refer to the famous pianist are not the same as their intentions to refer to the great statesman. If we take this view, we now distinguish occasions of use of a name by something very much like Fregean senses.

Although Frege himself never remarked directly on this sort of case, this might be just an oversight, because his response would seem so obvious: it is a case of names with multiple senses. If each occurrence of "Paderewski" in (6) is associated with a different sense, then while (6) would be of the form ⌜$\alpha = \alpha$⌝, the thought it expresses would be nontrivial, of the same type as that expressed by "Cicero is Tully." It is unlikely, however, that this is the response that Frege himself would have given, for it is unclear that Frege would allow a single name to be associated with more than one sense.

Frege makes two pertinent remarks. One is found in "The Thought" ([1918] 1977). There, Frege says that "we must really stipulate that for every proper name there shall be just one associated manner of presentation of the object so designated" (p. 12). Frege makes this remark in the context of his story of Herbert Garner and Leo Peter, both of whom are associates of Dr. Gustav Lauben. Garner knows nothing else about Dr. Lauben aside from when and where he was born; Peter does not know this, but knows other things about Lauben. This very fact, according to Frege, disqualifies Garner and Peter from speaking the same language, for in no language can a single name be associated with more than one sense. "Then as far as the proper name 'Dr Gustav Lauben' is concerned," Frege says, "Herbert Garner and Leo Peter do not speak the same language, although they do in fact refer to the same man with this name for they do not know that they are doing so" (p. 12).

Frege's other pertinent remark is found in the well-known second footnote of "On Sense and Reference" ([1892] 1970). He places the critical proviso at the head of the discussion when he says that "in the case of an actual proper name such as 'Aristotle' opinions as to the sense may differ." Now, according to Frege, in everyday life this might not be problematic, "so long as the reference remains the same" (p. 58), because this delimits how much people can disagree in their opinions about the sense they attach to the name. In a comparable way, two people may each see an object, although under very disparate circumstances. They may each properly describe what they have seen, but do so with distinct descriptions. It may turn out that these descriptions are so different that neither would think that they are describing the same object. But while each would think that the other had perceived a different object, it would of course be absurd to conclude that there *are* different objects. The situation with senses is no different, except that senses, being abstract rather than concrete, are grasped, not perceived (on Frege's preferred epistemology). We cannot conclude from a difference in description of the sense of an expression that there *are* different senses (and indeed when we shift to the milieu of a logically perfect language there is no issue, because we factor out speakers, who might have opinions). For Frege, since there can be only one sense of a proper name, if two people think there are different senses, someone is wrong about something. Either at least one of them is wrong in what they think the sense is, or wrong about the name with which it is associated. One of them, as Frege puts it in the "The Thought," is misled by false information. Frege's view was that each distinct sense (of the appropriate type) defines a distinct proper name. Hence, if (6) is of the form ⌜α = α⌝, it cannot be other than a logical truth.[46]

But is (6) of this form? What is compelling us to accept that conclusion? Only the assumption that it is names that stand beside the identity sign; what we have been searching for is some way to maintain this assumption, while seeking further "grain" elsewhere. But perhaps the best thing to do at this point would be to surrender the assumption, and adopt instead what we have urged, that it is *expressions* of names that stand beside the identity sign. The wisdom of this is reflected in our realization that (6) may be of a different form. Once we allow distinctive indices as marks of formal distinctiveness of expression, although not of referential distinctiveness, we can distinguish NP_i from NP_j, a fact that is independent of the lexical content of the expressions. Thus, we can distinguish as distinct expressions "[$_{NP}$ Paderewski]$_1$" and "[$_{NP}$ Paderewski]$_2$," just as we can distinguish "[$_{NP}$ Cicero]$_1$" and "[$_{NP}$ Tully]$_2$." But then, if "Cicero is Tully" is of the form ⌜α = β⌝ by virtue of this distinction, so too may "Paderewski is Paderewski" be of this form. Example (6) is now properly given as "Paderewski$_1$ is Paderewski$_2$."[47]

At this point, having reduced the puzzle of (6) to the standard puzzle of identity statements, we could conclude by reiterating the reasons for the informativeness of identity statements, now generalized, and be done with it. But this would be to miss an important, if somewhat subtle, difference between the cases. To see this, consider the circumstances under which a speaker would use two distinct expressions that are both phonologically and referentially nondistinct.

In the normal course of events, speakers operate under the assumption that any number of different people may bear a given name. In referring to each of these people, speakers will use expressions of this name, but they must be *different* expressions for each, since if they used the same expression, they would only succeed in having the expressions corefer, as a matter of grammar. Thus, in the case at hand, if speakers believe that there are two people each named "Paderewski," then they will use the distinct expressions—"Paderewski$_1$," and "Paderewski$_2$,"—to refer to them, and will believe the Assignment ""Paderewski$_1$," has the value Paderewski$_1$," and the Assignment ""Paderewski$_2$," has the value Paderewski$_2$." Let us assume that speakers may believe Assignments for distinct (i.e., noncoindexed) but cospelled expressions just in case they believe those Assignments are not equivalent; their use of expressions of a given name will then directly reflect their beliefs about how many values that name has.[48] Now this assumption, which we call *Singularity*, has a consequence. Speakers who, believing that "Cicero" and "Tully" are different names, believe a "Cicero"-Assignment and a "Tully"-Assignment, do not thereby automatically have any beliefs about how these Assignments are related. Given that there is no bar to a person having multiple names, whether the expressions corefer is an open issue, short of belief of a Translation Statement. Such beliefs, however, are idiosyncratic to speakers. On the other hand, speakers who believe two "Paderewski"-Assignments do so with respect to a general belief in Singularity, and hence *do* automatically have a belief about their relationship. They believe, given their belief in Singularity, that the expressions do *not* corefer. The effect of Singularity, therefore, is to eliminate the possibility of believing a Translation Statement of the form ⌜"NP$_i$," translates "NP$_j$,"⌝, where NP$_i$ and NP$_j$ contain the same name.

Now consider a sincere utterance of "Paderewski$_1$ is Paderewski$_2$." Given the context of Singularity, an interesting result follows: *no speaker is in a position to assert this consistently with his or her beliefs*. Certainly not someone, such as the speaker in the puzzle, who believes that there is only one person named "Paderewski," for the statement implies that there are two people named "Paderewski," because two distinct "Paderewski"-expressions are used. But also not someone whose beliefs are consistent with this implication; rather, that person would assert just the opposite, namely, "Paderewski₁ isn't Paderewski₂"—that is, a statement of the form ⌜α ≠ β⌝. It seems that we have run into something of an anomaly, an unassertable, yet informative, identity statement.[49]

We say "seems" because of an assumption implicit in the discussion: that the logical form of "Paderewski is Paderewski" is non–*de dicto*. This assumption gets us into trouble because for the assertion of such forms, the province of the Assignment Principle is the speaker; the Assignments believed are his, and are presupposed by his assertion. We have encountered, however, a way that a speaker has of shifting the purview of this principle to someone else, and remaining uncommitted, with respect to his utterance in context, to its implications. He can accomplish this by using a sentence whose logical form is *de dicto*, so that rather than being left unstated, Assignments are attributed. For "Paderewski is Paderewski," this will be (7):

(7) Paderewski₁ is Paderewski₂ ∧ g("Paderewski₁") = Paderewski₁ ∧ g("Paderewski₂") = Paderewski₂

To whom is the attribution being made by an assertion of (7)? A first-party attribution is inherently eliminated, and no third party is overtly specified, as with propositional attitudes; this leaves (7) as a second-party attribution. That is, in the case of identity statements (and nonattitude ascriptions in general), this attribution is normally to the addressee. In a sense, it is as if the speaker in uttering "Paderewski is Paderewski" *de dicto* says to the hearer, *your* "Paderewski"-expressions corefer.

The question now is what effect this information will have on the hearer. The intended effect is clear. The speaker's communicative goal (regardless of whether he is right or wrong about the facts of the matter) is to cause the hearer to alter his beliefs, so that his utterance is to act as a corrective to what are, from the speaker's point of view, the mistaken beliefs of the hearer. The speaker wants the hearer to believe that there is only one person named "Paderewski." A *de dicto* utterance of "Paderewski is Paderewski" will have this effect because of Singularity. A hearer accepting (7) will infer that his two "Paderewski"-expressions corefer (negating his previous view that they did not). But this does not square with Singularity, which proscribes distinct expression-types containing the same name from coreferring. In order for the hearer to bring his language back into conformity with this principle, the hearer has but one option. He must give up that there are two distinct "Paderewski"-expression types, and replace it with the belief that there is just one. But if this exhausts the hearer's inventory of "Paderewski"-expressions, it follows that he now believes there is only one person named "Paderewski."

Notice that the information that a hearer ultimately comes to believe from acceptance of "Cicero is Tully" *de dicto*—that two distinct expressions corefer (belief in a Translation Statement)—is different from what he comes to believe from acceptance of "Paderewski is Paderewski" *de dicto*—that, despite what he thought, there is only one "Paderewski"-expression. Nevertheless, the results for someone's overall epistemic states can be the same: beliefs that were previously taken to be about two people are now taken to be about one. This may require, as we have noted, quite a bit of housekeeping among beliefs. For instance, if someone previously believed that Paderewski had musical talent, and that Paderewski did not have musical talent, he is going to have to decide whether he does or he does not (or remain agnostic), just as if he had held that Cicero had poetic talent, but that Tully did not, prior to accepting "Cicero is Tully" *de dicto*. Thus, *de dicto* identity statements may be the distal cause of this sort of coalescence and reorganization of one's epistemic states, but, in this regard, we do not distinguish between "Cicero is Tully" and "Paderewski is Paderewski."

As it turns out, the analysis we have presented, and on which we will elaborate in the next chapter, was hinted at by Frege, in his story of Garner, Peter, and Lauben. He says there, revealingly, that he "shall suppose that Leo Peter uses the proper name 'Dr. Lauben' and Herbert Garner uses the name "Gustav Lauben"" ([1918] 1977, 12). Here Frege is searching for a notational way of characterizing that if Garner and Peter do in fact have different senses, then they are employing different names. Thus, someone who wanted to tell Garner or Peter that there is just one person Lauben would not say "Dr. Gustav Lauben is Dr. Gustav Lauben" but rather "Dr. Lauben is Gustav Lauben." In the context, this would be an informative identity statement, a statement of the form $\ulcorner \alpha = \beta \urcorner$; to utter "Dr. Gustav Lauben is Dr. Gustav Lauben" would be to say something trivial, of the form $\ulcorner \alpha = \alpha \urcorner$. Frege's point here is that what is confusing about this case is the assumption that we have an identity statement of the latter form. If only we had the analytic resources to set natural language straight, then we would see that the proper logical form of "Paderewski is Paderewski" or "Dr. Gustav Lauben is Dr. Gustav Lauben" is the same as "Cicero is Tully" or "Hesperus is Phosphorus." Frege, of course, did not think such resources were available. We, in contrast, do.

Notes

1. By "identity statements" we mean cases such as those in the text, as well as those with more prolix locutions such as "is the same as" (or "is the same P as," where P is some sortal term). The tense of the statement will be immaterial to our concerns; it will not be immaterial that the subject and object terms are proper names. Thus, we exclude from the present discussion cases in which one of the terms is a definite description, because such statements have significantly different properties; see Smullyan 1948. We also exclude from present consideration cases with demonstratives, but see the discussion in chapter 4.

2. Although the importance of this puzzle has come down to us from Frege, often bearing the moniker "Frege's puzzle," awareness of its significance can be found among his contemporaries. Lotze in his *Logic* of 1874 mentions it, as does Thomae, his colleague in Jena, in his *Elementare Theorie der analytischen Functionen einer complexen Veränderlichen* (1880; 2nd ed., 1898). Frege remarks on Thomae's formulation in the second edition in *Grundgesetze der Arithmetik* ([1903] 1997, §138).

3. Frege states the theory as follows, in sec. 8 of *Begriffsschrift* ([1879] 1972, 126):

Now let

⊢——$(A \equiv B)$

mean: *the symbol A and the symbol B have the same conceptual content, so that we can always replace A by B and* vice versa.

4. In contrast, with negative identity statements, when they are true they are about two things, and their relational nature is obvious.

5. Russell's conclusion in *The Principles of Mathematics* (1937, § 64) was that when identity holds between terms, those things signified by proper names, assertion of identity is "perfectly futile," because it is an assertion of an identity of a term with itself. Rather, Russell held that it is worthwhile to assert an identity only when there is a relation, either between a term and a denoting concept, or between two denoting concepts. While Russell was shortly to abandon the doctrine of denoting concepts for the theory of descriptions of "On Denoting," his view of identity as relational carried over, given his notion that names were no more than abbreviations for definite descriptions.

6. The relationships between the notions of *Begriffsschrift* and "On Sense and Reference" are remarked on by Angelelli (1967, 39-40) and Bynum (1972, 67–68). Mendelsohn (1982, 291) puts the matter aptly in regard to the *Begriffsschrift* theory when he observes that "Frege distinguished between that which identity

relates and that wherein the information conveyed by an [identity]-sentence resides, so in [*Begriffsschrift*], it now appears that although identity is to relate the terms flanking the identity sign, the information is to be that the same content is given by two ways of determining it."

7. Frege's preferred examples for showing difference in sense are either geometrical, which he employs in *Begriffsschrift* and in "On Sense and Reference," or perceptual, as in the examples of the mountains "Afla" and "Ateb" used in a draft of a letter to Jourdain, and "the evening star" and "the morning star" found in "On Sense and Reference." These are typical cases of what Frege would classify as synthetic truths, although he also took the analysis to apply to true arithmetic equalities, which he took to be analytic; see Frege [1914] 1979, especially 224ff.

8. Mendelsohn (1982, especially 289ff.) points out that without this assumption, there is little reason to include identity within logic (as opposed to natural language), and this is certainly the view Wittgenstein takes in the *Tractatus*, where he labels identity statements "pseudo-propositions," so as to indicate their inherent semantic uninformativeness. Wittgenstein (1922) remarks: "Identity of object I express by identity of sign, and not by using a sign for identity. Difference of objects I express by difference of signs" (5.53), concluding that "the identity-sign, therefore, is not an essential constituent of conceptual notation" (5.533). Wittgenstein then proceeds to show how propositions involving identity can be recast without it (5.531ff).

9. This case is to be distinguished from explicit definition, where the identity sign is used in introducing a term as an abbreviation for some other complex expression within the language. According to Frege ([1914] 1979, 244), once a term has been introduced in this manner, it is then "transformed into an independent sentence which can be used in the development of the system as a premise for inferences." But given that the defined term expresses the same sense as the defining term, all such an identity statement can do is provide clarity to proof, not information. Our case differs, for (i) we assume that "Max" and "Oscar" are names in common use, and (ii), since "Max" and "Oscar" are terms of equivalent complexity, one could not be used to define the other.

10. The point here could also be made using other well-known examples. Think of Putnam, who has no conceptual difference between elms and beeches, being told "elms are beeches." Similarly, suppose Kripke is right that Feynman and Gell-Mann are normally associated with the same mode of presentation ("a famous physicist"); yet utterances of "Feynman is Gell-Mann," if it were true, would convey information to those not up on the hagiography of modern physics.

11. Here the Black translation is rather stilted; the Feigl translation is better: "In different languages, and even in one language, the same sense is represented by different expressions" (Frege [1892] 1949, 86).

12. What the significance of the extrapropositional linguistic difference in identity statements of the form $\ulcorner \alpha = \beta \urcorner$ amounts to is open to a considerable difference of opinion. For instance, for Wettstein, this information pans out in how propositions are used; the informativeness of "Cicero is Tully" is to follow from

the fact that two distinct names are used in this statement. For Perry, informativeness results from how propositions are *constructed,* so that the informativeness of "Cicero is Tully" follows from the proposition it expresses being constructed by determining values for two distinct names. See also, for indexicals, Kaplan 1989. Another alternative is to see informativeness as a result of a *way of thinking* of a proposition, so that the informativeness of "Cicero is Tully" is to follow from there being distinct conceptions associated with the distinct names. See, for instance, Salmon 1985, although something very much like this latter view is discussed by Searle (1958, 166–173). The sort of epistemic/psychological notion we have in mind here has borne any number of monikers—dossier of information, body of knowledge, mode of presentation—aside from way of thinking of propositional constituents (see Evans 1973; Forbes 1990). Although they may be associated with somewhat different characteristics, what is common is that they all assume a compendium of conceptual information on which a speaker's use of a name is grounded. For instance, if we phrase the view in terms of dossiers of information, then an identity statement will convey that the information in the dossiers is about the same person—in other words, that the "name tags" on the dossiers corefer. Note that these notions are not be confused with Fregean senses, to which they bear a functional similarity. This is because unlike senses, they need not have an objective character. Indeed, virtually anything can contribute to someone's conception of an individual, including one's private experiences; one person's conception of an individual may bear only a fleeting resemblance to somebody else's. (Wettstein (2004), however, likens Frege's view in *Begriffsschrift* to direct reference accounts in that what an expression contributes to propositional content is just its reference (its "conceptual content"); the mode of determination with which it is associated is not part of this content, unlike Frege's latter notion of sense.)

13. The metalinguistic implication of taking names as "tags," and the divorce of the notion of informativeness from empirical information, were observed initially by Ruth Barcan Marcus; see Marcus 1963, 115.

14. On Russell's early views, Frege would be right in this rejection, for this would be to denote a reference without determining it; denotation would be, as Russell puts it, "linguistic through the phrase." (Unfortunately, according to Russell, this sort of argument can be turned on senses themselves (denoting concepts, in his terminology) with dire consequences; see Blackburn and Code's (1978) discussion of Russell's "Grey's Elegy" argument from "On Denoting.") Later, Russell (1929), holding the view that names are disguised descriptions, allows that "a description which will often serve to express my thought is 'the man whose name was *Julius Caesar,*'" the result then being subject to analysis via the theory of descriptions. Many issues arise with this view; see Kripke 1980, 68–70, 72, as well as section 3.2 below.

15. Another way of putting the issue for Frege is that he was concerned with what justifies having in a language multiple atomic terms for the same object; the answer he gives is that the distinct terms are each associated with distinct ways of determined the object in question. Our break with Frege is that we proceed from

the observation that there *are* multiple terms; we do not ask *why* there can be multiple terms.

16. That this follows as a theorem of modal logic was initially shown by Ruth Barcan Marcus; the significance of this result has been discussed by Marcus (1963) and Kripke (1980). See our discussion in the appendix to chapter 2, and in section 3.4 below. Note that if "the reference of '*a*' is the same as the reference of '*b*'" is parsed as a relation between expressions, then it would appear to express a contingent fact about expressions (that they corefer), not a necessary fact about things (that they are self-identical). See the remarks of Kripke (1971, 154–55).

17. The material in this section overlaps with that in the introduction, and in sections 1 and 2 of chapter 2. Readers already familiar with the presentation there may wish to skip this section and proceed to the next.

18. The weight speakers place on various distinguishing criteria may vary with context. This is highlighted by cases, unlike those in the text, in which there is a mismatch between phonological and orthographic distinctiveness. For instance, there are circumstances in which we would be content to say that "Jean" and "Gene" are the same, but there are others in which we may not be—for example, in legal documents. Or consider the opposite case, pointed out by Ruth Marcus, of "St. John," written only one way, but pronounced either "Saint John" or "Sinjin."

19. A name is a lexical item, something linguistic, yet we want to say that things are *named*. We make this connection as follows. "*a*" is a name of *a* for a community of speakers *iff* those speakers conventionally use syntactic expressions exclusively containing "*a*" to refer to *a*—that is, if they use such expressions in accordance with the Assignment Principle. Note that this does not prevent many people from having the same name.

20. Consider the following discourse: "He doesn't believe 'Wittgenstein' refers to Wittgenstein; he believes 'Wittgenstein' refers to Russell." This can describe, *de re,* the circumstance of the person confused about who Wittgenstein is. This, however, is not the relevant case of denying belief of an Assignment, for it leaves unaltered the assumption that the agent has the name "Wittgenstein" in his lexicon; indeed, the agent himself would deny that either attribution is true. Given this divergence, we must be careful to distinguish an attribution of an Assignment, at root a belief pertaining to the proper linguistic usage of words, from an attribution of a purely *referential* belief based on observation of how a speaker actually uses an expression. For some discussion, see chapter 4, section 3.8.

21. An Assignment is a relation between an expression and an individual. Any conception that speakers might have of an individual plays no role in any Assignment they might believe for that individual.

22. Henceforth, where no confusion will arise, when mentioning expressions we will omit labeled brackets.

23. Of course, a speaker could believe that they are the same word, having undergone some very strange sound changes; this may be implausible, but surely not impossible.

24. We continue to utilize indices in the manner developed in chapter 1. Coindexing indicates that the speaker believes that the tokens are of the same expression-type; noncoindexing, the belief that they are of different types.

25. In Fiengo and May 1994 we argue at length that pronominalization is, as we would put it here, an instance of (i); we called such cases "vehicle change."

26. If speakers believe that "Cicero" and "Tully" are translations, then from their belief that "Cicero" has the value Cicero, it could be inferred that they believe that "Cicero" has the value Tully. This would of course be so, but to attribute the latter to them would not be to attribute an Assignment in the sense we have defined.

27. More precisely, they are not believed to be the same expression. If one were also attributing to John the belief that "Cicero" and "Tully" were cognates—different forms of the same word—then substitution would be possible. See chapter 2, section 2.3, for discussion.

28. McDowell (1977) presents views somewhat similar to our own; however, he makes an assumption we do not make. He holds that Assignments (our terminology) are the *senses* of proper names. They are what a speaker *knows* when he knows a name. We hold something weaker, only that Assignments may be *believed* by a speaker when he knows a name. They are not senses, although, when attributed, they many play a role played by senses, the mode-of-presentation role. (McDowell does not contemplate the attribution of Assignments as we do.) We leave a fuller discussion of the differences between McDowell's "strong" theory and our "weak" theory for another occasion.

29. Intuitively, we may read g as "the reference of ___"; note that we can take Assignments to be functions only if the domain of Assignments is expressions, not names. See the discussion in chapter 1 and section 3.4 of this chapter.

30. Since Assignments are themselves sentential, our formulation allows Assignments to stand as primary clauses.

31. Although this information could be inferred from a non–*de dicto* logical form, if it is taken along with the (standard) assumption that speakers use their language in accordance with the Assignment Principle. While a non–*de dicto* form would then imply this information, it would not be entailed, as with the *de dicto* form, just from what shows in logical form.

32. The theory we are proposing encompasses when fully generalized four forms: the two we have been discussing in the text and two partially *de dicto* forms, in which there are Assignments to only one of the terms of the identity statement. Thus, we may also have the logical forms "$a = b \land g(\text{``}a\text{''}) = a$" and "$a = b \land g(\text{``}b\text{''}) = b$." While like their fully *de dicto* and non–*de dicto* counterparts, these partial forms, if true, are necessarily true (see section 3.4), all four convey distinct informational content. (These latter forms would be appropriate, for instance, when answering identity questions such as "Who is Cicero?" or "Who is Tully?") Notice further that "$a = a$" will only have two logical forms: "$a = a$" and "$a = a \land g(\text{``}a\text{''}) = a$." Again, both are necessary truths (like true "$a = b$"), but convey distinct informational content.

33. Sufficient grounds, that is, for believing a Translation Statement of type (ii). We can also have identity statements that provide sufficient grounds for believing translation statements of type (i), for instance if we were to assume that in "Venice is Venezia" the expressions are coindexed. Such a statement would express not only that the expressions corefer, but also that they contain the same name—that is, that "Venice" and "Venezia" fall within the limits of linguistic variation. (Compare this to the discussion in chapter 4 and section IV of this chapter of "Paderewski is Paderewski," where the terms on the sides of the identity sign are nondistinct.)

34. All this presupposes that the speaker believes that he and the hearer speak the same language. If an English speaker does not think that the hearer understands English, then he normally would not believe that he can informatively utter "Cicero is Tully" to him. But then he also would not think he could informatively say "John left" to him either.

35. Nothing in this picture says the speaker must be right. She might be wrong that Cicero is Tully, as she would be, for instance, if she held that Wittgenstein is Russell, but nevertheless she believes it, and wants the hearer to believe it as well. But this would not change the nature of the communicative interaction; the speaker would still be speaking sincerely. She would not be sincere, however, but deceitful, if she did not believe that Cicero is Tully, yet still want the hearer to believe this, and uttered "Cicero is Tully" to this end.

36. We mean here identities as they occur in formal proofs, not the identity statements that a speaker of a natural language would use to tell someone that two plus two equals four.

37. Identity statements differ from belief attributions, which ordinarily may be used in natural language either *de dicto* or non–*de dicto*. The reason is that identity statements are normally used for direct epistemic purposes—to inform someone of something. Belief attributions, on the other hand, are *indirect* reports of epistemic states; speakers may wish to attribute a belief but yet distance themselves from any particular claim about the terms under which agents would hold that belief.

38. Although our account is based on beliefs of speakers, and beliefs that they have about the beliefs of other speakers, our account does not reduce the content of identity statements to purely subjective beliefs of speakers. *Every* speaker who has "Cicero" in his or her lexicon believes that a "Cicero"-expression refers to Cicero; moreover, *every* speaker who accepts "Cicero is Tully" believes that "Cicero" and "Tully" corefer. But whether our account of the content of identity statements would be sufficiently *objective* for Frege is another matter. Nevertheless, there is a firm intersubjective assumption on the part of discussants that the expressions they use have the same referents.

39. One might inquire at this point whether *de dicto* and non–*de dicto* identity statements express the same proposition. This depends on how we are to individuate such entities. Let us say that a statement S expresses a proposition p if and only if the constituents of p are the values of the constituents of the logical form of the sentence used to make S. If we are to take the constituents of the

propositions to be the values designated by the terms of the identity, then if (true) "$a = b$" with a non–*de dicto* logical form expresses a proposition containing the object *a*/*b* and identity, then so too does it express this proposition under a *de dicto* logical form, since each of its conjuncts, including the Assignments, being identities, will contribute the same constituents. ("$g($"a"$)$" designates the same value as "a".) However, it might be held that a *de dicto* proposition also contains, in addition to these constituents, the function g and the linguistic expressions to which it applies as constituents, and would thus be a different proposition from a non–*de dicto* proposition, which does not contain these constituents. But regardless of which view of propositions is taken, identity statements, either *de dicto* or non–*de dicto*, if true, are necessarily true.

40. Something of the idea we have here is raised by Putnam (1954), and by Kripke (1980), who surveys the position, and even expresses sympathy with it, but does not actually adopt it. See the discussion in chapter 1.

41. Kripke stresses the point that, however the problem of names with multiple bearers is to be treated, rigidity, the central point he is concerned with, has "nothing to do with" the problem, which would arise in full force even if the naming conventions were such that no two individuals shared a name. Now that is perfectly true, as far as it goes. Much that is important and puzzling about rigidity is completely independent of the fact that, as it happens, different individuals may have the same name. But designation, be it rigid or not, is a relation between bits of language and individuals, and it can matter a great deal to the content of a theory of designation how these "bits of language" are defined and individuated.

42. While it is an independently interesting question whether such descriptions are rigid *de facto*, rigid *de jure*, or rigid in some third way, how this is adjudicated will not affect our argument.

43. As per the development in chapter 1, let "$[_m \alpha]$" stand for an expression-type containing a name α, such that for any discourse D, all tokens of $[_m \alpha]$ in D are coindexed, and no token of $[_m \alpha]$ is coindexed with any token of $[_n \alpha]$, $[_m \alpha] \neq [_n \alpha]$. Then, all tokens of $[_m \alpha]$ corefer, while tokens of $[_m \alpha]$ and $[_n \alpha]$ may or may not corefer.

44. We use the name "Paderewski" here in deference to this example's kinship to Kripke's (1979) belief-attribution puzzle; see the discussion in chapters 1, 2, and 4. The situation examined in the text is not limited to just the sort of communicative interaction described. It may arise, for instance, when someone wishes to know whether $a = b$, either when initially settling on one's beliefs, or when contemplating revising beliefs from a fixed, steady state. So suppose that Max develops an inkling of the truth about Paderewski, and, contemplating revising his beliefs, asks "Is Paderewski Paderewski?" Given that one wishes to straighten Max out, the appropriate answer will be "Yes, Paderewski is Paderewski," in which case he will revise his beliefs. In this case, the identity statement takes the form of an answer to a question, where no such overt prompt for its utterance was provided in the previous scenario.

45. Devitt, perhaps the most strenuous supporter of the causal theory, albeit understanding causal/historical chains as senses, notes the problematic nature of

examples like (6); see his "George" example in Devitt 1989. Devitt observes that chains, defined typewise by phonological and referential criteria, are insufficient. Rather, what is to account for informativeness with these examples is that a speaker may have multiple "files" all "grounded" in the same chain. But now what seems to be doing the work, in this case as well as in "Cicero is Tully," is the *nonchain* information in the file; but what information can this be other than descriptive information, for what other sort of information would keep, as Devitt tells us, the "networks distinct"? (This information must be able to distinguish *types* of chains, so utterance information would not be relevant, because it would distinguish only tokens.) But now the role of sense seems no longer to be played by chains themselves (they would be part of a *theory* of sense), but rather by descriptive information, à la Frege, although not strictly, since Devitt takes statements like (6) to be of the form ⌜α = α⌝; see the discussion below.

46. Frege's own views notwithstanding, we can envisage ways (6) might be analyzed that would fall roughly within the Fregean Weltanschauung. One option would be to seize on Frege's allowance that speakers of a natural language may differ in their opinions about the sense of an expression. If speakers can have an opinion about a sense, they can presumably have more than one, and not know that they are opinions about the same sense. A statement of the form ⌜α = α⌝ could then be uttered "informatively" as a corrective about such divergences of opinions. A second option would be to hold that there is a distinction between the sense of an expression in a language, of which there can be just one, and the senses speakers associate with an expression, of which there may be many. This way ⌜α = α⌝ would arguably be informative in the Fregean sense, because the two occurrences of "*a*" would be associated with different senses. Either way, however, speakers could *think* that there are two different senses associated with the name (type) "*a*." (At this point, one might drop talk of senses from the account, focusing on what speakers believe holds of the referent, on their *concept* of the referent. We would then have a view much like that embraced by direct reference theorists.) Frege himself, we would think, would not truck in such realms of analysis as these. For him, informativeness arises from differences in the way objects are objectively presented by senses; it is not a matter of what people believe about those senses, a domain infected by a hopeless psychologism.

47. We follow here the discussion of chapter 2, sections 3.4 and 3.5.

48. In chapter 2, we state this, relative to the indexing notation, as follows: *If cospelled expressions are covalued, they are coindexed.*

49. Adopting the sort of neo-Fregean view outlined in note 46 would not avoid this problem. Let us place ourselves in the position of people who might intend to utter a statement of the form ⌜a = a⌝ informatively. By the current hypothesis, in order for speakers to have such an intention, they must think that there are two senses associated with "*a*." Now, why would they think that? It could not be that they think there are two different people each named "*a*" (although this is what they would normally believe if they believed there were distinct senses), because then the speakers would never *assert* "*a = a*." As far as they are concerned, this sentence is false. So, it must be that the speakers think that the

two senses of "*a*" pick out the same reference. But even this will not be sufficient, simply because Max can utter "Paderewski is Paderewski" believing that he speaks truthfully, that there is only one person Paderewski, and that there is a unique sense associated with the name "Paderewski." The speaker believes there is one sense and one reference, so for him an assertion of "Paderewski is Paderewski" would be to utter a logical truth; the hearer believes there are two senses and two references, so what he would assert would be "Paderewski isn't Paderewski." Thus, some further auxiliary assumptions are needed, although it is unclear what they might be.

4

Paderewski

4.1 The Puzzle

Ignace Jan Paderewski (1860–1941) was by all accounts the most popular pianist of his time. Beginning his concert career in earnest in his late twenties, Paderewski's celebrity grew from his tireless touring over the next decades, in Europe, Australia, and the United States (during which Paderewski apparently developed a particular fondness for California, where he owned a ranch in Paso Robles, reported to have produced a more-than-adequate zinfandel). His recitals typically commenced with a sonata by Beethoven, and his repertoire showcased Chopin, Liszt, and his own works. Paderewski was a charismatic figure, both on the stage and off. Accounts comment on the "magnetism of his playing," which "shied away from . . . exaggerations and flashiness, stressing instead musical feeling and a faithfulness to the musical text," "his vast knowledge, intelligence, humor and fluency in several languages [that] left people deeply impressed" and note that "his stage presence, fine facial features and a shock of golden-red hair enchant women," so much so that the famed Polish actress Madame Modjeska was reported to have reminisced that Paderewski sitting at a piano gave an impression of a Botticelli or a Fra Angelico angel.

There was, however, another side to Paderewski. Always public spirited, having contributed substantially to numerous charities, as World War I loomed Paderewski became an outspoken advocate for the cause of Polish independence, his concerts typically including both musical offerings and speeches in support of the cause. As the most internationally famous activist for the Polish cause, Paderewski was intimately involved in organizing groups and raising funds, donating proceeds from his concerts as well as much of his personal fortune to famine relief. At the end of the war, with the success of their campaign in sight, Paderewski returned to Poland, where he was named prime minister and foreign minister in the transitional government. With the reestablishment of Polish statehood in 1920, Paderewski stepped down from these positions and returned with fervor to the concert stage, his celebrity undiminished, and even appeared in a Hollywood movie (the 1938 *Moonlight Sonata*). But with the invasion of Poland in 1939, Paderewski returned for the remainder of his life to his international activities in support of Poland, again raising money for famine relief and lobbying Western leaders for aid in Poland's struggle against Nazi Germany.

Paderewski entered the collective philosophical consciousness some four decades later, in a short passage in Saul Kripke's 1979 paper "A Puzzle about Belief." In that paper, Kripke was concerned to fend off the view that the failure of substitutivity of coreferential names in propositional-attitude contexts argued for some form of a description theory of names, perhaps along roughly Fregean lines, and consequently against the "Millian" view of names that he had espoused chiefly in "Naming and Necessity" (Kripke 1980). Kripke's counter runs roughly as follows. Suppose, given the facts about Padereweski's life we have surveyed, Peter comes to know of a pianist named "Paderewski" and of a Polish statesman named "Paderewski," but because of circumstances he does not realize that they are one and the same person. He believes rather that there are two different people, each named "Paderewski." Moreover, Peter has quite divergent views about the musical talent of pianists and politicians, taking the latter to lack what the former possess. Kripke then observes that just given our standard grounds for making belief attributions, a speaker fully apprised of the facts, in particular that there is only one person named "Paderewski," could attribute to Peter, without challenging his rationality, both the belief that Paderewski had musical talent and the belief that Paderewski did not have musical talent.[1] But which is it? Does Peter believe, or does he not, that Paderewski has musical talent? This is the puzzle. Its source, on Kripke's view, is to be found in a malfunction in the mechanics of belief attribution, not in a failure of substitution. We cannot even pose the question in this case of why "a believes that $P(b)$" does not follow from "a believes that $P(a)$," even though $a = b$, for unlike the failure to infer "Max believes Cicero was a Roman orator" from "Max believes that Tully was a Roman orator," where there is a linguistically apparent difference in their logical forms, in the case at hand such linguistic distinctions are neutralized. What we appear to have instead is an instance of the trivially *valid* inference from "*a* believes that *P*(*a*)" to "*a* believes that *P*(*a*)," given that *a* = *a*. Thus, whatever account we are to give for the genesis of the puzzle, it apparently cannot be attributed to a problem in the logical relations of the belief statements, and in particular to any specific assumptions about the logical form of proper names—for example, that they abbreviate descriptions.

It is a striking characteristic of the puzzle as just described that although the belief attributions

Peter believes Paderewski has musical talent.

and

Peter believes Paderewski doesn't have musical talent.

have logical forms that appear to imply that Peter believes an inconsistency, the belief that underlies these reports, that Peter believes there are two people, each named "Paderewski," is a perfectly consistent belief to hold, and does not indicate any lack of logical acumen. Indeed (as Kripke observes), no degree of logical acumen could lead Peter to reject the underlying belief, at least not without the interjection of some further premise that could cause him to revise his beliefs. But what would such a premise be? It could be supplied in the following way. Suppose that some benevolent speaker were to come along and, aware of Peter's predicament, says to him:

But Peter, Paderewski is Paderewski.

If Peter takes the point, he will now have good grounds for changing his beliefs, and if he does so, he will come to hold, as do the rest of us in the know, that there is only one person named "Paderewski," who is both a pianist and a statesman. Thus, the sentence above may be uttered by the speaker so as to impart information to the hearer that will be sufficient cause for the hearer to change his beliefs. But now the puzzle reasserts itself in a somewhat transmogrified form, for the sentence uttered appears to be nothing other than an *un*informative logical tautology of the form ⌜*a* = *a*⌝.[2]

Notice at this point that the puzzle, now framed in our preferred way as a (new) puzzle about identity statements, turns on a difference in the beliefs held by the speaker and hearer about how many people bear a given (proper) name: the *speaker* believes there is one person named "Paderewski," while the *hearer* believes there are two people, each named "Paderewski." What is perplexing is how the speaker's utterance, which apparently has only trivial objectual content, can cause the hearer's *linguistic* beliefs to become coincident with those of the speaker. This is the conundrum that we will attempt to resolve. Our tactic will be to argue that there may be more to the content of an identity statement than just objectual content, and it is this additional content—linguistic content, to tip our hand—that will do the heavy lifting. This linguistic puzzle, we should point out, is to be distinguished from another puzzle in which the relevant belief of the hearer is not the linguistic belief we have described, but rather the objectual belief that there are two people, which contrasts with the speaker's belief that there is just one.[3] But while the linguistic and the objectual puzzles are similar, and can even be found with superficially nondistinct linguistic forms, they nevertheless have quite distinct properties. There are, as we will see (at least) two Paderewski puzzles, neither of which should be subsumed under the other.

4.2 Linguistic Information

If there is a linguistic Paderewski puzzle, then the natural thing to do is to look for a linguistic account of the puzzle. Now, what would we expect such an account to consist of? At the most general level, we would expect that it would show how linguistic information can be semantically significant, and how this constitutes sufficient content to account for the failure of substitution and for the informativeness of identity statements. In putting together such an account, the natural first step would be to isolate relevant linguistic properties, as these are given to us by our best linguistic theory, and then explicate how these properties are manifest in a sufficiently finely articulated notion of logical form for sentences of the language. Davidson, in a passage from "Truth and Meaning" (1967, 32), articulated this step nicely: "It is consistent with the attitude taken here to deem it usually a strategic error to undertake philosophical analysis of words or expressions which is not preceded by or at any rate accompanied by the attempt to get the logical grammar straight." With this in place, the second step then would be to make explicit how the differences in logical form so isolated are sufficient for the purposes at hand, for instance, to invalidate substitution. Insofar as such an account could be carried through, it would give credence to the intuition that with pairs like "Max believes that Cicero is a Roman orator" and "Max believes that Tully is a Roman orator" the linguistic difference between "Cicero" and "Tully" is the cause of the failure of substitution, as well as the informativeness of "Cicero is Tully."

There is a tradition of skepticism about the prospects for an account of the sort just outlined, going back at least to Church's critique of Carnap's approach in *Meaning and Necessity*.[4] More germanely, the strategy described would seem to be stymied at the outset by the very case we want to analyze, for it could plausibly be taken as a moral of the Paderewski puzzle that *prima facie* there are no relevant linguistic distinctions to be drawn, since just the sort of linguistic distinctions we find in the Cicero/Tully case are neutralized. But given this, so the reasoning goes, the sound methodology would be to look elsewhere, in some nonlinguistic domain, for an account; a natural recourse, and one that has had considerable popularity, is to take the primary analytic posit to be the conceptions we harbor of things.[5] The operant observation in this way of looking at the matter is that having distinct conceptions does not imply that distinct things are being conceptualized. Someone may think of Paderewski in this way or that, but from this nothing follows whether he is thinking of one person or two. Since plainly we can conceive of something without thereby being able to name it, the affinity of this sort of approach with the objectual description of the puzzle should be apparent (for how else is one to think that there are two distinct people other than that he conceives of them as such?).

Our goal here, however, is not to undertake a critical exegesis of the conceptual view, although no doubt there is much to say; rather we want to consider the implications of simply denying the presupposition that underlies the view, namely that there are no relevant linguistic distinctions to be drawn. So suppose that we assume that in "Peter believes Paderewski had musical talent" and "Peter believes Paderewski doesn't have musical talent" or "Paderewski is Paderewski" we have two *distinct* linguistic forms. Or, as we would wish to say, that we have two distinct linguistic *expressions*. One way to express such a distinction would be by a spelling reform; this is what Frege gestures toward in "The Thought," when he suggests that coreferential occurrences of "Dr. Gustav Lauben" be distinguished as "Dr. Lauben" and "Gustav Lauben."[6] Now this approach has a distinct virtue, in that it provides a linguistic distinction on the order of that between "Cicero" and "Tully." It is in essence the approach we will follow, although we will not do so by spelling reform as such, for it is obvious that what is of relevance is not how the words are spelled, but only that they are spelled differently. In other words, what we are trying to capture is the numerical distinctiveness of linguistic expressions, and we can represent this in a most convenient and perspicuous way by the annotation of numerical indices. Accordingly, "Paderewski$_1$" and "Paderewski$_2$" are formally type-distinct linguistic expressions (just as "x_1" and "x_2" are formally distinct variables), as opposed to various occurrences we might find of "Paderewski$_1$," which are only token-distinct.[7]

The reason for representing numerical distinctiveness of expressions, and in particular, distinguishing type-distinctiveness from token-distinctiveness, was recognized early on; both Russell and Frege weighed in with apropos remarks. Russell comments in *Principles of Mathematics* (sec. 82) that "When an x is inserted to stand for the variable, the identity of the term to be inserted is indicated by the repetition of the letter x," while Frege elaborates on the point in the second volume of *Grundgesetze* (§99) as follows:[8] "Signs would hardly be useful if they did not serve the purpose of signifying the same thing repeatedly and in different contexts, while making evident that the same thing was meant. . . . In speaking of the same sign, the coincidence of the reference is transferred to the sign." What Russell and Frege are observing here is that if expression-occurrences are of the same type (coindexed under our notation), then they are necessarily coreferential, regardless of what the reference of the sign is. On the other hand, type-distinct expression occurrences (indicated by contraindexing) are under no such encumbrance; depending on their reference, they may or may not corefer.

The move we are contemplating here has a certain attractiveness, for it at least gives us a head start with the puzzle. This is because the belief reports will now take the form

Peter believes Paderewski$_1$ has musical talent.

and

Peter believes Paderewski$_2$ doesn't have musical talent.

from which we cannot extract anything flatly inconsistent—that is, of the form ⌜A & not-A⌝—and so are sentences that can be used to report rational beliefs. In a similar vein, our identity statement will be

Paderewski$_1$ is Paderewski$_2$.

which is of the form ⌜a = b⌝, standardly the form of informative identity statements, such as "Cicero is Tully." Note that in neither case is anything implied as a matter of the "spelling" of the linguistic terms as to whether the occurrences of "Paderewski" are coreferential.

While effecting this reduction is a great result, it really does not get us all that deeply into the problem posed by the Paderewski puzzle. As we have described the puzzle, it turns on beliefs of speakers about how many people bear a particular name, but as of yet we do not have any *connection* between the postulated difference in linguistic form and such beliefs. What we are still lacking is an account that, in some principled way, links these together; we have no grasp yet of how the linguistic differences correspond to beliefs about naming. At best we are in a position to answer an initial question as to what the linguistic information *is* that is brought into the equation. But we still have to answer the question of what governs the *beliefs* we can have about that linguistic information, our *de lingua* beliefs that so many people can bear a given name.

4.3 Bridging the Gap

What we are in search of is a bridge principle. To arrive at it, let us consider first the far end, the beliefs being bridged to; these would be beliefs that there are *x*-many people named α, for α a proper name.

What might be asked about such beliefs? Well, one thing that might be asked for is an explication of the main predicate, the term "named." A rough definition might be something like the following: *a* is named α iff *a* is designated by employing the lexical item α. But this definition begs a further one; what is the analysis of "employ a lexical item," and yet in turn, of "lexical item"? Well, a lexical item is an entry in a lexicon or vocabulary, and so we are down to a base notion in need of explication, that of a lexicon.

A lexicon is a list of entries, each distinct from all others, individuated by linguistic properties. Among these properties, a principle one is pronunciation, which we would more technically call a phonological spelling. The application of this property as an identity criterion is governed for speakers by a normative belief that if two items are pronounced differently, they are different items, up to limits of dialect and language. Thus, most speakers believe that "New York" and the native dialect's "Noo Yawk" are dialectical variants, and that "Venice" and "Venezia" are cognates, the English and Italian ways of pronouncing the same word. But a speaker could easily believe the contrary, that "New York" and "Noo Yawk" are pronounced so differently that they must be, in this speaker's view, different words (which nevertheless may still be taken to refer to the same place). Thus, when we speak of a lexicon, we mean a *speaker's lexicon,* built on beliefs about how the relevant linguistic criteria individuate the entries.

We can now fill in our definition, moving from lexicon and lexical item, to *employing a lexical item.* An employed lexical item is one that occurs as a constituent of sentence types. An employed lexical item is thus a lexical item under a syntactic description; it is a syntactic *expression* containing a lexical item. We notate such expressions by the standard technique of embracing the lexical items in labeled brackets: "[$_{NP}$Paderewski]" is a syntactic expression of the lexical item "Paderewski." So, finally, by *a is named by* α, we mean *a is designated by an expression of* α; by *a and b are named by* α, we mean *a and b are designated by expressions of* α, and so on.

By way of terminology, we will be using the term *name* to designate those lexical items by which things are named. There is an implication of our understanding of names that needs to be emphasized at this point: *names do not refer.* That is, reference is not among the linguistic properties that individuate lexical items. For suppose that reference did play this role; then a speaker would have in her lexicon as many names of the same phonological shape as she believed there to be things so named. Let us designate these now distinct names as "Paderewski$_I$," "Paderewski$_{II}$," and so on. Now consider the following statement, with respect to such a speaker's lexicon:

(N) There are many people named "Paderewski."

Obviously, this sentence could be true; but this is not what it turns out to be, since on the contemplated view there is no one named "Paderewski" at all, only someone named "Paderewski$_I$," someone named "Paderewski$_{II_5}$," and so on. Nor would matters be improved by replacing what stands between the quotation marks with one of these, for each of these can designate at most one person. Of course, if reference is not a criterion for lexical individuation, then no lexicon ever has more than one name "Paderewski." This one lexical item, however, can name any number of things. But bear in mind that reference, while not a property of names, *is* a property of syntactic expressions containing names, and these may be many, each with definite reference. In this way of looking at things, the statement above can be straightforwardly true, because indeed there may be many people designated by expressions containing the name "Paderewski." The thesis we have on the table thus has the following aspects: (i) syntactic expressions of names are the vehicles of reference; (ii) names are in a one-many relationship with their expressions. More precisely, (ii′) there is a one-many relationship between names and distinct expression-types, and (ii″) there is a one-many relationship between names and tokens of each expression type. We assume that the multiplicity implied by (ii) is indexed in syntactic structure (indicated by our use of subscripted (arabic) numerals[9]), and there are two cases to be distinguished: noncoindexing, corresponding to (ii′), and coindexing, corresponding to (ii″). "[Paderewski$_1$]" and "[Paderewski$_2$]" are (tokens of) distinct expression types, and *qua* being vehicles of reference, nothing follows whether their reference is the same or not. A stronger result holds, however, for multiple occurrences of one of these expressions; all of them corefer. Coindexing, in the natural interpretation, indicates sameness of expression-type; noncoindexing, difference of expression-type.

A question arises at this point with respect to the relation (ii); what fixes the cardinality of the expression-types for each speaker of the language? The answer is that a speaker will believe that there are as many expression-types containing a given name as she believes there are people bearing that name. This relation is bijective because while speakers assume that any number of different people may bear a given name, they do not normally believe that any one person can have one particular name more than once; Paderewski only has the name "Paderewski" once. Availing ourselves of our notational resources, we can encapsulate this *Singularity* as follows:[10]

Speakers believe that cospelled expressions corefer if coindexed, and that they do not corefer if not coindexed.

In a given discourse, a speaker's use of expressions of a name will directly reflect the speaker's beliefs about how many values that name has; in referring to each, a speaker will use different expressions, for only this will comport with his beliefs (otherwise his expressions would corefer). Thus, in accordance with Singularity, the speaker's use of x-many distinct but cospelled expressions will be based on his belief that there are x-many distinct people so-named. Singularity, therefore, is our bridge principle.[11]

4.4 The Puzzle Deepens

Let's take stock and see where we are with the puzzle, now that we can connect the expressions used to the relevant linguistic beliefs of speakers. Consider, in the context of Singularity, a sincere utterance of "Paderewski$_1$ is Paderewski$_2$." The immediate conclusion we come to is that *no speaker is in a position to assert this consistently with his beliefs.*

Why is this? On the one hand, for the speaker, who believes that there is only one person named "Paderewski," the statement implies that there are two people named "Paderewski," because two distinct "Paderewski"-expressions are used. On the other hand, someone such as the hearer, whose beliefs are consistent with this implication, would not assert this either. Rather, she would assert just the opposite, namely, "Paderewski$_1$ isn't Paderewski$_2$,"—that is, a statement of the form ⌜$a \neq b$⌝. So, we now at least have a more subtle description of what is going on in the puzzle: "Paderewski is Paderewski" is usable and informative but not assertable consonant with anyone's beliefs.

That this should be so is odd to say the least, especially given that Singularity licenses the following bit of reasoning. The hearer, by assumption, believes (1):

(1) $\exists x \exists y\, x \neq y$ (x is named "Paderewski" $\land$ y is named "Paderewski")

From (1) we can infer (2), by Singularity—that is, that there are two "Paderewski"-expressions that do not corefer.

(2) $\exists x \exists y\, x \neq y$ (x is referred to by "Paderewski$_1$" $\land$ y is referred to by "Paderewski$_2$")

Now, from (2) and "Paderewski$_1$ is Paderewski$_2$," it ought follow that (3):

(3) $\exists x \exists y\ x=y$ (x is referred to by "Paderewski$_1$" $\wedge$ y is referred to by "Paderewski$_2$")

By Singularity we then proceed immediately to (4):

(4) $\exists x \exists y\ x=y$ (x is named "Paderewski" $\wedge$ y is named "Paderewski")

which entails (5):

(5) $\exists x$ (x is named "Paderewski")

which, again by Singularity, implies (6):

(6) $\exists x$ (x is referred to "Paderewski$_1$")

Now, if the hearer's acceptance of "Paderewski$_1$ is Paderewski$_2$" is sufficient by this line of reasoning for her to reject (1), the result will be that her beliefs will come into conformity with those of the speaker. But the question remains: How does the speaker's utterance give rise to the reasoning outlined? After all, the "Paderewski"-expressions are used, not mentioned, so how is sufficient linguistic information provided in order for the hearer to change her beliefs in the way described? So far, we have no answer to this.

The problem we are facing harks back to the remark of Davidson's that we cited above; we still do not have the logical form quite right yet. To see why this is so, we need to make explicit something that has been at best only implicit thus far. Consider a speaker who utters the sentence "[$_S$ Paderewski was a Pole]." Among the things we can say about that speaker is that he uses the syntactic expression "[$_{NP}$ Paderewski]," and that with such use he believes he can accomplish the goal of speaking of that about which he intends to speak. A speaker who wishes to speak of Paderewski will use the expression "[$_{NP}$ Paderewski]" because he believes that "[$_{NP}$ Paderewski]" refers to Paderewski, so that by using this expression he may refer to Paderewski. Following the usage we have established, we call these sorts of beliefs, for instance, that "[$_{NP}$ Paderewski]" refers to Paderewski, beliefs of *Assignments*.

In the normal course of sincere speech, a speaker standardly presupposes such beliefs of Assignments; this is the effect of the Assignment Principle, introduced in chapter 2. Thus, a speaker who sincerely asserts "Paderewski was a Pole" believes (among other things) that (i) Paderewski was a Pole and (ii) "Paderewski" has the value Paderewski. But while (ii) is normally implicit, part of background assumptions of discourse, as we argued in chapters 2 and 3, Assignments may also be made explicit, as part of what is said, or if you wish, part of the content of the proposition expressed. In the terms we find congenial, what we are suggesting is that there is a systematic ambiguity of logical form, one containing an assignment, the other not. "Paderewski is a Pole," for example, will have the logical forms (*D*) and (D):

(*D*) *P* (Paderewski$_1$)

(D) *P* (Paderewski$_1$) $\wedge$ *g*("Paderewski$_1$") = Paderewski$_1$

In giving (D), we have formalized Assignments as functions from expressions to values; we can think of *g* for our purposes here as the reference function.[12] Note that (D) entails (D'):

(D') *P* (*g*("Paderewski$_1$"))

that is, that the reference of "Paderewski$_1$" is a Pole.

Now why would a speaker deviate from the normal course of events and utter a sentence with a logical form such as (D)? When would it serve his communicative purposes? One main reason, perhaps *the* reason, is that in this way the speaker can attribute Assignments to someone other than himself, and in doing so make what we might rightly call a *de dicto* attribution. By itself such an attribution might not amount to very much, saying no more than, say, someone believes that "Cicero" refers to Cicero. But when placed in coordination with the attribution of other, nonlinguistic, beliefs, the effect of such attribution can be considerably greater. So consider the following logical form, with the assignment given colloquially:

(DB) Max believes [Cicero$_1$ was a Roman, and "Cicero$_1$" has the value Cicero$_1$]

A speaker who utters this sentence with this logical form says that Max believes that a person referred to by "Cicero" is a Roman. To say this, however, is to lay in a rather restrictive claim regarding Max's belief, for by doing so the speaker is refraining from attributing the belief that Cicero was a Roman with respect to any other way of naming Cicero. So, for instance, it cannot be inferred from (DB) that Max also believes that a person referred to by him as "Tully" was a Roman—that is, (DB) does not imply (DB'):

(DB') Max believes [Tully$_2$ was a Roman, and "Tully$_2$" has the value Tully$_2$]

The inference to (DB') fails because ""Tully$_2$"" cannot be substituted for ""Cicero$_1$."" These expressions are not coreferential; unlike "Tully$_2$" and "Cicero$_1$," which denote the same person, they denote different *expressions* of the language.

Notice here that Assignments are semantic beliefs that speakers can confidently and reliably attribute to agents. Indeed, there may be nothing of semantic relevance in the current context other than such beliefs that can be attributed with such certainty, certainly not the beliefs that an agent associates with his representation of a person or object (given that there even are any), for these are not the sort of beliefs to which anyone other than oneself has particular access. An Assignment can be attributed even if the speaker is in no position to attribute to the agent any descriptive or qualitative grounds on which the agent associates that name with that value.[13]

The circumstances we are observing are really no different with the following pair, those of the puzzle:

Peter believes [Paderewski$_1$ has musical talent, and "Paderewski$_1$" has the value Paderewski$_1$]

Peter believes [Paderewski$_2$ doesn't have musical talent, and "Paderewski$_2$" has the value Paderewski$_2$]

Here, however, another factor comes into play; given Singularity relative to what is being attributed to Peter, it follows that he believes that there are two people, each named "Paderewski," one of whom has musical talent, the other not, and of course there is nothing inconsistent about this. But to echo Kripke, does Peter, or does he not, believe that Paderewski has musical talent? The answer depends on how we take the question. If it is *de dicto*, then once we have clarified which "Paderewski" expression is being used, there is a yes or no answer to be had. But this is not the way Kripke intends it to be taken. Rather, the puzzle arises, putting it in our terms, from posing the question non–*de dicto* in the context of *de dicto* attributions. But given the clash of beliefs about how many people are named "Paderewski" between the speaker and the agent, the question is inevitably unanswerable as asked.

4.5 The Identity Puzzle

Like Kripke, it is our view that the puzzle as just outlined arises from aspects of belief attribution. But we differ, given our articulation of the "logical grammar," in the principle at stake; it is from Singularity that the puzzle arises, not from disquotation in Kripke's sense. The utility in looking at things our way arises in part from its applicability to other aspects of the puzzle. So, with our current understanding, let us return to the identity puzzle: How can "Paderewski is Paderewski" be an informative identity statement?

As we left matters, we had gotten as far as analyzing "Paderewski is Paderewski" as being of the form $\ulcorner a = b \urcorner$, which gave rise, as we saw, to certain unfortunate consequences, since the relevant Assignments were presupposed attributed to the speaker. But now we have another option: the *de dicto* logical form:

Paderewski$_1$ is Paderewski$_2$, and "Paderewski$_1$" has the value Paderewski$_1$, and "Paderewski$_2$" has the value Paderewski$_2$.

That is, identity statements too are ambiguous; they also have logical forms that contain Assignments, schematically

$(D=)\ a = b \wedge g("a") = a \wedge g("b") = b$

from which it follows directly that

$g("a") = g("b")$

So, given the logical form above, it follows that the reference of "Paderewski$_1$" is the same as the reference of "Paderewski$_2$." But now the question arises: to whom are the Assignments contained in a logical form of the form $(D=)$ being attributed? A first-party attribution is inherently eliminated by the fact that the Assignments are explicit, and no third party is overtly specified (as in belief attributions). Rather the attribution is to the second party—that is, normally to the addressee. It is as if the speaker, in uttering "Paderewski is Paderewski" *de dicto* says in effect to the hearer, *your* "Paderewski"-expressions corefer, and this can be asserted consistently with the speaker's beliefs about how many people are named "Paderewski."

The existence of *de dicto* logical forms is a general phenomenon, not bounded to any particular linguistic context. We have previously, in chapter 2, discussed their occurrence in propositional-attitude contexts; their occurrence embedded in modal contexts is another example. Suppose a speaker is faced with an interlocutor who is highly reticent about revising any of his beliefs, a person for whom the best strategy would be to have him just entertain that there is only one person named "Paderewski." To this person, the speaker may say, *de dicto* in our sense, (P):

(P) It is possible that Paderewski is Paderewski.

(P) entails:

It is possible that the reference of "Paderewski$_1$" is the reference of "Paderewski$_2$."

as entailments hold within modal contexts. What is not entailed by (P) is

The reference of "Paderewski$_1$" is the reference of "Paderewski$_2$"

correctly so, given the invalidity of inferring p from $\Diamond p$, in contrast to its unembedded counterpart, which does have this entailment. Where they do *not* contrast, however, is in what their usage tells us about what the speaker and hearer believe; this is the same. Since both involve attributions, usage of either will conform to the hearer's beliefs; it is his beliefs of Assignments, and consequently about how many people are named "Paderewski," that are presupposed in the discourse. A speaker can respect these presuppositions because his beliefs do not come into play; his presuppositions are just not on the table, reflecting a general property of using language attributively.[14]

We now have an important result. Identity statements can contain linguistic information, and this information can be attributed to the hearer by the speaker. (Note that this does not undermine the necessity of true identity statements, for (D=) is a conjunction of identities, and a conjunction of necessary truths it itself a necessary truth; see the discussion in the appendix to chapter 2, and in chapter 3.) This refines the puzzle for us, to the question of how this information can be *informative*—that is, what is the effect of this information on the epistemic states of the hearer, such that it will be causal of a change in his belief states?

Well, let's follow through the logic of the communicative interaction of the speaker and hearer. The speaker's communicative goal is to cause the hearer to alter his beliefs; the speaker wants the hearer to believe that there is only one person named "Paderewski," just as he does. As such, he makes his utterance. The hearer accepting "Paderewski is Paderewski" *de dicto* will infer that his "Paderewski"-expressions corefer, thereby negating his previous view that they did not. This, however, is unstable, for it does not square with Singularity, there being too many expressions given his (interim) revised belief of coreference. To bring his language back into conformity, the hearer has but one option—give up that there are two distinct "Paderewski"-expression types, and replace it with the belief that there is just one. If this exhausts the hearer's inventory of "Paderewski"-expressions, it follows that he now believes there is only one person named "Paderewski." The speaker's desired result has been achieved; he has brought the hearer's beliefs into conformity with his.[15]

It should be clear that this description of the informativeness of "Paderewski is Paderewski" is just an informal rendering of what we gave as (1) through (6) above, and we now have a grasp on the question that we posed there. The speaker's utterance gives rise to the reasoning outlined because the linguistic information conveyed in the *de dicto* logical form is sufficient information to cause the hearer to adjust his linguistic beliefs in the manner described (or, if modally embedded, to contemplate adjusting). Making this change of course may require some housekeeping in the hearer's overall epistemic states, since beliefs that were previously taken to be about two people, are now taken to be about one. If someone previously believed that Paderewski had musical talent, and that Paderewski did not have musical talent, he is going to have to decide whether he does or he does not (or remain agnostic). This last step is the ultimate effect of the information that the speaker has conveyed to the hearer by his utterance of "Paderewski is Paderewski."[16]

4.6 Informativeness and the Reverse Puzzle

Let us dwell for a few moments on the remarks in the paragraph that concluded the previous section. As we have it, we can think of the epistemic result of a hearer's acceptance of "Paderewski is Paderewski" as an instruction to merge his beliefs about Paderewski, to form the union, if you will, of his "Paderewski$_1$"-beliefs and his "Paderewski$_2$"-beliefs, while resolving whatever conflicts or inconsistencies this would engender. Now this joining of disjoint sets of beliefs into one presumably has an inverse, an operation splitting one set of beliefs into two. Indeed this is just what a speaker would want a hearer to do if, in reversing the initial scenario, it is the *speaker* who believes there are two people named "Paderewski," while the hearer believes there is just one. The puzzle here is what could the speaker say in order to instruct the hearer to divide his unary "Paderewski" beliefs into two?

The answer that comes immediately to mind is: say the opposite of what was said before, not "Paderewski is Paderewski," but rather "Paderewski isn't Paderewski." But uttering this in the context seems very odd indeed. The hearer believes there is only one person named "Paderewski," so the only relevant identity statement he would hold to be true would be "Paderewski$_1$ is Paderewski$_1$," a sentence of the form ⌜$a = a$⌝. But then the initial reaction of the hearer to the speaker's utterance of "Paderewski isn't Paderewski" is that it is the negation of this, that the speaker had uttered a logical falsehood. At this point the hearer might walk away left with doubts about his interlocutor's sanity. He may, however, be more charitable, for knowing the linguistic options, he could recognize that it is possible that the speaker's intention was to utter a sentence of a different form, namely, "Paderewski$_1$ isn't Paderewski$_2$." This is a perfectly reasonable thing to say, and if this is what the speaker did assert, so the hearer would reason, it would only be because he believes there are two people named "Paderewski." Now, the hearer continues, why would the speaker tell me, the hearer, about his beliefs in this way? Well, presumably because he wished to highlight the differences in our beliefs, and perhaps he did so, given the context, because he thinks I'm wrong about there being only person named "Paderewski." *Ergo*, the point of the speaker's utterance was that he wants me to change my beliefs to be like his.

Well, our goal has been reached, but in a way that is much different (and weaker) than before. In the prior case, the hearer's reasoning got off the ground because the sentence the speaker uttered was a denial of what the hearer holds; belief revision then results solely from the hearer's reflections on his own epistemic states. In this latter case, however, if there is an inconsistency, it is ineffectual. Rather, the hearer's reasoning is generated by his benevolent desire to give a sensible reconstruction of the speaker's speech act, and reason it through to a likely conclusion as to cause. As a result of these reflections in part about the *speaker's* epistemic states, the hearer may indeed alter his beliefs, and hold that there are two people named "Paderewski."

Now suppose that a hearer, by this more indirect route, does change from believing that there is one person named "Paderewski" to that there are two. But now the hearer is stuck. Since the hearer has one set of (nonlinguistic) beliefs about Paderewski, the task that faces him now is to cleave this set into two; this is the consequence, given Singularity, of his newfound belief. But he is left in the dark as to how to proceed; he does not have sufficient information on where to make the cut. In this regard, the speaker's utterance cannot be said to be informative, for it cannot cause any stable reorganization of the hearer's nonlinguistic beliefs. For this, more information is needed; it would be in line for the hearer, having reasoned through from the speaker's utterance of "Paderewski isn't Paderewski," to respond "Oh, how are they to be distinguished?" In contrast, no comparable request would be needed in the initial case; the hearer may respond to the speaker's utterance of "Paderewski is Paderewski" with nothing more than "Oh, I see." Further information is not required, because there is sufficient information to unify previously distinct sets of beliefs to arrive at a new, stable set of beliefs (again, short of having to resolve conflicts and inconsistencies, or at least remaining agnostic about such).

If "Paderewski isn't Paderewski" is ultimately uninformative in the reverse context, is there some way that information can be provided that would allow for the division of beliefs? There is a minimal way of changing things that would have this result: replace the proper names with definite descriptions. The speaker might rather say, for instance, "The pianist isn't the statesman." Accepting this—"Oh, I see" again seems an appropriate response—the hearer will now have a handle on things, for a wedge as to where to split his beliefs has been provided, between those relevant to being a pianist and those relevant to being a statesman. What we see here, then, is a difference emerging between names and descriptions; names, in the context, are informationally "weak"; descriptions, informationally "strong." In the standard context, in which information is needed to join beliefs, weak information is sufficient, so of course stronger information will suffice as well. But not in the reverse case; here nothing less than strong information will do.

It will perhaps not have gone unnoticed that lurking in these remarks is an argument against reducing names to descriptions, for if names in some sense carried descriptive information, we would expect them to be informative in the reverse context just like descriptions. This conclusion is of course nothing new, but it does differ from the standard arguments in that it arises from epistemic rather than modal considerations. But while both sorts of considerations lead to the same conclusion about names and descriptions, it turns out that they do not carve the referential joint in exactly the same way. So consider a speaker, in the reverse context, saying to the hearer "That guy isn't that guy," uttering the first demonstrative while pointing to the pianist in the concert hall, then very slowly saying "isn't" as they quickly dash outside to the political rally in the town square, and demonstrating the orating politician while uttering the second demonstrative. This utterance *is* informative; "strong" information, it appears, can be supplied contextually as well as linguistically. Demonstratives, therefore, fall on the side of the fence with descriptions, in opposition to proper names. This divergence between name and demonstrative expressions stands in contrast to well-known arguments that names and demonstratives cluster together, as opposed to descriptions, as devices of rigid (or direct) designation, which are based on the properties of these expressions in modal contexts.[17] The modal arguments are intended to show that reference is not the same as satisfying a description, and this is true of reference made by the use of either names or demonstratives. Our epistemic argument, in contrast, pertains to how different referential vehicles can be used by speakers in the service of effecting changes in the belief states of their interlocutors. In this regard names and demonstratives do not form a natural class; rather demonstratives cluster with definite descriptions, in that they can overtly carry information on which the hearer can base the revision of his beliefs, something names, in the circumstances described, cannot do.

4.7 A Demonstrative Puzzle

To this point, we have dwelled on the linguistic Paderewski puzzle, the puzzle that turns on linguistic beliefs of the speaker and hearer. At the outset, however, we remarked that this is to be distinguished from a different puzzle, one that is not linguistic in character; now that we have brought demonstratives into the picture, we are in a position to broach this puzzle, albeit only briefly and rather sketchily.

The setting for this puzzle is much like the original; the twist is that the linguistic information is removed. So suppose that the speaker and hearer know of the pianist and the statesman, the speaker believing they are one and the same, the hearer that they are not. However, neither the speaker nor the hearer know his name—the name "Paderewski" is not to be found as an entry in either of their lexicons.[18] The speaker now utters to the hearer "That guy is that guy," pointing first to Paderewski as he plays the piano on the concert stage, then while slowly uttering "is," they dash outside, somewhat preceded by Paderewski, and pointing to him, now on the political rostrum exhorting the crowd, finishes the utterance.[19] Clearly this can be an "Oh, I see" case; the speaker's utterance can be informative, effecting a revision in the beliefs of the hearer. No longer will he believe there are two people; now he will believe there is just one.

To understand this "demonstrative" form of the puzzle, and to see how it differs from the "linguistic" form of the puzzle we have been considering, we need to be clear first about the logical form of "That guy is that guy," and how it differs from the logical form of "Paderewski is Paderewski." For, as we will see, only the logical form of the latter is subject to Singularity, and it is from this that the distinction between the puzzles emerges.

To unfold this, recall that we have taken it that for names, expression-types are projected from lexical items, and that tokens of these types are what occur in syntactic structures. We annotate tokens by indexing, so that all tokens of a given type will bear the same index, and tokens of different types will always bear different indices. Moreover, as we understand what it means to be a token of a syntactic type, it directly follows that all tokens of an expression-type are covalued; all tokens (in a given discourse) of "[Paderewski]$_1$," will corefer, *as a matter of grammar*. It is a characteristic of natural language, however, that there may also be expression-tokens whose relevant syntactic contents are spelled the same—they all contain the name "Paderewski"—but yet are not covalued. An immediate consequence of this observation is that syntactic tokening cannot be of names, for if it were, all expressions containing the same name would have to be covalued. Thus, our insistence that what are syntactically tokened are expressions of names (and our practice of appending indices to syntactic expressions—that is, to NPs, and not to the names they contain)—and our insistence that, properly speaking, it is expressions, not names, that refer. Moreover, since expression-tokens that contain the same name but that are not covalued must be tokens of different expression-types, namely, tokens of "[Paderewski]$_1$" and "[Paderewski]$_2$," we can take the position that the relation from expression-type to value is a function.[20]

Now what about expressions that rather than containing names, contain demonstratives like "that man"? Tokens of such expressions contain orthographic occurrences of the word "that" and orthographic occurrences of the word "man." But does it follow from this coincidence that these are tokens of a demonstrative expression-type "that man"? Can we say of them just what we have said of name-expressions? The quick answer is no; the reason, roughly, is that syntax underdetermines demonstrative expression tokening. This answer, however, is a bit cryptic; to flesh it out, we need to spell out some our understanding of the linguistic characteristics of demonstratives.

Demonstratives, we propose, introduce functions from contexts to indices. So suppose that we think of demonstratives, as delivered syntactically, as doubly incomplete, containing a place for a context and an index. Then, in a context C^i, the index "1" might be determined, and we will have the expression-token "[$_1$ that α (C^i)]," while in context C^j, $i \neq j$, the index "2" might be determined, and we will have the expression-token "[$_2$ that α (C^j)]."[21] C^i and C^j need not, however, determine different indices. There is no bar to occurrences of demonstratives in distinct contexts determining the same indices—that is, to coindexing—so that we can also have "[$_1$ that α (C^i)]" and "[$_1$ that α (C^j)]." The determination of the index by the function introduced by a demonstrative serves as its definition; typically a successful definition involves demonstrating an object, the demonstration being part of the context that determines the index.[22]

The characterization of demonstrative expressions we have just given is meant to encompass their *linguistic* properties. As such, it is to be distinguished from a common view that demonstratives introduce functions from demonstrations to values; we differ in what we take to be both the domain and range. For reasons that will become increasingly clear as we proceed, demonstrations cannot take the place of contexts, nor values of indices; we can observe at this point that these notions are not coextensive—there may be any number of demonstrations in a context held fixed, and there may be any number of distinct indices (more precisely expressions bearing distinct indices), with the same value. This is not to deny, however, that demonstrations play a role in the overall account. It is just that we see this role as ancillary to the information needed for a sufficient linguistic description. Demonstrations, and the relation they bear to their demonstrata, are part of the definition of context; all that is required linguistically is that this definition characterize the domain of the demonstrative function onto indices.

The possibility of this last case raises the following question: Are "$[_1$ that α $(C^j)]$" and "$[_1$ that α $(C^j)]$" tokens of the same expression-type, a type we may represent as "$[_{(\,)}$ that α$(\,)]$" so as to indicate its incompleteness with respect to context and index? Now if it is central to the type-token distinction that two tokens of the same expression-type be coindexed and therefore have the same value, then, since these are coindexed, and therefore covalued, it might be said of these two cases that they are indeed tokens of the same type. But in general this will not do, since "$[_3$ that α $(C^k)]$" is, on this view, *also* a token of the expression-type "$[_{(\,)}$ that α$(\,)]$," and "$[_1$ that α $(C^j)]$" and "$[_3$ that α $(C^k)]$" are not only not coindexed but might not even be covalued. The terminological tension should be clear. On the one hand there is a notion of "token-of," special to linguistics, that suggests "derived from." This sort of talk appears elsewhere in linguistics, as when it is said that two phonetically distinct allophones are tokens of the same phoneme. The other sort of talk focuses rather on the question of whether we have repetitions of the same thing, where the expression "same thing" may be taken more or less strictly. These usages may diverge; in the case of allophones, it is perfectly legitimate to say that two phonetically distinct allophones are tokens of (derived from) the same phoneme (-type), but that they are not repetitions of the same thing (they are phonetically distinct).

The former usage, the linguistic one, though harmless, is not the one we have been adopting so far. We have said that there is an expression-type "[₁ Paderewski]," and that it has tokens. And we have said that the value of the expression-type "[₁ Paderewski]" is Paderewski and that the values of all of the tokens of the expression-type "[₁ Paderewski]" are Paderewski. So types with values have tokens with values. The type-token distinction, as we have been deploying it, is a relation between expressions with values. But it makes no sense to talk of the value of "[₍₎ that α( )]." A value can only be determined when a context is specified and an index derived. But in the type-token talk we have been engaged in, the point has been that tokens of the same type are (1) coindexed, and (2) have the same value as that type. But as just discussed, there are no demonstrative expression-types that have values. Even if we wish to call "[₍₎ that α( )]" a demonstrative expression-type (in the linguistic "derivational" sense), it nevertheless has no value. So we must revise our type-token talk accordingly. So far we have said: coindexed NPs are tokens of the same type. Now we must add the proviso: *if they have a type*. So far we have said: coindexed expressions have the same value as the type they are tokens of. Now we must add the proviso: *if they have a type*.

Importantly, notice that having added these provisos, we *still* may say: coindexed expressions are covalued. That is, if expressions are coindexed, they are covalued; this is an extensional property of the semantics. The semantics, if you will, does not care about the genesis of this coindexing, whether it arises from the different ways in which name-expressions and demonstrative-expressions are projected. Covaluation—coreference in the case at hand—is a matter of grammar, indeed the *same* matter of grammar, regardless; the semantics need look no further than that there is coindexing to determine that token-expressions have the same value. Coindexed demonstrative-expressions will have the same value (demonstrata); when they are not coindexed, they are not so compelled. But this is no more (or less) than what we can say of name-expressions, at least from the perspective of grammar.

Notice that nothing we have said so far disallows multiple occurrences of a fully determined demonstrative-expression; all we have said is that in the relevant sense they are not tokens of the same type. Thus a representation such as the following ought to be allowed:

[that guy (C^i)]₁ saw [that guy (C^i)]₁

But there is yet another question lurking, pertaining to how fine contexts are sliced. Clearly, in this sentence we have two demonstrative expression-tokens, and that when uttered, they occur at different times. And it must be admitted that difference in time alone *can* distinguish contexts, as can spatial differences alone. But *must* they? If they must, then the sentence given may never be uttered. But before we draw that conclusion, we must be clearer about what contexts are. What plainly they are not are complete representations of the actual conditions of utterance, for speakers are rarely, if ever, in a position to apprehend the total objective conditions of utterance. Rather, speakers employ a much more labile and subjective notion of context, which depends on their beliefs about the objective conditions, and their views of the relevance to their speech act of the various aspects of utterance context. Thus, a context, as it figures in the determination of demonstrative-expressions, will be, more often than not, partial, and not complete. So, for instance, while objectively the time of utterance is different for each utterance of a demonstrative-expression, a speaker may or may not believe that this is a relevant factor. If change of time is paramount to the speaker, then context will be taken to change; if it is not, the speaker will consider the current context to be unchanged (and *ceteris paribus* for other aspects of context). Returning to the sentence above, it will be on this view utterable, with the meaning that with respect to an unchanging context, the person demonstrated saw himself.[23]

With this much under our belt, we are now in a position to return to the issue that set us down the present path: What is the logical form of "that guy is that guy"? There are two possibilities:

[that guy (C^i)]$_1$ is [that guy (C^i)]$_1$

in which context is invariant, and:

[that guy (C^i)]$_1$ is [that guy (C^j)]$_2$

in which context changes. (What we cannot have is

[that guy (C^i)]$_1$ is [that guy (C^i)]$_2$

if the relation from contexts to indices is a function.) Of these two logical forms, clearly it is the latter that could be uttered in the puzzle context. Not only is it of the form "$a = b$" (the other being of the form "$a = a$" and analytic relative to the context), but it also represents an essential aspect of the demonstrative puzzle so described, namely, that each demonstrative-expression is uttered in a different context, one in the concert hall, the other at the rally. Our attention is therefore directed toward this logical form as the logical form of "That guy is that guy," as uttered in the context of the puzzle.

The reason for our continued scrutiny is that we have still not settled whether an utterance of the sentence in question, with this logical form, will suffice for the speaker's communicative purposes as described above. This is pertinent, for as we have seen, a sentence with a logical form comparable with respect to indexing but containing name-expressions did not suffice. Recall that in this latter case—"Paderewski$_1$ is Paderewski$_2$," (non–*de dicto, sans* Assignments)—it would follow from Singularity that a speaker of this sentence believes that there are two people each named "Paderewski," so that it would be unsuitable for use in a circumstance such as that of the initial puzzle in which the speaker believes there is only one person so-named. But this is not the conclusion to be drawn about "That guy$_1$ is that guy$_2$," in the case at hand. The reason for this is not hard to see, once we recognize that under the logical form proposed, *utterances of a sentence of this sort are not constrained by Singularity*. Singularity, at heart, is a condition that constrains speakers' beliefs about the relation of linguistic types; it says that if spelling is invariant, then different types, and hence their respective tokens, have different values. It is thus applicable just where we are willing to say that there are types that syntactic occurrences are tokens of. But demonstrative-expressions, as we have seen, are of no syntactically determined type, and so Singularity simply does not come into the picture. Since Singularity is bypassed, "That guy$_1$ is that guy$_2$," does not imply that two people are demonstrated, only at most that there are different contexts, and this is compatible with a speaker uttering this sentence perfectly well believing that he is demonstrating the same person twice over, as is the case in the above scenario. Therefore, what the speaker says, and what the hearer takes him to be saying, is that the person demonstrated in the first context is the same person as demonstrated in the second. But since this denies what the hearer would have taken to be the case in the circumstances—that the demonstrations are of different people—the hearer will have gained information sufficient to cause him to consider altering his beliefs.

At this point, the difference between the two Paderewski puzzles should be emerging with some clarity. In the puzzle with demonstratives, the speaker, on the basis of his own beliefs about how many people there are (i.e., just one), can make an informative assertion non–*de dicto,* and by doing so bring the hearer's otherwise divergent beliefs into accordance with his own. The puzzle here *is* objectual; there is no issue as to variant linguistic beliefs of the speaker and hearer. In contrast, it is just such beliefs that are at issue in the puzzle with proper names. In this case, the speaker cannot make an informative assertion based on his own beliefs about how many people are named "Paderewski," but can do so on the basis of his beliefs about the hearer's beliefs about how many people are so-named. The logical form of his utterance must be, as we have said, *de dicto*. This puzzle is linguistic.

4.8 Demonstrative Reference

At this juncture we make an observation: the demonstrative puzzle does not depend on the speaker and hearer not having the name "Paderewski" in their lexicons. For we need only notice that the puzzle would have continued apace in the scenario described above if the speaker had uttered not "That guy is that guy," but "That Paderewski is that Paderewski," or even, with accompanying ostension, "Paderewski is Paderewski." Either of these latter utterances too would be informative. So, even though the speaker and hearer have the name "Paderewski" in their lexicons, there is apparently no impediment to the speaker uttering a sentence with the logical form "Paderewski$_1$ is Paderewski$_2$," all the while believing that there is only one person *named* "Paderewski," so long as his utterance is demonstrative, and thus Singularity is not in play.[24]

The picture that emerges from this observation when combined with our previous results is that expressions of names have a dual status, so that when expressions of names are used successfully there are two routes at the disposal of speakers by which the same value can be secured, one via semantic reference, the other by demonstrative reference. Semantic reference is reference based on semantic beliefs of speakers; these beliefs may perseverate over time, and may be the basis, by the use of a name, for repeated references to a given individual. By way of contrast, demonstrative reference is more ephemeral in nature; it is inherently dated, located, and oriented, with referential value being obtained through demonstration. Demonstrative reference and semantic reference are independent, and they are canonically associated with different linguistic vehicles. Normally, speakers will use demonstrative expressions to make demonstrative reference, and name-expressions to make semantic reference (or descriptions, where names are either unavailable or inappropriate). However, demonstrative reference at least is not inherently tied to a particular type of linguistic expression. While speakers will use proper names semantically when context is insufficient to support demonstration, demonstrative reference can predominant when context warrants, in which case proper names can be used as the linguistic vehicles of demonstration. Such is the case in the demonstrative Paderewski puzzle.

As might be expected, demonstrative uses of proper names conform to general conditions on demonstrations that license the use of demonstratives. These conditions are quite flexible; speakers know that hearers are forgiving when it comes to demonstration, and do not require that the referent be the proximate demonstratum. All that is absolutely required of a speaker is that he believe that whatever is proximately demonstrated will be associated by the hearer with the appropriate object. For instance, pointing to a picture of Paderewski may be sufficient to demonstrate Paderewski, in which case the speaker may utter either "That guy is a pianist" or "Paderewski is a pianist," and pointing to a picture of him as an adult and then to one of him as a baby may be sufficient to demonstrate Paderewski twice, the different pictures providing sufficient diversity of context to support uttering either "That guy is that guy" or "Paderewski is Paderewski." What holds for pictures holds more diversely, for both single and multiple uses of demonstratives; with the latter, for instance, doing different things, wearing different costumes, having different identities, as well as bring depicted differently may be sufficiently divergent contexts to support multiple indications of the intended referent. But regardless of how the demonstration is accomplished, there is an additional encumbrance on the demonstrative use of names, for (keeping to our example) an utterance of "Paderewski is a pianist" implies a belief that it is a picture of *Paderewski* being demonstrated, and this has to come into the mix somewhere. So, unless the speaker believes it is a picture of Paderewski, and believes of the hearer that he believes it is a picture of Paderewski (or at least believes that the hearer believes that the speaker believes that the picture is a picture of Paderewski[25]), a proper name cannot felicitously be used demonstratively. Of course, the point generalizes; so long as it is believed that, relative to the context, the *demonstration* is of Paderewski, a proper name can be used demonstratively.

What we can now see is that if context is held constant, and the aforementioned epistemic condition is met, demonstrative-expressions and name-expressions are interchangeable; either may be used to the same communicative ends as vehicles of demonstrative reference, and this is to be distinguished from the use of name-expressions as vehicles of semantic reference. Failing to heed this dual nature of name-expressions can lead to confusion of cases; here is one that from our point of view would be particularly egregious. Consider Frank, a bright, if somewhat naive, student at Cambridge in the halcyon days of the early twentieth century. Frank, we may assume, has the name "Russell" in his lexicon, so that (1) holds:

(1) Frank believes that "Russell" refers to Russell.

But although Frank's linguistic usage conforms with this belief—his intention in using the name "Russell" is to refer to Russell—Frank's behavior belies a different truth. When he says he is going to Russell's lectures, he in fact goes to Wittgenstein's, and when he sees Wittgenstein on the street, he points to him and says "There goes Russell." It thus seems that (2) holds:

(2) Frank believes that "Russell" refers to Wittgenstein,

so that (3) is the case:[26]

(3) Frank doesn't believe that "Russell" refers to Russell.

But how can (1) and (3) both be true?

One answer, of course, is that they cannot be, if (3) is true, then (1) is false. This result, however, would seem to undermine one of our central claims. Example (1) appears as a belief of an assignment, and (3) as the denial of such belief. Example (3), however, does not imply that Frank is incompetent in his linguistic usage. Linguistically, he uses the name properly, to refer to the person he believes to be named "Russell," but he has misapplied it, for he is mistaken as to who Russell *is*. But if the falsity of (1) does not imply that Frank lacks such linguistic competence, then, the argument goes, it cannot be that beliefs such as (1) reflect a speaker's linguistic knowledge of a name in the way that we have described it, and so such beliefs cannot play the central explanatory role we have ascribed to them. Clearly, this is not a result that we are prepared to embrace, and indeed we should not, for it traffics in just the confusion we warned against.

The problem with this argument stems, we believe, from the rendering of (1), which runs roughshod over an important distinction, collapsing two quite distinct sorts of beliefs in one wording. One, roughly that "Russell" means Russell, is a belief of an assignment; the other, which can be paraphrased as "That's Russell," is an *identificational* belief. To see how these might be confused, suppose that Frank was asked to identify the person he has in mind when he uses the name "Russell" and he does so by in fact demonstrating Russell (not Wittgenstein). We could then say that:

(I) Frank believes that "Russell" refers to that person.

But since the demonstrative picks out Russell, the context would be such that we could also have (I'):

(I') Frank believes that "Russell" refers to Russell.

(I') is equivalent to (I), differing only in that it contains the demonstrative name "Russell" instead of the demonstrative "that person." Now the similarity of the identificational belief (I) rendered as (I') to a report of a belief of an assignment will be innocuous, so long as Frank properly identifies whom he means to refer to by his use of the name "Russell." The coincidence, however, can break down, and when it does the two sorts of beliefs split apart. Thus, if Frank (mis)identifies Wittgenstein, not Russell, as the reference of "Russell," then (1) above is false, and (2) and (3) true, where (1) through (3) are *identificational* beliefs—in each case, the (used) name being a demonstrative name. But nevertheless, Frank still believes an assignment; as noted, linguistically he uses the name properly, to refer to the person he believes to be named "Russell," and this is unaffected by his misidentification. So if (1) is understood as attributing a belief of an assignment, it remains true, even though (3) is false, for (3) is the denial of an identification, not of an assignment.

To recap, what the present considerations emphasize is the importance of keeping clear two quite distinct uses of proper names, to each of which there is a corresponding puzzle. Although both the linguistic puzzle and the demonstrative puzzle can turn on utterances of "Paderewski is Paderewski," under analysis what is said in each case is quite different. In only the former case is what is said *de dicto*. These cases are not to be conflated, for this would be to confuse the puzzles, and to be confused, at a more basic level, about linguistic beliefs fundamental to our grasp of reference as an aspect of our linguistic competence.

4.9 Concluding Remarks

To conclude, what the intricacies and subtleties of the Paderewski puzzle lead us to is the view that there is not one puzzle, but two, one fundamentally linguistic in nature, the other not. In arriving at this conclusion, we have, of course, been sketchy at times, and rather blithely skipped over many details, some of which have been covered in previous chapters. These include our initial stipulation regarding the distinctiveness of "Paderewski"-expressions, the relations of the Paderewski puzzle and the Pierre puzzle, and of the identity puzzle given here to the traditional puzzle of "Cicero is Tully." In the later two cases, considerations of the equivalence of Assignments come into play; see our discussion in chapters 2 and 3. Moreover, a number of further matters are discussed in those chapters that extend the observations here, including the embedding of identity statements in propositional attitude reports, giving a sort of "double" puzzle, and the reduction of certain aspects of the notion of a causal referential chain to anaphora in discourse. Additional issues, for instance, regarding the mechanisms of belief revision, remain outstanding. Our goal here, however, has been more modest—to give at least a plausibility argument for the linguistic character of the connected problems of substitution and informativeness, as this is highlighted by the Paderewski puzzle.

Notes

1. Nor would the speaker be calling his own rationality into doubt were he to report that Peter both did and did not believe that Paderewski had musical talent, all the while supposing that the speaker is aware of the pertinent fact regarding Paderewski—that is, aware that there is only one such person so-named.

2. This "new puzzle" of identity was originally introduced in Fiengo and May 1998, 2002 (reprinted as chapters 2 and 3). Devitt (1989) briefly mentions a similar example, although he employs the example to rather different ends; for remarks, see chapter 3, note 45.

3. Notice that the belief of the hearer is not that there are two people Paderewski, and of the speaker that there is just one, since the proposition that there are two people Paderewski is necessarily false (presuming one does not dismiss it *tout court* as a use/mention confusion). One might be tempted to avoid this conclusion by holding that the term "Paderewski" is ambiguous as used in "There are two people Paderewski." But this would appear to imply that "There are indefinitely many people Paderewski" is indefinitely ambiguous, a rather unsatisfying result.

4. Initially in Church 1950, where he employs the so-called translation argument. Also see Church 1956, in which he outlines his case for language-independent propositions.

5. We lump together here what has gone under a number of rubrics, including ways of thinking, dossiers or files of information, modes of presentation (at least on one understanding of the notion), and body of knowledge. While there may well be differences of detail if not substance among these notions, there is a common core in that they all assume that a speaker's use of a name is based on a compendium of conceptual information.

6. The only alternative, Frege thought, was that if there were two cospelled expressions with different senses, they would have to be expressions of different languages. This is because for Frege a language is a system of signs, pairings of formal symbols and senses; different systems of signs constitute different languages. Thus, his protagonists in "The Thought," Leo Peter and Herbert Garner, if they each have the name "Dr. Gustav Lauben" with different senses, so they are different signs, would each speak different languages. Spelling reform allowed Frege to escape this conclusion, even if this has, in Frege's context, a certain artificiality.

7. This is just a brief rehearsal of points we make at length in chapter 1.

8. Frege, importantly, points out that the operant notion of *same sign* goes beyond mere typographical coincidence. In continuing the passage cited in the text (1903, [1970] 194), he remarks that "we shall understand by 'signs of similar shape' those intended by the writer to have similar shapes in order that they may designate the same thing." Frege is right to emphasize the intentionality at play here; we turn to it in the next section.

9. As above, presence of a subscript will indicate an expression, absence a name: "Paderewski$_1$," indicates a syntactic expression, "Paderewski" the name.

10. Our formulation here differs from that in chapter 1 merely in making explicit that speakers believe Singularity.

11. Beliefs stemming from Singularity are normative and defeasible; one can imagine nonstandard scenarios that make sense precisely because Singularity is set aside. So, suppose that baby Ignace is kidnaped. The kidnappers, ignorant of the child's name, bestow one; they name him "Ignace." If one knows this, it seems

that one would believe that one person has the same name twice, "Ignace" as bestowed by his parents and "Ignace" as bestowed by the kidnappers, and on the basis of this belief could assert "Ignace is Ignace" informatively. In this case, there would be good cause for holding that the norm, as fixed by Singularity, does not obtain.

12. We hedge here because of nondenoting name-expressions. While there are any number of ways of treating such expressions (e.g., as having some sort of abstract denotata, or as standing as disguised descriptions of fiction), as we pointed out in chapter 2, whatever approach is adopted, it will remain orthogonal to the issues that arise from the attribution of Assignments; these are constant across denoting and nondenoting names.

13. It might be thought that the role played by attributed Assignments could be filled not by attributing specific descriptive or qualitative conditions to the agent, but by a weaker attribution, just that there are such conditions, while leaving their particular content unspecified. Presumably, this would attain the sort of epistemic neutrality that accrues to attributed Assignments, given that having some such conditions is constitutive of having a name in one's language. We are dubious, however, of this latter claim. One may have no idea whatsoever what conditions are satisfied by the reference "Cicero" or "Tully." But that would be no bar to accepting the truth of "Cicero is Tully"—say it was uttered by George Washington, who is compelled to unimpeachably speak the truth—and hence coming to know that "Cicero" and "Tully" corefer. All that is needed for this, and hence for having a name in one's language, is that these are names, and that they can be employed in expressions that have a semantic value; see the discussion below and in chapter 3. Moreover, it is central to our proposal that there are clear and precise identity conditions provided by the grammar that distinguish Assignments; the parallel problem of conceptual individuation is notoriously murky.

14. So whether a speaker believes Pegasus exists or not, or is agnostic, is no bar to his attributing that Pegasus exists to someone else. A speaker can say "Max believes Pegasus exists" even if he believes that there is no such thing as Pegasus. Speakers' beliefs are immaterial in governing a speaker's usage in attributive contexts, including those we are discussing in the text. Thanks to Jeff King for discussion of these points.

15. We should perhaps point out here something that should have been apparent as we proceeded. The puzzle as we have described it is, in part, to analyze (i), and to show how one can be dislodged from such a belief by an utterance of "Paderewski is Paderewski."

(i)　*Believe*[a, $\exists x \exists y\ x \neq y$ (x is named "Paderewski" $\wedge$ y is named "Paderewski")]

Since the quantifiers are inside the propositional attitude, it does not matter for the puzzle whether the facts of the matter are such that the speaker or hearer is right. The speaker may be wrong that there is only one person and the hearer might be right that there are two people named "Paderewski." All that is relevant is that the speaker wants the hearer to have the same *beliefs* as him.

16. We have perhaps somewhat oversimplified the mechanisms of belief revision here, for we might suppose that change in belief states is normally weighted. If a comes to believe that p where he previously believed that $\neg p$, then given the context, a will retain belief that $\neg p$ to some degree. Suppose a speaker who believes that Paderewski is not Paderewski, accepts a speaker's utterance of "Paderewski is Paderewski." The hearer, as described in the text, will revise his beliefs, but we may assume, will leave a 10 percent chance that $a \neq b$—that is, that his initial belief was correct. But note that the negation of this, $a = b$, is not what the hearer now believes is 90 percent certain. What the speaker now believes is, given Singularity, $a = a$, and that is 100 percent certain. Note that it could be that the hearer is now 90 percent certain that there is one person named "Paderewski," leaving a residual 10 percent certainty that there are two people so-named. But these clearly are not complementary; the belief that there aren't two people named "Paderewski" does not even imply that there is one person so-named.

17. Putting together observations stemming from Kripke 1980 and Kaplan 1989.

18. We stipulate this lack of knowledge to simplify the puzzle; as will become apparent, it is by no means required.

19. This example is modeled on an example of Kaplan's (1989). Of course, accomplishing such an utterance may take considerable time, so as to allow Paderewski to change his location, but this is not necessary for the sentence *That guy is that guy* to be informative. Imagine that one seeks to deny that someone has been instantaneously replaced by his doppelgänger; then one can utter this sentence in normal time while demonstrating the person in question as he stands rigidly before the interlocutors.

20. We would only be prevented from taking this position if tokens of the same type could be distinctly valued, but this is precisely what is not possible, given the relation of expression-type to expression-token. See the discussion in chapter 1.

21. The schematic letter ranges over whatever else may occur in the nominal with the demonstrative word "that" ("this," "those," and so on). Thus, we take the account to generalize over both simplex and complex demonstratives.

22. Note that there is no requirement that an index be defined *de novo* for each occurrence of a demonstrative; if it is already defined, then we have anaphoric occurrences, in which demonstrative expression picks up both the indices and context of an antecedent demonstrative. By way of illustration, consider a speaker who utters "That guy saw that guy" only to be contradicted by another speaker, who says "No, that guy didn't see that guy." Clearly, the force of the second utterance derives from its dependence on the demonstratives in the first utterance; the second speaker intends to speak about the same individuals in the same contexts as did the first speaker. Another anaphoric use of demonstrative expressions in when they play the role of bound variables, as in "Every guy thinks that guy is handsome."

23. Note here that a speaker may believe that a context is invariant with respect to occurrences of demonstrative expressions, even though each of those expressions may be associated with a distinct demonstration. Indeed, insofar as demonstrations are actions at unique space/time coordinates, any demonstration will be

distinct from any other, regardless of whether a speaker believes that context has shifted or not. If this is so, then demonstrations could not serve in place of context as our operant notion, for they would be too finely individuated.

24. That there is a difference in identity statements of the sort we are discussing is recognized by Kaplan in "Demonstratives," although he recognizes that this poses a difficulty for his approach. The reason is that the informativeness of identity statements results from a variance in the way character delivers a content with respect to a context when demonstrative terms flank "be"; but proper names have constant character with respect to context, so any two proper names with the same reference have the same character, and thus "the informativeness of ⌜$\alpha = \beta$⌝, with α and β proper names, is not accounted for" (Kaplan 1989, 562).

25. That is, the speaker need not believe that the picture is a picture of Paderewski so long as he believes that it is believed *of* him that he believes that it is a picture of Paderewski.

26. We exclude the case in which (1) and (2) are taken together to imply that Frank believes "Russell" refers to both Russell and Wittgenstein.

References

Angelelli, I. 1967. *Studies on Frege and Traditional Philosophy*. Dordrecht: D. Reidel.

Bilgrami, A. 1992. *Belief and Meaning*. Oxford: Blackwell.

Blackburn, S., and A. Code. 1978. "The Power of Russell's Criticism of Frege." *Analysis*, 38: 65–77.

Bynum, T. W. 1972. "Editor's Introduction." In G. Frege, *Conceptual Notation and Related Articles*. Oxford: Oxford University Press.

Carnap, R. 1947. *Meaning and Necessity*. Chicago: University of Chicago Press.

Chomsky, N. 1965. *Aspects of the Theory of Syntax*. Cambridge, MA: MIT Press.

Chomsky, N. 1981. *Lectures on Government and Binding*. Dordrecht: Foris.

Chomsky, N. 1986. *Knowledge of Language: Its Nature, Origin and Use*. New York: Praeger.

Chomsky, N., and H. Lasnik. 1995. "The Theory of Principles and Parameters." In N. Chomsky, *The Minimalist Program*. Cambridge, MA: MIT Press.

Church, A. 1950. "On Carnap's Analysis of Statements of Assertion and Belief." *Analysis*, 10: 97–99.

Church, A. 1956. "Proposition and Sentences." In *The Problem of Universals*. Notre Dame, IN: University of Notre Dame Press.

Davidson, D. 1967. "Truth and Meaning." In D. Davidson, *Inquiries into Truth and Interpretation*. Oxford: Clarendon Press, 1984.

Davidson, D. 1984. "Belief and the Basis of Meaning." In D. Davidson, *Inquiries into Truth and Interpretation*. Oxford: Clarendon Press.

Devitt, M. 1989. "Against Direct Reference." In P. A. French, T. E. Uehling, Jr., and H. K. Wettstein, eds., *Midwest Studies in Philosophy, Volume 14: Contemporary Perspectives in the Philosophy of Language II*. Notre Dame, IN: University of Notre Dame Press.

Evans, G. 1973. "The Causal Theory of Names." In G. Evans, *Collected Papers*. Oxford: Clarendon Press, 1985.

Evans, G. 1977. "Pronouns, Quantifiers, and Relative Clauses (I)." In G. Evans, *Collected Papers*. Oxford: Clarendon Press, 1985.

Evans, G. 1980. "Pronouns." In G. Evans, *Collected Papers*. Oxford: Clarendon Press, 1985.

Fiengo, R., and R. May. 1994. *Indices and Identity*. Cambridge, MA: MIT Press.

Fiengo, R., and R. May. 1996. "Anaphora and Identity." In S. Lappin, ed., *The Handbook of Contemporary Semantic Theory*. Oxford: Blackwell.

Fiengo, R., and R. May. 1998. "Names and Expressions." *Journal of Philosophy*, 95: 377–409.

Fiengo, R., and R. May. 2002. "Identity Statements." In G. Preyer and G. Peter, eds., *Logical Form and Language*. Oxford: Clarendon Press.

Forbes, G. 1990. "The Indispensability of *Sinn*." *Philosophical Review*, 99: 535–563.

Frege, G. 1879. *Begriffsschrift: A formula language, modeled upon that of arithmetic, for pure thought*, translated by S. Bauer-Mengelberg, in J. van Heijenoort, ed., *From Frege to Gödel: A Source Book in Mathematical Logic*. Cambridge, MA: Harvard University Press, 1967. Also translated by T. W. Bynum as *Conceptual Notation: A Formula Language of Pure Thought Modelled upon the Formula Language of Arithmetic*, in G. Frege, *Conceptual Notation and Related Articles*. Oxford: Oxford University Press, 1972.

Frege, G. 1892. "On Sense and Reference." Translated by M. Black, in P. Geach and M. Black, eds., *Translations from the Philosophical Writings of Gottlob Frege*. Oxford: Blackwell, 1970. Also translated by H. Feigl as "On Sense and Nominatum," in H. Feigl and W. Sellars, eds., *Readings in Philosophical Analysis*. New York: Appleton Century Crofts, 1949.

Frege, G. 1893. *The Basic Laws of Arithmetic: Exposition of the System*. Translated by M. Furth. Berkeley: University of California Press, 1967.

Frege, G. 1903. *Grundgesetze der Arithmetik, Volume 1: Selections* (sections 55–67, 138–147, appendix), translated by P. Geach and M. Beaney. In M. Beaney, ed., *The Frege Reader*. Oxford: Blackwell, 1997.

Frege, G. 1914. "Logic in Mathematics." Translated by P. Long and R. White, in H. Hermes, F. Kambartel, and F. Kaulbach, eds., *Posthumous Writings*. Chicago: University of Chicago Press, 1979.

Frege, G. 1918. "The Thought." Translated by P. T. Geach and R. H. Stoothof, in G. Frege, *Logical Investigations*. Oxford: Blackwell, 1977.

Frege, G. n.d. "Frege to Jourdain." Translated by H. Kaal, in G. Frege, *Philosophical and Mathematical Correspondence*. Chicago: University of Chicago Press, 1980.

Geach, P. 1962. *Reference and Generality*. Ithaca, NY: Cornell University Press.

Geach, P. 1976. "Back-Reference." In A. Kasher, *Language in Focus*. Dordrecht: D. Reidel.

Grice, H. P. 1989. *Studies in the Way of Words*. Cambridge, MA: Harvard University Press.

Haïk, I. 1984. "Indirect Binding." *Linguistic Inquiry*, 15: 185–223.

Heim, I. 1982. *The Semantics of Definite and Indefinite Noun Phrases*. Doctoral dissertation, University of Massachusetts, Amherst.

Higginbotham, J. 1983. "Logical Form, Binding and Nominals." *Linguistic Inquiry*, 14: 395–420.

Higginbotham, J. 1985. "On Semantics." *Linguistic Inquiry*, 16: 547–594.

Kamp, H. 1984. "A Theory of Truth and Semantic Representation." In J. Groenendijk, T. M. V. Janssen, and M. Stokhof, eds., *Truth, Interpretation and Information*. Dordrecht: Foris.

Kaplan, D. 1989. "Demonstratives." In J. Almog, J. Perry, and H. Wettstein, eds., *Themes from Kaplan*. Oxford: Oxford University Press.

Kaplan, D. 1990. "Words." *Proceedings of the Aristotelian Society, Supplementary Volume* 64: 95–119.

Koster, J., and E. Reuland, eds. 1991. *Long-Distance Anaphora*. Cambridge: Cambridge University Press.

Kripke, S. 1971. "Identity and Necessity." In M. K. Munitz, ed., *Identity and Individuation*. New York: New York University Press.

Kripke, S. 1979. "A Puzzle about Belief." In A. Margalit, ed., *Meaning and Use*. Dordrecht: D. Reidel.

Kripke, S. 1980. *Naming and Necessity*. Cambridge, MA: Harvard University Press.

Lasnik, H. 1976. "Remarks on Coreference." *Linguistic Analysis*, 2: 1–22.

Loar, B. 1972. "Reference and Propositional Attitudes." *Philosophical Review*, 81: 43–62.

Lotze, H. 1874. *Logick*. Leipzig: S. Hirzel. (Translated by Bernard Bosanquet as *Logic*. Oxford: Clarendon Press, 1888.)

Marcus, R. B. 1963. "Discussion." In M. Wartofsky, ed., *Boston Studies in the Philosophy of Science*. Dordrecht: D. Reidel.

McDowell, J. 1977. "On the Sense and Reference of a Proper Name." *Mind*, 86: 159–185.

Mendelsohn, R. 1982. "Frege's *Begriffsschrift* Theory of Identity." *Journal of the History of Philosophy*, 22: 279–299.

Neale, S. 1990. *Descriptions*. Cambridge, MA: MIT Press.

Neale, S. 1992. "Paul Grice and the Philosophy of Language." *Linguistics and Philosophy*, 15: 509–559.

Perry, J. 1988. "Cognitive Significance and New Theories of Reference." In J. Perry, *The Problem of the Essential Indexical and Other Essays*. New York: Oxford University Press, 1993.

Putnam, H. 1954. "Synonymy, and the Analysis of Belief Sentences." *Analysis*, 14: 114–122.

Quine, W. V. O. 1953. "Reference and Modality." In W. V. O. Quine, *From a Logical Point of View*. Cambridge, MA: Harvard University Press.

Reinhart, T. 1983. *Anaphora and Semantic Interpretation*. London: Croon Helm.

Richard, M. 1983. "Direct Reference and Ascriptions of Belief." *Journal of Philosophical Logic*, 12: 425–452.

Russell, B. 1929. "Knowledge by Acquaintance and Knowledge by Description." In B. Russell, *Mysticism and Logic*. New York: Norton.

Russell, B. 1937. *The Principles of Mathematics*. 2nd ed., New York: Norton.

Russell, B. 1948. *Human Knowledge: Its Scope and Limits*. New York: Simon and Schuster.

Salmon, N. 1985. *Frege's Puzzle*. Cambridge, MA: MIT Press.

Saul, J. 1997. "Substitution and Simple Sentences." *Analysis*, 57: 102–108.

Schiffer, S. 1990. "The Mode-of-Presentation Problem." In C. A. Anderson and J. Owens, eds., *Propositional Attitudes: The Role of Content in Logic, Language and Mind*. Stanford, CA: Center for the Study of Language and Information, Stanford University.

Searle, J. 1958. "Proper Names." *Mind*, 67: 166–173.

Smullyan, A. 1948. "Modality and Description." *Journal of Symbolic Logic*, 13: 31–37.

Stanley, J. 2000. "Context and Logical Form." *Linguistics and Philosophy*, 23: 391–434.

Thomae, J. 1880. *Elementare Theorie der analytischen Functionen einer complexen Veränderlichen*. Halle: L. Nebert. (2nd edition: 1898.)

Wettstein, H. 1991a. "Cognitive Significance without Cognitive Content." In H. Wettstein, *Has Semantics Rested on a Mistake? And Other Essays*. Stanford, CA: Stanford University Press.

Wettstein, H. 1991b. "Turning the Tables on Frege, or How Is It That 'Hesperus is Phosphorus' Is Trivial?" In H. Wettstein, *Has Semantics Rested on a Mistake? And Other Essays*. Stanford, CA: Stanford University Press.

Wettstein, H. 2004. *The Magic Prism*. Oxford: Oxford University Press.

Wittgenstein, L. 1922. *Tractatus Logico-Philosophicus*. London: Kegan, Paul.

Index

Anaphora, and syntactic identity, 33
Angelelli, I., 129n6
Attributed assignments, 63–65
 and de dicto belief, 63–65
 and implicatures, 65–67
Assignments, 11, 15–17, 11–14,
 60–63, 65–68, 70–81, 108–110,
 112–113, 115, 117, 126–127,
 149–151, 153, 163, 166–168
 admissible, 113
 belief of, 60–62
 propositional status, 82–93
 status as senses, 81–82
Assignment Principle, 62, 108

Belief attribution, 11, 61, 63–69, 82,
 140, 152
 de dicto, 22, 34, 64, 66–69, 70,
 72–73, 76–78, 80–82, 111–112,
 117, 119, 127–128, 150–154, 168
 and empty names, 67–68
 non-de dicto, 67–68, 70, 77,
 111–114, 117, 119, 127, 151,
 163–164
Bilgrami, A., 97n17
Binding Theory, 35, 57
Blackburn, S., 131n14
Bynum, T., 129n6

Carnap, R., 143
Causal theory of reference,
 121–122, 168
 historical chains, 123

Chomsky, N., 14, 35, 47n5,
 48nn13, 14
Church, A., 143, 169n4
Code, A., 131n14
Cognitive value, 99
Conversational implicature, 41, 43
Coreference, 25ff, 198
 grammatically determined, 37
 and speakers' intentions, 38–40

Davidson, D., 1, 42, 48n18, 142, 149
De dicto puzzle, 68–70
Definite descriptions, 156–157
De lingua belief, 10, 24, 25, 145
Demonstratives, 27, 157, 159–160,
 164–166
 and context, 159–163
 and singularity, 183
Devitt, M., 136n45, 169n2
Disquotation principle, 21–22, 152

Empty names, 68
Evans, G., 29–33, 47n8, 49n21,
 131n12
Expression identity, 54–56
Expressions, of names, 15–20
 and coreference, 19–20
 identity of expressions, 16–19,
 54–56
 in conversation, 23–24
 independence from name-
 identity, 18
 rigidity, 114

Fiengo, R., 48nn12, 15, 49nn19, 21, 22, 50n23, 133n25, 169n2
Forbes, G., 131n12
Frege, G., 13, 21, 51, 60, 81, 85, 94, 99–103, 105–106, 112, 116–117, 124–125, 129n3, 130nn7, 9, 131n15, 140, 143–144, 169n8
  account of identity statements, 101–105

Geach, P., 49nn20, 21
Grice, P., 8

Haïk, I., 49n21
Heim, I., 49n21
Higginbotham, J., 30, 32, 48n12

Identificational beliefs, 167–168
Identity puzzles, 75–80
  de dicto, 76–77, 116–118
  Paderewski puzzle, 75–78, 80
  Pierre puzzle, 78–80
Identity statements, 44–46, 99ff
  de dicto and non-de dicto, 114–118
  Frege on, 99–103
  informativeness of, 104–105, 115–116
  linguistic puzzle, 142–145
  logical form, 112–115
  metalinguistic, 99–100, 103–104, 106
  as necessary truths, 118–119
  singularity, 126–127
  thought expressed, 99–103, 105
  translation statements, 115–116
Indices, 16–17
Indexicals, 27–28

Judgeable contents, 99

Kamp, H., 49n21
Kaplan, D., 47n8, 70. 131n12, 171nn17, 19, 172n24
Koster, J., 48n15
Kripke, S., 16, 20–21, 56, 72–73, 80, 82, 120, 123, 130n10, 131n14, 132n16, 135nn40, 41, 44, 140–141, 151–152, 171n17

Language use, as tool use, 7–9
Lasnik, H., 29, 47n5, 10, 48n13
Lexical competence, 14
Lexicon, 14, 17–18, 52–53, 71, 75, 107–109, 112, 115, 145–147, 158, 164
Linguistic competence, 166
Loar, B., 95n10
Lotze, H., 129n2

Marcus, R. B., 131n13, 132n16
May, R., 48nn12, 15, 49n19, 21, 22, 50n23, 133n25, 169n2
McDowell, J., 133n28
Mendelsohn, R., 129n6, 130n8
Millianism, 21, 140
Mode of presentation, 51–52, 81, 101

Names
  ambiguous, 12–13
  identity criteria, 52–54
  as lexical items, 145–147
  with multiple bearers, 119–121
  senses expressed by, 123–125
Names and expressions, 13–15, 51ff
Neale, S., 49n21
Non-coindexing, 40
Non-coreference, 29–31
  implicature, 41–44

Paderewski Puzzle, 20–23, 72–73, 75–80, 122–129, 139ff
  de dicto, 149–153
  demonstrative puzzle, 158–164
  informativeness, 152–154
  reverse puzzle, 154–157
  and singularity, 74–75
  uninformativeness, 155–157
Perry, J., 104
Phrase-markers, 34
  and syntactic identity, 34–36
Pierre puzzle, 73–80
Possible worlds, 121
Propositional attitudes, 20, 25, 111
Putnam H., 135n40

Quine, W., 95n10

Reference, 11–12, 14–16, 29, 55–56,
    81, 146–147, 150, 157, 159,
    164, 165
  and context, 26–28
  demonstrative, 164–167
  of expressions, 16

Referential dependency, 32–33
Reinhart, T., 50n23
Reuland, E., 48n15
Richard, M., 48n15
Rigid designators, 119–122, 157
  asyntactic theory, 120–122
  syntactic theory, 122–123
Russell, B., 27, 100–101, 129n5,
    131n14, 144

Salmon, N., 131n12
Saul, J., 94n9
Schiffer, S., 51, 97n18
Searle, J., 131n12
Singularity, 71–82, 126–127,
    147–148, 151–152, 154, 156,
    158, 163
  and Paderewski puzzle, 72–73
  and Pierre puzzle, 73–75
Smullyan, A., 129n1
Stanley, J., 47n7
Substitutivity of identicals, 20, 51,
    59–60, 66, 68, 111, 116, 140,
    142–143
  failure, 65–66
Syntax, 17, 18, 107, 154

Thomae, J., 129n2
Translation, 56–59, 69–71, 109–110,
    115, 117, 126, 128
  and de dicto belief attribution,
    68–70
  and indexing, 57–59
  and substitution, 59–60
  translation statements, 56–57

Wettstein, H., 104, 131n12
Wittgenstein, L., 130n8